9780861902187
£5.50

WEST GERMANY

OFF
THE BEATEN TRACK
WEST GERMANY

MPC

Published by:
Moorland Publishing Co Ltd,
Moor Farm Road,
Ashbourne,
Derbyshire
DE6 1HD
England

British Library Cataloguing in
Publication Data:
Aldridge, Janet
    West Germany. --- (Off the beaten
    track).
    1. West Germany - Visitor's guides
    I. Title II. Speaight, George
    III. Wood, George, 1922- IV. Collins,
    Martin, 1941-
    V. Series
    914.3'04878

ISBN 0 86190 218 1 (paperback)
ISBN 0 86190 217 3 (hardback)

Colour origination by:
Scantrans, Singapore

Printed in the UK by:
Butler and Tanner Ltd, Frome,
Somerset

Cover photograph:
Burg Eltz, Mosel (*MPC Picture
Collection*).

Black and white illustrations have been
supplied as follows:

J. Aldridge: pp165, 169, 171, 179, 182,
183, 184, 193, 198, 199, 201, 205, 256,
258, 260, 262, 263, 265, 269, 283; Furth
im Wald Tourist Office: p197; German
National Tourist Office: pp15, 27, 67,
69, 127, 131; Georg Holtl: pp173, 174-5,
189; MPC Picture Collection: pp72, 239,
240, 241, 245, 251, 252, 271, 273;
Munich Tourist Office: pp212, 213, 215,
217, 219, 221, 223, 229, 230, 233;
Oberbayern Tourist Office: pp243, 274,
275; Regensburg Tourist Office: p161;
G. Speaight: pp17, 295, 296, 300, 301,
303; B. C. Walker: p246; G. Wood:
pp35, 39, 45, 46, 48, 53, 84, 86, 89, 93,
95, 97, 111, 112, 115, 117, 137, 140, 142,
144, 145, 147, 149; P. Wood: pp139, 151.

Colour illustrations have been
supplied as follows:

J. Aldridge (*Wies Church pulpit*); Georg
Holtl (*chapel, Museumdorf*); Der Senat
der Hansestadt Lübeck (*Holstentor*);
Mittelmosel Bildarchiv (*Bremm*); MPC
Picture Collection (*Wine selling in the
Mosel, Enkirch, Linz am Rhein,
Rüdesheim*); Oberbayern Tourist Office
(*Maria Gern, Ramsau*); G. Speaight
(*Ediger-Eller*); G. Wood (*Deidesheim,
Siebeldingen, Dörrenbach, Stuppach
parish church, Saar Valley, Schloss
Weikersheim, Bad Mergentheim, Creglin-
gen, Arnsberg, Aub*).

Acknowledgements
Janet Aldridge would like to ac-
knowledge the assistance of Klaus
Kreher, Susanne Westiner, Petra
Jonas, Fremdenverkehrsverband
München-Oberbayern, Georg
Holtl, Herman Plotz and the
Grafenau Tourist Office.

George Speaight would like to
acknowledge the assistance of
Heinrich Meinhard for advice and
information on German wines.

George Wood would like to acknowledge the assistance of his
wife and Professor Wilhelm
Brockhaus.

Quotations from *The German Lesson*
by Siegfried Lenz, are reproduced
with the permission of Methuen,
London.

Contents

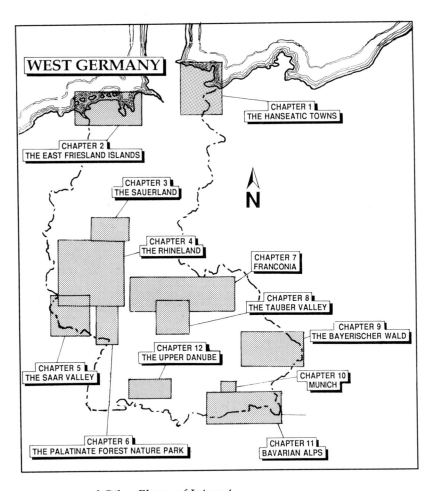

WEST GERMANY

CHAPTER 1
THE HANSEATIC TOWNS

CHAPTER 2
THE EAST FRIESLAND ISLANDS

CHAPTER 3
THE SAUERLAND

N

CHAPTER 4
THE RHINELAND

CHAPTER 7
FRANCONIA

CHAPTER 8
THE TAUBER VALLEY

CHAPTER 9
THE BAYERISCHER WALD

CHAPTER 12
THE UPPER DANUBE

CHAPTER 5
THE SAAR VALLEY

CHAPTER 10
MUNICH

CHAPTER 6
THE PALATINATE FOREST NATURE PARK

CHAPTER 11
BAVARIAN ALPS

Museums and Other Places of Interest
Throughout the Federal Republic, State museums are, in general, closed on Mondays and public holidays. The tourist information bureaus can provide up-to-date lists of museums and other places of interest, with addresses and times of opening.

Note on Maps
The maps for each chapter, while comprehensive, are not designed to be used as route maps, but to locate the main towns, villages and places of interest.

Introduction

Western Europe is a continent of great diversity, well visited not just by travellers from other parts of the globe but by the inhabitants of its own member countries. Within the year-round processes of trade and comerce, but more particularly during the holiday season, there is a great surging interchange of nationalities as one country's familiar attractions are left behind for those of another.

It is true that frontiers are blurred by ever quicker travel and communications, and that the sharing of cultures, made possible by an increasingly sophisticated media network, brings us closer in all senses to our neighbours. Yet essential differences do exist, differences which lure us abroad on our annual migrations in search of new horizons, fresh sights, sounds and smells, discovery of unknown landscapes and people.

Countless resorts have evolved for those among us who simply crave sun, sea and the reassuring press of humanity. There are, too, established tourist 'sights' with which a country or region has become associated and to which clings, all too often, a suffocating shroud — the manifestations of mass tourism in the form of crowds and entrance charges, the destruction of authentic atmosphere, cynical exploitation. Whilst this is by no means typical of all well known tourist attractions, it is familiar enough to act as a disincentive for those of more independent spirit who value personal discovery above prescribed experience and who would rather avoid the human conveyor belt of queues, traffic jams and packed accommodation.

It is for such travellers that this guidebook has been written. In its pages, no more than passing mention is made of the famous, the well documented, the already glowingly described — other guidebooks will satisfy the appetite for such orthodox tourist information. Instead, the reader is taken if not to unknown then to relatively unvisited places — literally 'off the beaten track'. Through the specialist knowledge of the authors, visitors using this guidebook are assured of gaining insights into the country's heartland whose heritage lies largely untouched by the tourist industry. Occasionally the reader is urged simply to take a sideways step from a site of renowned tourist interest to find one perhaps less sensational, certainly less frequented but often of equivalent fascination.

From wild, scantily populated countryside whose footpaths and byways are best navigated by carefull map reading, to negotiating the side streets of towns and cities, travelling 'off the beaten track' can be rather more demanding than following in the footsteps of countless thousands before you. The way may be less clear, more adventurous and individualistic, but opportunities do emerge for real discovery in an age of increasing dissatisfaction with the passive predictability of conventional holidaymaking. With greater emphasis on exploring 'off the beaten track', the essence of West Germany is more likely to be unearthed and its true flavours relished to the full.

Martin Collins
Series Editor

1 • The Hanseatic Towns

The history of Germany is, until the nineteenth century, the story of separate kingdoms, dukedoms, and principalities, and even of individual self-governing towns. During the Middle Ages a number of these towns, mostly in the north of the country, joined together to protect their commercial interests in what was called the Hanseatic League. From the thirteenth to the fifteenth century this league, which was never more than a loose confederation, exercised a powerful influence in the north of Europe. It had a diet that met as occasion required and raised armed forces when its power was threatened. The cities upon which it was based expanded with docks and warehouses while the merchant families who directed its commerce grew rich.

Though the power of the league has long disappeared, the cities that built it up remain centres of commercial activity, with great civic treasures and a spirit of independence that, it seems, is somewhat different to anything found elsewhere in Germany. These towns are in no way off the beaten track, but they are largely unvisited by English speaking tourists and contain much that is well worth seeing. As a change from the lakes and mountains for which Germany is famous, the traveller with a feeling for the excitement of exploration might well consider a visit to a few of these historic towns.

Hamburg, the largest of these towns and a *Land* of the Federal Republic of Germany (Bundes Republik Deutschland) in its own right, lies at the end of the long estuary of the river Elbe. The best way to approach it is by the ship service from Harwich. As the ship moves up the estuary the dykes lining the banks, the marshy land and fields beyond them, the busy shipping, the multitude of small yachts on a summer weekend, the rows of fishermen's cottages that are now clearly gentrified for commuters to Hamburg, and the industrial developments that crowd increasingly along the shore, all prepare you for the great city that lies ahead. The ship berths at a quay right in the heart of the city.

It must be said at the start that one does not go to Hamburg to look at buildings. A large part of the town was burnt down in 1842 and the city suffered a terribly destructive air raid in 1943 which set a fire storm sweeping through the streets with a temperature of up to 1,000 °C (1,832 °F) killing in one night some 40,000 of its citizens. Everything is rebuilt now, and the six spires, which are the landmark of Hamburg, once more reach into the sky. Almost the only ruin still to survive is the remains of a U-boat bunker in the harbour, which all the high explosives of the Royal Air Force could not totally destroy! The most impressive building in the city, as one would expect, is not a cathedral or a palace but the town hall, the Rathaus, built in 1886 and boasts some fine rooms for civic ceremonies.

The docks of Hamburg have been affected by the growth of containers for commercial shipping and the dock area, like other dock areas, is seeking other uses for its vast warehouses. But if, in some respects, Hamburg seems run down, in other cases it is still vibrant with commercial life. In particular it is the chief city in the Federal Republic for journalism and contains the publishing offices of most of the picture magazines that decorate the news stands, and whose exposures of scandals (and inventions of scandals) have rocked society in recent years.

It is a very political city too, with a strong socialist tradition, and was one of the last cities in Germany to surrender to the Nazis. Chancellor Helmut Schmidt, who led the Social Democratic Party for so long is a Hamburger, and the type of cap which he always wore can be seen on the heads of many Hamburg citizens today.

But if one has an idea that this is just a bleak commercial city it will soon be dispelled if one was to make a tour from the river front, with its lively shipping activity, along a half ring of parks and gardens to the huge Alster lake whose edge lies only a few yards from the town hall. You can walk for 8¹/₂ miles (14km) round this lake by the Alsterwanderung if you like. There are boat trips, which can be taken on the lake and cafés and restaurants on its banks. In a few years time, when water purification measures are completed, bathing will be allowed in its waters.

As one would expect, the merchant princes of Hamburg were not going to be outdone by the royal princes of other German states and so they bought fine paintings and other works of art for the civic galleries and museums. The objects that are the most impressive in the museums of Hamburg are probably the nineteenth-century ones that would have appeared on the market after the affluent period of the great royal collectors in the German states had ended.

The Kunsthalle holds no less than eleven paintings by Caspar

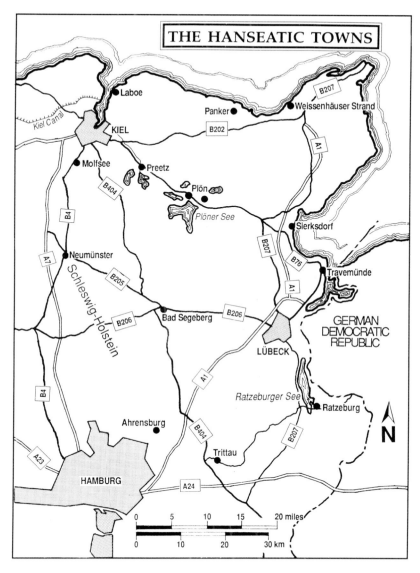

THE HANSEATIC TOWNS

David Friedrich. Only the Nationalgalerie in Berlin has more. Friedrich was a pioneer of early nineteenth-century Romantic painting. His typical canvas depicts a man standing in a vast landscape of mountains brooding, it seems, upon the nature of the universe. It may be a man and woman gazing from the edge of a forest at the moon in a blood-red sky or a boat crew shipwrecked on a wide

expanse of ice. He was fascinated by the landscapes of the Hartz
mountains and by the atmosphere of the Baltic coast but, by intro-
ducing a strange, unexplained human presence into his art, he lifts
them into a realm beyond mere paintings of scenery and gives them
a universal quality, a sense of man's smallness and helplessness
against the forces of nature. The paintings of Friedrich were almost
forgotten after his death, but have now been rediscovered and are
widely appreciated as forecasting what has been called 'the existen-
tial isolation of the twentieth century'. Unless you go to Berlin or
Dresden, the Kunsthalle in Hamburg is almost the only place where
the visitor can study a number of his works together. These paintings
alone make a visit worthwhile.

The other main gallery in Hamburg is the Museum für Kunst und
Gewerbe, the art and craft museum. The chief attraction here is
probably an extraordinarily rich collection of the style that the Germans call *Jugendstil* but which is also known as Art Nouveau. Much
of this was purchased by the far-seeing museum director, Justus
Brinkman, at the Paris exhibition of 1900. There is glass, pottery,
carpets, furniture, books, and anything else one can think of displayed, not as individual items, but in entire rooms furnished in this
style. This enables one to wander round them and really imagine
those years when the fusty nineteenth century seemed to be blown
away by the fresh, clean look of the new age, and with no warning of
the horrors that this new age was to bring. In this collection the work
of William Morris and other English designers of that school is well
represented.

One other museum that may be missed as it is not well known is
the Jenisch-Haus, reached from Klein-Flottbek on the *S-Bahn*. This
was the home of a Hamburg banker and senator which he built as a
summer residence in the 1830s. He gave receptions here for the high
society of the day. The furnishings and decoration give a good idea
of the taste and style of life of a successful, cultivated business man
of the early nineteenth century. The house stands in a beautiful park
that was laid out 'in the English style' as an ornamental farm. The
Englischer Garten in Munich represents a similar taste. The garden
architect was a Scotsman, William Booth.

If you have an interest in gardening you might well study the
work not only of William Booth but of other members of his family
who made a major contribution to the horticulture of the Hamburg
area with the founding of a nursery in 1795. They introduced many
foreign trees and shrubs to Germany, including rhododendrons,
conifers and orchids. They were followed by another Scotsman,

Peter Smith, who founded a business here in 1848. At the right season of the year every restaurant in Germany seems to offer asparagus specialities, *Spargel-Spezialitälen*, and Scottish visitors especially may like to remember that this, like many other vegetables, was originally introduced into Germany by these Scottish gardeners in the early decades of the nineteenth century.

One other excursion from the centre of Hamburg that is well worth pursuing is to the Hagenbeck Zoo (*U-Bahn* Hagenbecks Tierpark). Carl Hagenbeck was a fish dealer who found that the net of one of his fishing boats had caught six seals. Rather than throw them back into the sea, he put them on show and found that they attracted much public interest. He went on from this to collect more animals and in 1907 his son opened a zoo in the suburb of Stellingen as the first in the world in which animals were displayed in natural surroundings and not behind bars. The zoo has been greatly extended, and is laid out with remarkably effective lakes, hills and landscape features, so that you really feel you might be on safari rather than a few miles from the centre of a city on the North Sea. The Hagenbeck family also started a circus that became one of the best known in Germany and led the way in the training of animals by kindness and rewards.

It is difficult to write about Hamburg without mentioning the Reeperbahn in the St Pauli district. For some visitors this is so far from being off the beaten track that it is the only object of their visit. But others may need some kind of guide.

Like all sea ports, there grew up in Hamburg the facilities that sailors are supposed to look for on shore: bars and brothels. St Pauli has always provided these, and the present administration of the city recognises that they will exist whether legally or not, and so sensibly provides some control over the way they are made available. There are said to be 3,000 licensed prostitutes in the area. If, between the river and the Reeperbahn, you chance upon a side street barricaded off with notices banning women and juveniles from entering, you will know that this is the street where the 'ladies' sit in the windows. It is believed that this is the only place in Germany where this custom, which is well established in Holland and Belgium, can be found.

Elsewhere there are bars for homosexuals and bars for transvestites and bars for other variations that could well qualify as off the beaten track, but one is assured that there are plenty of bars where one can take the wife or girlfriend without any problems. In 1962 The Beatles first made their reputation at one of these — the Star Club, at 39 Grosse Freiheit, which leads off the Reeperbahn.

One place of entertainment that is unique to Hamburg is the

Hansa Theatre in Steindamm behind the railway station. This is a theatre offering a variety programme of singers, jugglers, comedians and acrobats of a type that unfortunately seems to have disappeared elsewhere. The audience sits in two- or five-seater well-upholstered benches, with a good view of the stage and a table in front, at which food and drink can be served. This theatre was originally opened in 1894, and the rather old-fashioned atmosphere is very attractive.

There is one further visit that the English speaking visitor may like to make. Near the Ohlsdorf Station is the largest cemetery in Europe, which provides a fine display of funerary art. But there are two things here that have a special involvement for British visitors. At B1-Bk59 are the graves of 2,500 British soldiers who died in the two world wars, which are looked after by the British War Graves Commission. At Bu-Bq66 is a mass grave and monument for the 55,000 citizens of Hamburg who were killed in British air raids on the city during World War II. No Englishman of any sensitivity can visit Hamburg without some feeling of discomfort. When this memorial was unveiled in 1952 the then Bürgermeister, Max Brauer, spoke the following words:

> These are not victims of a natural catastrophe. Their death was — like the death of the peaceful citizens of Guernica, Rotterdam and Coventry — the work of men. Because our people had lost their freedom, they were led by a foul dictator to the slaughter. Bombs and fire were rained over foreign cities. Then, in its turn, our own city went up in flames. Our dead exhort us: Let no new dictator come over you! Seek peace and undertstanding between peoples! Think on it, lest there may come some other form of total war, whose victims in the future may be even more numerous than those before whose graves we stand today.

Lübeck and Kiel

A folk song of this area runs as follows:

> *Hamborg, Lübeck, Bremen,*
> *sie brauchen sich nicht zu schämen;*
> *denn sie sind eine freie Stadt,*
> *wo Bismarck nichts zu sagen hat.*

which can be translated as:

> Hamburg, Lübeck, Bremen,
> have nothing to be ashamed of;
> for they are a free town,
> where Bismarck has nothing to say.

This illustrates the independent spirit of these Hanseatic towns, and places Lübeck next to Hamburg. Indeed, these two cities took it in

The Holstentor, Lübeck

turn to lead the Hanseatic League over the centuries with Hamburg commanding the North Sea and Lübeck the Baltic. In **Lübeck**, known as the Queen of the Hansa, there is plenty for the traveller to see.

From the fifteenth-century gateway, topped by twin turrets, you enter the old town, entirely encircled by water. Fine buildings, predominantly built in brick between the fifteenth and the eighteenth centuries, are on every side: the town hall, with its decorated Renaissance façade, churches, with their soaring spires, hospitals, warehouses and merchants' dwellings. Among these is the Buddenbrooks House, owned in the nineteenth century by the ancestors of Thomas Mann, where he was born and the inspiration of his great novel, *Buddenbrooks*. There are museums, some in old churches, some in citizens' houses, and a particularly attractive and little-known museum of puppets adjoining the small puppet theatre in Kleine Petersgrube. There are restaurants too: in the Rathaus cellar which, as everywhere else in Germany, provides food and drink; in the historic fraternity house of the Schiffergesellschaft, where the captains of the sailing ships used to meet and where models of their ships now hang over the tables; and in the rococo hall of the nineteenth-century Haus der Gesellschaft zur Beförderunggemeinsamer Tütigkeit (a typically Germanic mouthful which when translated means the Public Welfare Work Society). There are also shops selling

Lübeck marzipan, a speciality of the town. Everywhere one can see stepped gables and arched buttresses, narrow passageways and ostentatious façades witnessing to the pride, wealth and good taste of the city and its merchants. If the visitor has a feeling for architecture, days can be spent exploring this city with the aid of a detailed guide book, but it will have to be in German, for the British have never heard of Lübeck!

If you tire of architecture there is the idyllic fishing village of Gothmund nearby and the seaside resort of Travemünde offers bathing, sailing, a casino and a colourful night life. Beyond, on the other side of the estuary, lies the German Democratic Republic. In recent times a handful of desperate and courageous East Germans braved the mines, searchlights and the guard boats every year to seek a new life in the other Germany. Today happily, improved relationships between the two Germanies are leading to a better atmosphere and to some exchange of family and tourist visits. If you are tempted to taste the experience of a visit to the German Democratic Republic, you will find that life there lacks many of the amenities that make the Federal Republic such a pleasant country. But there are things to be seen and experiences to be enjoyed in communist Germany that are worth the journey. The main disadvantage is that it seems essential to travel with an organised party or as a government guest. The idea that one might want to just drive along or get out at a railway station and find a welcoming Gasthaus seems to be beyond the comprehension of the East German bureaucrats.

Some 40 miles (64km) to the north is **Kiel**, the capital of Schleswig-Holstein. This was a small Hanseatic town but gained importance in 1895 with the building of the Kiel Canal, which the Germans call the Nord-Ostsee-Kanal. It used to be a major naval base but is now largely rebuilt and is a pleasant example of German post-war reconstruction, with its pedestrian precinct, university, parks, museums, theatres and concert hall, and above all the quays alongside which lie the liners that provide a service with Norway and Sweden. Unlike many major ports, where the harbour area is hidden away behind rows of warehouses, the ships here lie right beside the main street and bring the atmosphere of the sea to the centre of the town.

The canal itself lies a few miles up the Kieler Förde and cannot be seen from the town. It carries more traffic (though not a higher tonnage) than any other canal in the world. An interesting excursion is to watch the operation of the huge Kiel-Holtenau locks at Schleusen. The new bridge here offers a good view of the canal and the Förde.

The fraternity house of the Schiffergesellschaft in Lübeck, now a restaurant

Kiel, on its sheltered Förde, is a great place for yachting. The high spot of the year is Kiel Week in June, when the town is full and regattas of every kind are held. What began in the nineteenth century as a society event has now developed into a hugely popular festival.

A few miles up the Förde, where it broadens out into the open sea, is the impressive Marine Memorial at Laboe, from the top of which one can see as far as the Danish islands. On the beach here a U-boat of World War II is preserved, and the interior can be visited. For any one of the now diminishing number of Englishmen who knew what it was for their ships to be sunk by one of these vessels, such a visit can be an uncanny experience.

In the other direction, to the south at Molfsee, is the Freilicht Museum, the open-air museum for Schleswig-Holstein. Here some sixty-five buildings from all over the area have been re-erected: farmhouses, cottages, barns, windmills, a bakery, a forge, a weaving mill, a pottery, and so on. Bread, wool, pottery, iron work and other craft objects are made by local craftsmen, and farm animals are reared on the site. Since its foundation in 1961 this has grown into one of the most important open-air museums of its kind.

The Countryside

There are many more conventionally scenic areas of Europe than Schleswig-Holstein, but if you come here to look at the towns you might find that you stay to savour the country round them. It is a rich, fertile countryside, with brick-built, half-timbered thatched farmhouses and the occasional grand mansion. On the way from Hamburg towards Lübeck, for instance, the visitor soon comes to **Ahrensburg**, with its Renaissance Ahrensburg Schloss, open to the public and surrounded by a pleasant park. Further on there is a nature reserve, Naturschutzgebiet Forst Hahnheide, at **Trittau**, with wide forests, a lake, and many attractive walks. Ratzeburg lies on an island in an extensive lake. At one end of the island is the twelfth-century Romanesque cathedral, Ratzeburg Dom, with a fine medieval altarpiece and beautiful cloisters. In a corner of the cloisters is a striking sculpture of a crippled man by Ernst Barlach, the Expressionist artist, and the Ernst Barlach-Haus Museum devoted to this work is in the town. From here you can take a boat to Lübeck, which would provide a suitable approach to this maritime city.

Between Lübeck and Kiel there are no less than eleven nature reserves along the coast with sands, dune grasses, and a rich bird life. But if the visitor seeks a different kind of pleasure, there are holiday resorts here with every kind of attraction: at **Weissenhäuser Strand** there is the longest water slide in Europe — all of 150yd, and the Hansapark at **Sierksdorf** boasts what looks like a truly terrifying switchback called the Loopingbahn 'Nessie'. A more direct route passes through the vast lake area at **Plön**, which does not need the ridiculous title of the Holsteiner Switzerland for its beauties to be appreciated. The Plöner Schloss here, which served first as a summer residence for the Danish kings and then as a training academy for Prussian military cadets, recalls the long dispute between Denmark and Germany for the possession of Schleswig-Holstein; it is now a boarding school. At **Panker** the Landgrave of Hesse built a country house at the beginning of the eighteenth century which is still inhabited by his descendants. They have established here a stud for breeding Trakehner horses, whose gleaming bay coats may be admired in the paddocks surrounding the house. This is a traditional East Prussian breed, whose survival was ensured by its transference here before the advancing Russian army in the last months of the war. Almost everywhere you will find Heimatmuseums illustrating the local history traditions and occasional unexpected special collections of the work of some enthusiastic collector which is itself like the Circus Museum at **Preetz**, the site of a thirteenth-century monastery, the Preetzer Kloster, and is charmingly situated on a river on which one can paddle a canoe all the way down to Kiel.

On the way back to Hamburg you might call at the open-air zoo, the Tierpark Neumünster, at **Neumünster**, where you can see animals that once roamed across Germany but are now no longer found here, like aurochs (European bison), bears, lynx, wild horse, and wolves. At **Bad Segeberg** there is an open-air theatre, Segeberg's Freilichttheater, in a rocky setting that is the site of unique performances of the 'Western' adventure stories of Karl May, with hundreds of Red Indians galloping in on their horses and the air reeking with the smell of gunpowder.

A special interest that might be profitably pursued in Schleswig-Holstein is that of organ music. The composer Buxtehude was the organist at the Mariankirche in Lübeck at the end of the seventeenth century and his reputation attracted visits from Bach and Handel. The present organ, built in 1968, is dedicated to his memory but while most of the older organs in the big cities were destroyed in the war, almost every village church can boast a fine instrument. All through north Germany, from the border with Holland to that with Denmark, a wide and truly popular appreciation of organ music developed in the baroque period, encouraged by the congregational participation of the Lutheran church liturgy. Today many organ concerts are given on these instruments and a visit could be built round attending them. The Amt für Kirchenmusik at 76 Uhlandstrasse, Hamburg 76, publishes a two-monthly programme for the Hamburg area and other concerts are advertised locally.

Further Information
— The Hanseatic Towns —

Museums

Alstertalmuseum
65 Wellingsbüttler Weg 79g-h
Open: Saturday and Sunday, 11am-1pm and 3-6pm.

Automuseum Hillers
1 Kurt-Schumacher-Allee 42
Open: daily 10am-5pm.

Ernst Barlach-Haus
52 Baron-Voght-Strasse 50a
Open: daily 11am-5pm, except Monday

Bischofsburg
(in Gemeindehauses St Petri)
1 Speersort 10
Open: Monday to Saturday, 10am-1pm.

Johannes-Brahms-Gedenkräume
36 Peterstrasse
Open: Tuesday and Friday, 12noon-1pm, Thursday, 5-6pm.

Deutsches Maler- und Lackierer-Museum
74 Billwerder Billdeich 72
Open: Saturday and Sunday 9am-1pm. In summer also open on a Wednesday.

Das Museum der Elektrizität
76 Klinikweg 23
Open: Tuesday to Sunday, 9am-5pm.

Gedenkstätte Ernst Thälmann
20 Tarpenbekstrasse 66
Open: Tuesday to Friday, 10am-7pm, and Saturday and Sunday 10am-1pm.

Geologisch-Päläontologisches Museum, Universität Hamburg
13 Bundestrasse 55
Open: Monday to Friday, 9am-6pm and in term time, Saturday, 9am-12noon.

Hamburgosches Museum für Völkerkunde
13 Rothenbaumchaussee 64
Open: daily 10am-5pm, except Monday

Heine-Haus
50 Elbchaussee 31
Open: Tuesday to Friday, 11am-7pm, Saturday, 11am-6pm.
Closed summer.

Jenisch-Haus
52 Baron-Voght-Strasse
Open: summer, Tuesday to Saturday 2-5pm. Sunday, 11am-5pm. Winter, Tuesday to Saturday, 1-4pm, and Sunday 11am-4pm.

Krameramtswohnungen
11 Krayenkamp 10-11
Open: Tuesday to Saturday, 10am-5pm

Kunsthalle
1 Glockengiersserwall
Open: daily, 10am-5pm except Monday

Kunsthaus
1 Ferdinandstor 1
Open: Tuesday to Sunday, 10am-6pm.

KZ-Gedenkstätte Neuengamme
(Concentration Camp Memorial)
80 Neuengammer Heerweg
Open: Tues to Sunday 10am-5pm.

Luftwaffenmuseum Uetersen
2081 Appen/Unterlinde
Hauptstrasse 140
Open: Tuesday to Friday, 3-5pm, Saturday and Sunday, 10am-5pm in summer. Winter, open Saturday and Sunday 10am-3pm.

Mineralogisches Museum der Universität Hamburg
13 Grindelallee 48
Open: Wednesdays, 3-7pm.

Museum der Elbinsel Wihelmsburg mit Milchmuseum
93 Kirchdorfer Strasse 163
Open: Sundays 4-6pm in summer.

Museum für Kunst and Gewerbe
1 Steintorplatz 1
Open: daily 10am-5pm, except Monday

**Museum für Hamburgische
Geschichte**
36 Holstenwall 24
Open: daily 10am-5pm, except Monday

Museum Mana Kumaka
70 Kramerkoppel 42
Open: Saturday & Sunday 11am-5pm.

Museum Rade am Schloss Reinbek
Reinbek
Schlossstrasse 4
Open: Saturday & Sunday 10am-6pm.

Museumsdorf Volsdorf
67 Im Alten Dorfe 48
Open: daily, except Tuesday & Thursday, 9am-12noon, 2pm until dusk.

Panoptikum (waxworks)
4 Spielbudenplatz 3
Open: Monday to Friday 10am-9.30pm.
Saturday, 10am-midnight, and Sunday, 10am-9.30pm.

Planetarium
60 Hindenburgstrasse
Open: Wednesday and Friday 4-6pm.
Sunday 10am-9.30pm and Saturday, 10am-midnight.

Postmuseum
36 Stephansplatz 1-5
Open: Tuesday to Friday 10am-2pm, Thursday, 10am-4pm.

Tourist Offices

Ahrensburg
Ahrensburger Fremden- und
Verkehrsverein
Rathaus
2070 Ahrensburg
☎ 2070

Bad Segeberg
Tourist-Information
Oldesloer Strasse 20
2360 Bad Segeberg
☎ (0 45 51) 57-2 33

Hamburg and Schleswig-Holstein
Fremdenverkehrszentrale Hamburg
1 Bieberhaus am Hauptbahnhof
Hamburg
☎ 248700

Kiel
Verkehrsverein der Landeshaupt-stadt
Kiel
Auguste-Viktoria-Strasse 16
2300 Kiel 1
☎ (04 31) 6 22 30

Lübeck
Touristbüro des Lübecker
Verkehrsvereins
Am Markt
Lübeck
Schleswig-Holstein
☎ (04 51) 72300

Neumünster
Verkehrspavillon Grossflecken
2350 Neumünster
☎ (0 43 21) 4 32 80

Plön
Kurverwaltung
Schwentinehaus
Am Lübschen Tor 1
2320 Plön
☎ (0 45 22) 27 17

Preetz
Fremdenverkehrsverein
Mühlenstrasse 14
2308 Preetz
☎ (0 43 42) 22 07

Ratzeburg
Amt für Fremdenverkehr und Kultur
Am Markt 9
Alte Wache
2418 Ratzeburg
☎ (0 45 41) 80 00 81

Trittau
Gemeinde Trittau
Europaplatz 5
2077 Trittau
☎ (0 41 54) 20 61

Weissenhaüser Strand
Kurverwaltung
Seestrasse
2440 Weissenhaüser Strand
☎ (0 43 61) 49 07 31

2 • The East Friesland Islands

This group of islands lying off the coast of north Germany, to the west of Denmark, was immortalised for many English readers by a book called *The Riddle of the Sands* by an Anglo-Irish writer, Erskine Childers, published in 1903. It is a classic sea story, with a spying background, describing how a pair of English yachtsmen, sailing a boat for pleasure in these waters, discovered preparations for the invasion of England by flat-bottomed troop-carrying barges to be concealed under cover on these islands until the time for invasion came.

Whether such a plan was militarily feasible in the Kaiser's Germany of 1903 is doubtful; it was certainly not considered in the vastly different conditions of Hitler's Germany in 1940. But the attraction of the book, which still exercises a powerful appeal on many readers, lies in its description of the islands, of the seas round them, and of the maze of sandbanks and mudbanks that lie between them and the coast.

These islands are known to discriminating Germans, who appreciate their remoteness from the busy mainland, their quietness (motor cars in general are forbidden), the invigoration of the air which is recommended for sufferers from coughs and catarrh, and their natural beauty. But to English speaking visitors they are indeed, off the beaten track.

These are, of course, not places to go to if one's wish is to lie in Mediterranean heat on a sun-baked beach with a thousand others turning their white skins pink. But if there is a feeling for subtler pleasures where the sea meets the sky a great discovery can be made here. There are indeed many visitors during the high summer, but other seasons can offer their own special qualities when the place is much less crowded.

Why should the English, who have their own North Sea coast, bother to visit the North Sea coast of Germany? It is probably because the conditions there are totally different. The English east coast has, indeed, its own charms, but it lies sheltered from the prevailing west

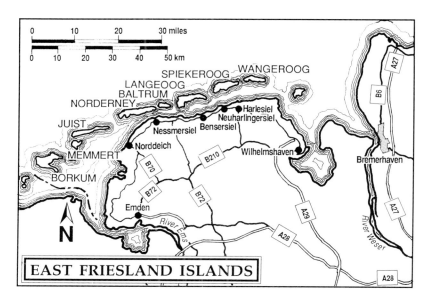

EAST FRIESLAND ISLANDS

winds. The German north-west coast has received the full force of the west winds for thousands of years, sweeping from the Atlantic up the Channel and piling the seas up on the stretch of coast between the mouths of the Ems and the Elbe. The land here has been ribboned and lacerated by gale and storm, leaving a line of what are really little more than sandbanks a few miles offshore which were rescued, by the fourteenth century, from the encroaching sea and have supported a cluster of houses and a church each ever since.

Between the islands and the mainland lies the area of part mud, part sand for which the German name is *Watt*. It is necessary to recognise this word if one is ever to go here and to give a general description of the area there is no better way than to quote the account in *The Riddle of the Sands*.:

> This singular region…is a low-lying country, containing great tracts of marsh and heath, and few towns of any size…. Seven islands lie off the coast. All, except Borkum, which is round, are attenuated strips, slightly crescent-shaped, rarely more than a mile broad, and tapering at the ends; in length averaging about 6 miles, from Norderney and Juist, which are seven and nine respectively, to little Baltrum, which is only two and a half. Of the shoal spaces which lie between them and the mainland, two-thirds dry at low-water, and the remaining third becomes a system of lagoons whose distribution is controlled by the natural drift of the North Sea as it forces its way through the intervals between the islands. Each of these intervals resembles the bar of a river, and is obstructed by dangerous banks over which the sea pours at every tide scooping out a deep

pool. This fans out and ramifies to east and west as the pent-up current frees itself, encircles the islands and spreads over the intervening flats. But the further it penetrates the less scouring force it has, and as a result no island is girt completely by a low-water channel. About midway at the back of each of them is a 'watershed', only covered for five or six hours out of the twelve.

Erskine Childers and his friend (for his book is clearly based on a personal visit) explored the *Watt* in a boat with a draught of 4ft (1.2m), and a centre board to let down in deeper water. They were regularly stranded on the sand at low tide, but they chose sheltered places and came to no harm. A special type of flat-bottomed fishing boat, known as an Ewer, has been developed for use in the *Watt*, which abounds in crustaceans and shell fish. There are channels between the sandbanks which are marked — not always very accurately — by lines of saplings as booms, indicating somewhat deeper water, but it will be obvious that this is no place for normal yachting. The *Watt* can be explored on foot at low tide and its fascinating animal and vegetable life studied. There are some marked routes from one island to another, but the visitor must take care. The sea comes in very quickly, and the tide has a rise and fall of some 9ft (3m). Visitors should never venture unaccompanied for any distance from land. There are organised walks, guided by experienced locals, which are strongly recommended. A good experience is to take a ride in one of the high-wheeled horse-drawn wagons which make trips across the sands at low tide. A tide calendar is an indispensable reference for every islander.

For the visitor who looks for activity, the attractions that the islands can offer may be summed up as bathing, sports, camping, fishing and birdwatching. Bathing can be enjoyed on many beaches on the seaward side of the islands. The Germans still like to talk, in a rather Victorian way, of the health-cure that sea bathing offers, and the earliest popularity of these islands for visitors was, indeed, as health-cure resorts in the nineteenth century. The air temperature averages 19°C (69°F) at mid-day in July and August, and the sea temperature is only a degree or so lower. Nudist and topless bathing has not yet made much headway in these areas, but there are beaches on Borkum and Norderney that are reserved for this purpose. Rather more care than usual should be taken when swimming in these waters in view of the tides and the deeply scoured nature of the sea bed. Warning signs are displayed on the beaches when weather conditions render bathing not recommended. There are several enclosed swimming baths, with warmed sea water and artificial waves, which are always open.

Sports that can be practised on the islands include sailing at all times on the seaward side of the coast and in the lee of the islands at high tide; horse-riding on the sand, gymnastics on the beach, tennis, table tennis, and windsurfing can all be pursued here.

Camping sites are provided on several islands and reservation is essential. However caravan trailers are generally not permitted. As always in Germany, camping outside designated sites is only allowed with the permission of the owner, and non-existent as far as these islands are concerned.

Fishing is good. Plaice, sole, turbot, mackerel, smelt and cod are caught in the North Sea; flat fish, crab, mussels, cockles, shrimps and prawns are found in the *Watt*. All these will be served, fresh from the sea, at tables in local restaurants. A famous delicacy is Heligoland lobster, from the island far out in the North Sea. Be warned that *Ostfrieslands Krabeen* in a local restaurant may not signify crabs but prawns — however none the less delicious for all that. The local name for crabs is *Granat*, which has led to the joke that this coast has been called the Costa Granata!

Substantial North Friesland dishes are *Eintopf aus Birnen, Bohnen und Speck* (hot-pot with pears, beans and bacon) and *Labskaus* (salt meat with herring and gherkins, served with fried egg). Beer is the local drink, often preceded by a *Schnaps* (strong liquor), and tea is drunk everywhere, usually with candy sugar and milk and sometimes with a spoonful of cream.

Birdwatching is the great speciality that these islands can offer. All the islands have bird sanctuaries and the whole area has been declared a National Park. Birds that may be seen include gulls of all kinds — black-headed, black-backed, herring, common, and occasionally the rare glaucous; terns and oyster catchers, sandpipers, plovers, pewits, moorhens, ducks and geese. When the colder weather begins great swarms of migratory birds settle on the *Watt* on their way from Scandinavia to warmer climes.

If a beginner would like to combine a little birdwatching with a foreign holiday, all that is needed is a pair of binoculars with 8x, 9x or 10x magnification, a pocket-sized guide to identifying birds (all the species that are seen on these islands are found in the British Isles as well) and some suitably drab weather-proof camouflage clothing. If you are an experienced birdwatcher you will know this already, but there is a book, *A Guide to Birdwatching in Europe* by J. Ferguson-Lees, which opens up the whole of the continent as an area for the observation of birds. Human intruders are, of course, barred from the bird sanctuaries, but tours of some of them are arranged. If you join one of these it is as well to remember that birds often use their droppings as bullets to deter invaders, and therefore a head covering and old clothes are recommended. It is not only birds that find sanctuary here. Seals, in particular, may be seen on a number of sandbanks. If a visitor encounters one he or she is asked not to try and touch or disturb it in any way.

But activities do not have to be pursued. It is enough merely to pace the dunes or sit in one of the basket chairs (a Korb) that are a feature of German beaches. You need to hire one for the length of your stay. There is a choice as to where it should be situated and it can be turned so that it acts as a shelter from the wind, or gives sun or shade. This is your private castle for as long as you desire.

All the islands are connected to the mainland by regular ship services, but the times of these are generally dependent on the tides. Motorists must usually leave their cars at car parks or garages at the ports of departure. There are air connections from the mainland to some of the islands, and light aircraft link all the islands (except Spiekeroog) together. Although some people may regret the noise of the aircraft, the view of the islands, from the air, lying between the sea and the *Watt* is a striking one.

The economy of the islands now depends mainly on their holiday visitors. The number of beds available for visitors is usually about double the number of permanent residents and every island has a choice of hotels. There is still a local community and the inhabitants are true Frieslanders — a race of quiet, self-reliant individuals whose motto indicates their character, 'God made the sea, the Frieslanders made the dykes'. They feel the influence of the sea in their bones, and according to local experience life comes and goes with the tides: babies are born as the tide comes in, and people die as it goes out.

The Islands

Visitors can travel to **Borkum** by car-ferry and ship from Emden. There is a limited access for cars on this island and a small airport provides a service for inter-island flights. One may be interested in visiting the dyke and aquarium museum of North Sea fish life, the Nordseeaquarium, and the Heimat Museum of local fishing and seafaring life, in the daytime; for evening entertainment there is a casino. For a totally relaxing holiday there are bathing beaches on the island and a nature reserve, the Landschaftsschutzgeheit Greune Stel.

No cars are permitted on the island of **Juist** but there is means of reaching it by ship from Norddeich; the island transport is by horse

The island of Norderney from the air. The harbour is nearest the camera with a deep-water channel dredged in the Watt

coaches. The coastal museum of marine biology, Küstenmuseum, is highly recommended, or one may wish to take a visit to Memmert, an uninhabited sandbank to the south-west which is the largest bird sanctuary in Germany, where thousands of herring-gull pairs breed. The unbroken sandy beaches stretch along the entire north side of Juist and the Hammersee is the only sweet-water lake to be found on the islands.

Norderney is the most developed of the islands but like Borkum has a very limited access for visitors' cars. There is a car-ferry from Norddeich and with the mainland, there is an airport which provides a link. Unusually for these islands, Norderney has a fair amount of deciduous and coniferous trees. This was a fashionable resort in the nineteenth century with many eminent visitors, including European royalty. Indeed, there is a variety of facilities to cater for the interests of the visitors: a fishing and local history museum, the Fischerhaus-Museum — the Kurtheater which stages varied performances throughout the year and golf courses which can be found on the dunes. For those wishing to relax under the sun there is a bathing beach. A bird sanctuary is here and also a camping site.

Baltrum, being the smallest of the islands, does not have much to offer although there is an airport and bathing beach. Ships provide a service from Nessmersiel and Norddeich. Yet again cars and bicycles are not permitted and so transport on the island is by horse coaches.

Probably one of the most eye catching features of **Langeoog** is its dunes, the highest of all the islands, which tower to a peak of 30ft (9m)! There is a small airport, bathing beach and bird sanctuary here, not forgetting a large yacht harbour. Cars are not permitted but there is a shipping service from Bensersiel.

Spiekeroog, known as the 'Green Island' because of its small clumps of trees, was a refuge for pirates in the fifteenth century. In the Napoleonic period a military garrison was based here which, in 1812, repulsed an attempted British landing. A bus service was established here in 1949 but horse coaches still run. No cars are allowed but bicycles have limited access. The Inselkirche is a good Renaissance building of 1696 with a model of the flagship of the Spanish Armada (wrecked here in 1588) hanging in the nave and a medieval *pieta* that came from this ship. A place of interest on the island is the local natural history museum, the Inselmuseum. There is a ship from Neuharlingersiel to Spiekeroog and half of the island is a nature reserve.

Wangerooge is a highly developed health resort complex. A ship from Harlesiel gives access to the island for no cars are allowed. There is a small airport, bathing beach, seabird sanctuary and camping site here.

The Mainland

Attractive though the islands are, the coast of the mainland behind them should not be neglected. A long line of dykes stretches a hundred yards or so in from the shore all along the coast. These are some 25ft (8m) high, with a path along the top which provides a splendid walk, far more extensive than can be obtained on any island. Below, on one side, lies the *Watt* with the islands in the distance. On the other side the fields are intersected with draining ditches, with perhaps a row of alders or poplars, brick farmhouses here and there, and maybe an old windmill. Some black and white cattle may graze in the fields perhaps, while covered with tarpaulins to protect them from the cool night air. The security offered by the dykes has only been preserved by constant care and repair: as recently as 1962 and 1976 severe storms have breached the dykes and let the sea in.

Striding along the top of the dyke one feels, indeed, on top of the world. Whether it is a summer day, with swallows diving over the hot sand; or a clear day in spring, when the wind shifts to the north-east and burns the skin; or an autumn evening with the mist rising in banks, making the farmsteads seem to float off the ground like boats on a rising tide; or even winter, with the ditches frozen over and a north-westerly wind howling at the farms, bending the trees over and whipping up the seas, so that you are hard put to it to keep your feet, there is something special about this coast.

The Riddle of the Sands is not the only book which may arouse interest in this area, for there is another more recent book which conveys the atmosphere equally vividly from the standpoint of the land rather than the sea. This is *The German Lesson* by the contemporary German novelist, Siegfried Lenz. The story deals with the harassment of a distinguished impressionist painter by the Nazis during the last year of the war, and the deliverance of the district by the British troops. But the great thing about this book is not so much the story but the way it evokes the landscape. The story is actually located in the North Friesland islands, which lie somewhat to the north of the East Friesland islands, on the west coast of the Schleswig-Holstein peninsula. There is no better way to create an impression of the feel of this area than by quoting a few passages. The book really should be read and is beautifully translated by Ernst Kaiser and Eithne Wilkins. The atmosphere of the *Watt* is well caught:

> There is the murky sadness of the flats, low clouds in the west, gusts of wind curling the water in the runnels and pools, and causing the sea-birds feathers to bristle; in the distance there is the faint hum of a lonely airplane…. In these flats, here in this expanse of mud-grey wilderness, hollowed and dotted by shallow puddles, here the emergence of life is supposed to have begun…. The rushing noise out there in the flats was the incoming tide. It came foaming shorewards, across the sand, filling up the runnels and moving in bubbling tongues across the flats, filling all the pools and water-holes, bringing with it grass and shells and bits of wood, covering up the traces that the sea-birds had left, and our own tracks. It came in northward right up the shore, quickly covering an expanse of grey clay…. Every flood-tide carried in some other booty. One cast up on the beach masses of roots washed bone-white by the sea, another one pieces of cork and a battered rabbit-hutch; lumps of seaweed, shells, and torn nets were lying about, and iodine-coloured plants that looked like grotesque trains torn off dresses.

Above all, it is the particular quality of the light that gives to these islands their unique character:

> It is always rewarding here in our countryside to watch somebody moving into the distance under our sky: one simply stands still of one's

own accord and turns all one's attention to the interplay of space and movement, and one always marvels at the oppressive dominance of the horizon.

Further Information

— The East Friesland Islands —

Places of Interest

Baltrum
Inselglocke
An ancient Dutch ship's clock washed ashore here and has been incorporated into the island's coat of arms.

Borkum
Alte Leuchtturm
Old lighthouse, 1576, 213ft (65m) high.

Neue Leuchtturm
New lighthouse, built 1879, commanding a good view.

Inselmuseum Dykhus
Collections on the island's history and local life, and the animal, bird and marine life of the region.

Nordseeaquarium
Displays of the under-water life of the North Sea.

Juist
Küstenmuseum
Collections on marine biology, the pre-history of the region, fishing and sea services, wrecks and lifeboat services, and the extraction of North Sea gas.

Naturschutzgebiet Bill mit Hammersee
A bird sanctuary adjoining the sweet-water lake.

Langeoog
Melkhorn-Düne
The highest point of the islands, offering a good view.

Norderney
Inselmühle
The only windmill on the islands, built 1862.

Leuchtturm
Lighthouse, 213ft (60m) high, with good view.

Fischerhaus-Museum
Collections on the life of the islanders, history of fishing, and development of seawater bathing as a medical cure.

Spiekeroog
Inselkirche
Dates from 1696.
Inselmuseum
In 'Haus Hero', with collections on the history of the island, animal and plant life, the development of shipping, fishing and bathing, as well as the sea rescue service.

Wangerooge
Inselmuseum
In old lighthouse, with collections on local life and shipping.

Neuer Leuchtturm
New lighthouse, built in 1933, with adjoining youth hostel.

Tourist Offices

Fremdverkehrsverband Nordsee-
    Niedersachsen-Bremen
Gottorpstrasse 18
Postfach 1820
2900 Oldenburg
☎ (0441) 1 45 35

Baltrum
Kurwaltung
2985 Baltrum
☎ 0 49 39/161

Borkum
Kurwaltung
Goethestrasse 1

Postfach 1680
2972 Borkum
☎ 0 49 22/303/1

Juist
Kurwaltung
Strandstrasse 5
2983 Juist
☎ 0 49 35/89 10

Langeoog
Kurwaltung
Hauptstrasse (Rathaus)
2941 Langeoog
☎ 0 49 72/555

Norderney
Kurwaltung
Postfach 240
2982 Norderney
☎ 0 49 32/89 10

Spiekeroog
Kurwaltung
2941 Spiekeroog
☎ 0 49 76/235

Wangerooge
Kurwaltung
2946 Wangerooge
☎ 044 69/411

3 • The Sauerland

A sk the average English-speaking person where he or she will find the Sauerland and you will probably be met with a blank stare. Yes, he or she has heard of the Black Forest and of Bavaria but the Sauerland, no. So where is it? Well, it is a marvellously picturesque area lying east of Cologne (Köln) and the industrial Ruhr in the Federal State of Nordrhein-Westfalen. In the rather flowery terms of the tourist organisations it is described as the Land of a Thousand Mountains and even though the visitor may be inclined to think of them as hills rather than mountains — the highest is just 2,765ft (843m) — this at least makes it clear that it is by no means a flat and uninteresting landscape. Little known to overseas visitors it may be, but it is a deservedly popular area with the Germans, especially those living in the Ruhr megalopolis who can reach it very quickly. The Dortmunder, for example, could be well into the Sauerland by car or train within half an hour. From further afield the Dutchman or Belgian can reach here in 3-4 hours driving time and this makes it evident that for the traveller from Britain there is no excessive journey to be faced once he or she has crossed the Channel or North Sea. The Dutch have made the Sauerland particularly their own and come here in vast numbers during the summer holiday period.

The international visitor arriving at Cologne or Frankfurt airports can be at his or her destination in $1^1/_2$-$2^1/_2$ hours by public transport or can, of course, hire a car and complete the journey at his or her own pace. For the rail traveller from Britain the overnight crossing from Harwich to the Hook of Holland is ideal and will enable the visitor to reach the Sauerland around mid-day or if preferred one can travel via Ostend to arrive at about the same time.

There are several theories as to the origin of the name Sauerland. Unlike Schwarzwald (Black Forest), there is no English version. Some people say that the name stems from the fact that Karl der Grosse (Charlemagne) conducted particularly 'sour' campaigns against the Saxon inhabitants. Be that as it may, there is certainly

The Holstentor Lübeck, is the most famous town gate in Germany and is depicted on the 50DM. banknote

The Glockenturm, Arnsberg, the Sauerland

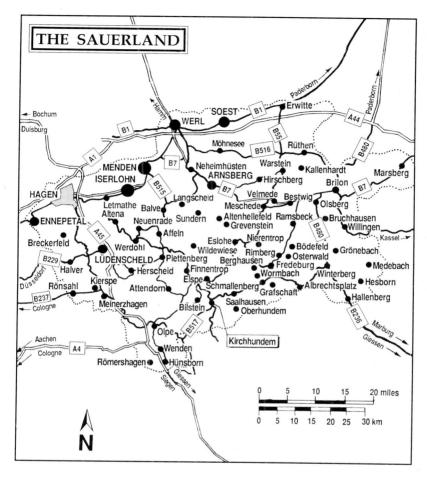

nothing sour about the welcome the visitor receives today. Because of its popularity with the locals and people 'in the know' there is an enormous amount and variety of holiday accommodation available. There are some well established and quite sophisticated resorts but in general it is a land of small towns and villages where farmhouse and self-catering holidays are widely available and offer excellent value for money.

There is no lack of opportunity for leisure activities either. The many lakes — they are mostly enormous reservoirs — dominate the landscape almost as much as the hills and water-orientated activities of every kind feature prominently in this area. It is possible to bathe either in the natural places or in the dozens of indoor and outdoor swimming pools. Sailing, windsurfing, boating and other activities can be enjoyed as well and in the summer there are steamer trips on a number of the lakes.

There are two German words which should be mastered. The first is *Talsperre* (*Tal* means valley, *Sperre* means barrier), the word for the mighty walls or dams which create the reservoirs. It is often combined with the name of the river which is dammed, thus Henne-talsperre, the dam across the valley of the river Henne. The word for reservoir is *Stausee* (*Stau* means dammed back water, *See* means lake); again it is often combined with the river name although the *Stau* bit is then often omitted, thus Möhne(stau)see, the lake created by the damming of the river Möhne. Incidentally, *Stau* is also the word used to describe a traffic jam on the *Autobahn* (motorway).

On land every other sporting activity is catered for with riding, cycling and tennis being especially favoured. There are many museums, caves, pleasure parks and theatres to be visited and the charming towns and villages with their black and white timbered houses will delight many a photographer. But it is for the simple pleasure of rambling in the countryside that many people come here and this activity is made all the more enjoyable by the many camp sites and youth hostels as well as plenty of simple bed and breakfast accommodation everywhere. The Sauerland visitor must not expect to find mighty cathedrals like those in Cologne or Freiburg, the towering Alps (although there is plenty of snow in winter), the fantastic palaces of King Ludwig II or the vineyard slopes of the Rhine or Mosel. The pleasures of this area are all its own and perhaps all the more approachable through being on a more modest scale.

There is no major river or designated tourist road to provide a logical pattern of exploration and therefore it is helpful to imagine the country divided into segments like a clock face with the centre point near Grevenstein in the Homert Nature Park and tour the area in a clock-wise direction. Begin in the south-west, for this is where the visitor from abroad is very likely to enter the Sauerland. The *Autobahn* (A4) from the Cologne direction joins the north-south A45 at Olpe south junction and the first stop should be made in the nearby town of **Olpe**. With its outlying district around the Biggesee reservoir this *Kreisstadt* (administrative centre of the district) lies in charming surroundings of woodland and water in the Ebbegebirge Naturpark and is an ideal place for outdoor activities. There are around 155 miles (250km) of waymarked footpaths and a number of long-distance trails cross here. North of the town things are dominated by the Biggesee, Westphalia's biggest reservoir. There are five

The old town hall which now houses the local museum, Attendorn

recognised bathing beaches around the lake, rowing and sailing boats and pedalos to hire and also four steamers for lake cruises from Easter until the end of October. The visitor will find several open-air swimming pools (*Freibad*), and an indoor one (*Hallenbad*), with a giant chute in the town. Because there are well over eighty of them, not every public swimming pool in the Sauerland will be mentioned in the text but readers may be sure that they will never be far away from one. Here in Olpe there is a more than adequate selection of accommodation in hotels, inns (*Gasthöfe*) and pensions; there are numerous camp sites, a youth hostel in the part called Stade and also a hostel of the CVJM (equivalent to the YMCA). Olpe is certainly ideal for families; in 1986 in a national competition it achieved special mention for its welcome to family groups and the favourable offers made to them.

Imagining the clock-face in the segment between 25 and 20 minutes to the hour, continue in a north-easterly direction along the Biggesee and come, near the north end, to the little town of **Attendorn**. This is an old town of the Hanseatic League and a number of historic buildings remind one of its past. The old Rathaus now houses the district Heimatmuseum (museum devoted to local history, folklore, etc) and is the only secular Gothic building in southern Westphalia. The mighty Burg Schellenberg is open to the public and noted for its display of old weapons. The Catholic parish church (twelfth-fourteenth century) enjoys the honorary title of Sauerland Cathedral (*Dom*). The modern Civic Hall (*Stadthalle*) serves for exhibitions and conferences and the facilities available include a fully automatic bowling alley and a restaurant with wonderful views —

as well as excellent food, of course. The Attahöhle claim to be the biggest and most beautiful stalactite caves in Germany; certainly they are well worth a visit. As at Olpe, there is ample provision for leisure activities here and the accommodation available includes a youth hostel and camp sites. Accommodation prices generally appear to be very modest.

Continuing in the same direction reach, in another 5-6 miles (8-10km) the town of **Finnentrop**. Much of the population lives outside the town so it is by no means a big place. It lies between the Homert and Ebbegebirge Naturparks and its environs extend into both. In the summer months outdoor activities include sports and shooting contests and in the winter there is a varied programme of cultural events in the *Festhalle*. The indoor pool complex includes solarium, sauna and restaurant.

Administrative changes in recent years have created a situation in regard to addresses and locations which may well be confusing to the foreign visitor. Very large areas have been formed into a single unit and given a title such as Stadt Finnentrop, taking the name of the principle centre of population within the area. The areas are predominantly rural and the visitor arriving at Finnentrop for instance by train, may well be surprised to find that the 'Finnentrop' address for which he or she is aiming is 9-12 miles (15-20km) away. In some cases, take Lennestadt for example, there is no place or railway station with that name which makes the matter even more confusing. The situation applies to a greater or lesser degree throughout Germany but for some reason appears to be particularly evident in the Sauerland.

As in Finnentrop, there is a youth hostel in **Plettenberg** about 6 miles (10km) to the north-west. Otherwise accommodation in the latter place is on a rather more limited scale and the tourist without an advance booking might have to go a little afield at busy seasons. However, the area should certainly not be overlooked and there are a number of sights to interest the visitor. A significant church building is the Protestant Christuskirche (about 1200) and the Böhler Kapelle, a little chapel endowed in 1422 which is noted for its glass painting. The village church in the part called Ohle dates from around 1050-1100 and has some early wall paintings; the ruins of the castle complex Schwarzenberg (approximately 1301) justify a little time. There is a well marked network of paths and a popular walk is that to the viewpoint on the Hohe Molmert (1,882ft, 574m) a few kilometres to the west. About 6 miles (10km) in the opposite direction the 1,791ft (546m) high Schomberg also has fine views.

The former domain of the Counts of the Mark — Märkisches Sauerland — was at one time noted for its many narrow-gauge railways, some of them passenger-carrying lines and others purely for freight. The Märkische Museumseisenbahn (Museum Railway) was founded in 1982 by enthusiasts anxious to record the history of these little lines. They are gradually assembling a collection of locomotives and rolling stock, some of which runs on a $1^{1}/_{2}$ mile (2km) line at **Hüinghausen** between Plettenberg and Herscheid. The museum also has a workshop in the old boiler-house of Firma Graeka at **Eiringhausen** near Plettenberg. Due west of Finnentrop lies **Herscheid** at the foot of the highest point in the chain of the Ebbegebirge, the 2,175ft (663m) high Nordhelle. Several of the smaller lakes are within easy reach and there are many kilometres of footpaths providing rambling opportunities for every degree of effort. In winter the skiing area has facilities for beginners as well as for the more experienced skier. Before leaving this section, the town of **Meinerzhagen** deserves attention. It lies west of the A45 close to the western extremity of the Sauerland. The thick forests close to the town make it easy for the hiker to use this as a base and his or her walks could embrace visits to some of the smaller reservoirs. There is a Protestant church from the thirteenth century and Schloss Badinghausen which may be visited. In winter there are various theatrical productions and other entertainments; here close to the highest parts of the Ebbegebirge, there is ample opportunity for skiing although the activity is not highly organised. In and around the town there is a reasonable amount of accommodation including a youth hostel.

The most important town in the next segment of the clock-face is **Lüdenscheid**, one of the biggest Sauerland centres. It is the *Kreisstadt* of Märkisches Sauerland and lies on the forested ridge between the valleys of the rivers Lenne and Volme. It is not really the place to look for holiday accommodation, although there is a ninety-six-bed youth hostel here, but rather a place to be visited for shopping or sightseeing. There are frequent theatrical and musical productions, the latter no doubt influenced by the fact that there is a music school in the town. The Stadtmuseum is housed in a building of unusual style which was awarded the 'architectural prize for concrete' in 1983. The museum shows the history of the town and region and has an unusual collection of historic buttons. There is also a museum of fire-fighting with many interesting exhibits. The Bremecker Hammer is a museum of technological culture and the history of the iron industry. Schloss Neuenhof, 2 miles (3km) south of the town centre, is famed for its elaborate wrought-iron gateway. The present moated *Schloss* was built in 1643 and has not been altered since 1693. The Protestant parish church is a neo-classical hall building which replaced a twelfth-century basilica in 1826. The west tower is mainly Romanesque and the neo-classical pulpit-altar is worth seeing. There are two indoor pools in the town and an open-air *Wellenbad* (pool with artificial waves).

North-west of Lüdenscheid the little town of **Breckerfeld** has, in its Protestant parish church of St James (fourteenth century) an outstanding carved altar in oak depicting Mary, St James and St Christopher. The Catholic parish church dedicated to the same saint — confusing surely — is also worth seeing. Six miles (10km) south and close to the Sauerland border is **Halver,** a town which combines tourism and industry. It is surrounded by forests in which there are many waymarked paths but every kind of leisure activity can be indulged in here. There is a *Hallenbad* and a fine open-air pool while half a dozen man-made lakes are within each reach. A short distance to the south-east, is **Kierspe,** a health resort in the Ebbegebirge where the *Hallenbad* has a sauna and also medical baths. There are medieval churches in Kierspe and in nearby **Rönsahl.** In addition to the inevitable reservoirs there is the Wasserschloss Haus Rhade (a moated palace). Neither Halver nor Kierspe have very much holiday accommodation although there are a few *Ferienwohnungen* (holiday flats) mainly in the latter place. It has to be remembered that here in the west of the Sauerland, very close to the industrial Ruhr, these resorts probably cater more for day visitors than for long-stay guests.

East of Lüdenscheid and in this sector the neighbouring communities of **Werdohl** and **Neuenrade** can be considered. The former is mainly an industrial town in a charming setting and has the usual leisure facilities and a reasonable amount of accommodation. The Protestant Christuskirche (1868) and the Catholic St Michaelskirche (1901) are both built in neo-Gothic style and the latter has an old crucifixion group dating from the early sixteenth century. Neuenrade has more to offer the visitor but not a great deal of accommodation in the centre. Swimming instruction is available at the heated *Freibad* and there is also a *Hallenbad*. The surrounding woods have a nature trail and a keep fit circuit as well as many kilometres of marked paths and cross-country ski routes. There are many fine old trees in the town park including a reputedly 1,000-year-old *Lindenbaum* (lime tree).

The thirteenth-century village church in nearby **Affeln** contains a rare treasure in its colourful 'Antwerp' altarpiece. This was carved

Burg Altena

in Antwerp in 1525 and was intended for a church in Norway but the Reformation caused the cancellation of the order and the residents of Affeln were able to purchase this masterpiece at a bargain price.

Continuing the clock-wise circuit, come in 7 miles (12km) from Lüdenscheid to the old town of **Altena** straddling the river Lenne and a favourite excursion goal for the residents of the industrial areas to the west. The town is dominated by the romantic castle Burg Altena, the seat of the Counts of the Mark and now the home of the museum of that family. This is not the only museum here, however, for there is also the German Wire Museum to tell the history of that local industry with which is combined the Smithy Museum complete with the workplace of a medieval blacksmith. Burg Altena has another claim to fame for it was the first of the world's youth hostels and the complex includes a museum of youth hostelling and rambling. The old dormitories are of interest but today's hostellers are accommodated in a more modern building nearby. There is another youth hostel down in the town where the swimming pools and sporting facilities are to be found. There is a citizens' centre in Burg Holtzbrinck (seventeenth century) where concerts and theatrical productions take place. The town art gallery is in Haus-Köster-Emden at 93 Lennestrasse. In fairness it must be said that Altena itself is a rather scruffy industrial town with the wire works and other industries rather prominent along the valley road. There is, however, a pleasant pedestrian precinct.

The holiday area centred on **Balve** is about 10 miles (17km) east of Altena and lies in the picturesque and historically interesting Hönnetal between the Balver Forest and the Sorpesee, one of the large reservoirs which has steamer services between May and September. The caves near Balve have an area of 20,000ft² (2,000m²) and are quite spectacular. They are called *Kulturhöhle* which means that they are prehistoric dwelling places as distinct from *Tropfsteinhöhle* which are stalactite caves such as those near Attendorn. The caves now provide the venue for various events including an annual jazz festival in June and a shooting contest in August. In Balve the Romanesque parish church of St Blasius has a rather striking interior and there are parts dating from the end of the twelfth century with frescoes from about the middle of the thirteenth century. The Museum für Vor- und Frühgeschichte has minerals and fossils of great antiquity together with finds from some of the caves in the area. Schloss Wocklum is a nobleman's two-winged moated house from around 1700 south of which is the 1,259ft (384m) high Burgberg which has remains of old fortifications with walls, gateways and the graves of early occupants. At the foot of this hill the Luisenhütte is a foundry and mining museum. The rambling possibilities of the area are considerable and there are numerous places of interest — castles, caves, dams and so on — creating goals to aim for. Balve and its neighbouring villages have a fair amount of guest accommodation including a good proportion of *Ferienwohnungen*. The indoor pool is called the *Schwimmhalle* and includes a sauna.

The iron industry established in the Middle Ages is still important in the economy of **Iserlohn** but let it not be thought that this in any way detracts from the many attractions there are for the visitor. It is a favoured residential town and has a worthwhile amount of accommodation mainly in hotels and *Gasthöfe*. Sights of interest in the town include the late Gothic upper town church of St Marien (fourteenth century) which contains a carved altar (around 1400), probably Dutch and is an important work of the period; there is also the Protestant Pankratius Church, originally a Romanesque pillared basilica but altered in late Gothic style. Nearby a patrician house (1763) with external staircase has become the Haus der Heimat with administrative offices and the interesting Heimatmuseum.

Just to the west of the town towards Letmathe between the A46 and B7 are the extensive stalactite caves called the Dechenhöhle which are well worth a visit. Iserlohn is surrounded by forests and provides well for sporting and leisure activities. It would be an ideal centre for a weekend break.

Hagen is the Sauerland's biggest city. With its suburbs it covers a large area which is crossed by four rivers. The Lenne flows northwards along the east side of the city to add its waters to the Ruhr, a hitherto picturesque rural river which now continues westwards to give its name to Westphalia's huge industrial area. West of the city the Ennepe and Volme combine and after a short distance they too make their contribution to the Ruhr which, for practical purposes, forms the Sauerland boundary in this north-west corner. The visitor may be surprised to find that Hagen presents him or her with a townscape unusual in Germany for around the turn of the century this was a centre of early *Jugendstil*, largely due to the initiative and patronage of the industrialist Karl Ernst Osthaus.

Architects like Henry van der Velde and Peter Behrens and the painter Thorn Prikker lived and worked here and their thinking and artistic attitudes have had a marked influence. The *Hauptbahnhof* (main railway station) for example, has a monumental entrance hall with windows depicting *The Obeisance of the Crafts before the Artist*, Thorn Prikker's first work in glass. The Eduard Müller Crematorium is an important work by Behrens. The Hohenhof built by van der Velde after 1906 has been acquired by the town and restored to contain some of the surviving furnishings designed by the architect and contributions by other artists of the period including Matisse.

The oldest parts of Schloss Hohenlimburg date from 1230 but the palace has suffered many modifications over the centuries. The central feature is the inner courtyard which has a high wall with passages and turrets. The fine half-timbered oriel and wrought-iron fountain are attractive features. The Heimatmuseum is to be found here. The Karl-Ernst-Osthaus Museum has a collection of twentieth-century art. The entrance hall survives from van der Velde's interior. The Hagen Freilichtmuseum is an open-air museum tracing the history of technology and crafts, the working of metals, timber and paper with more than seventy early workshops and industrial plants. Various musical and other entertainments take place in the 'village' square of the museum, a visit to which can be recommended.

Needless to say, Hagen is not entirely composed of cultural attractions and leisure and sporting activities are not forgotten as is evidenced by the presence of four indoor and four heated outdoor swimming pools. The countryside with its forests, lakes and rivers is never far away. The railway enthusiast, finding him or herself in this area, could be forgiven for venturing a little over the Sauerland boundary to **Oberwengern** about 6 miles (10km) west of Hagen city centre to travel in the historic 'museum' train which runs west along a pleasant 13 miles (21km) stretch of line closely following the river Ruhr. The track is mostly a freight line of the Federal Railway (Deutsche Bundesbahn) and the train consists of carriages dating from 1893 onwards drawn by a historic diesel locomotive (1939), the precurser of the later successful series of locomotives of class V36. The locomotive and vehicles belong to the big railway museum in Bochum not far away.

Another interesting excursion would be that to **Wuppertal** (about 20 minutes by train from Hagen) where the unique *Schwebebahn* is an elevated railway with suspended cars which serves the commuters of the Wupper valley. For much of its route the railway straddles the river Wupper and although modern vehicles have now been provided, the system, with its eighteen stations, is essentially that which has been operating safely and efficiently for more than 60 years. In Wuppertal there is a tramway museum and also a museum of historic timepieces. Hagen claims to have beds for 1,000 visitors and there is a large youth hostel.

About 6 miles (10km) south-west of Hagen the town of **Ennepetal** in the valley of the river Ennepe has many attractions but will be mentioned here only for its remarkable caves, the *Kluterthöhle*. Although the caves are millions of years old, little is known of them before the sixteenth century. They comprise an imposing system of caverns and passageways of which nearly 4 miles (6km) are so far accessible. They are a wonderful natural monument but more surprising is that in the last few decades they have been found to have a climate which is very beneficial to sufferers from asthma and similar complaints and since they are officially recognised by the leading authorities as a place of medical treatment, certain areas have been set aside for sufferers.

North of Iserlohn the countryside is noticeably less hilly but still quite well wooded as far as **Menden** 7 miles (12km) away. There is a youth hostel here and ample opportunity for rambling in the surrounding countryside in which there are a number of places of interest. In adjoining **Lendringsen** there is a big leisure centre with a heated *Freibad* and other facilities. In Menden itself there is a *Hallenbad* and three more open-air pools. The huge hostelry on the Wilhelmshöhe has seats for some 1,000 guests. There are churches from the fourteenth and seventeenth centuries in the town where there is a religious procession on Good Friday. There is also a Whitsun church fair here as there is in many other places. There is a museum of natural history and one dealing with the local and cultural history of the area. The river Hönne flows northwards through the town, shortly to join the Ruhr. Cross that river to reach the town of Werl 11 miles (18km) to the north-west and nearly on the northern fringe of the Sauerland. The route is through fairly flat, mostly agricultural, land. **Werl**, although by no means a holiday resort, has quite a lot to interest the sightseer who may join the 250,000 visitors who come each year to the Franciscan pilgrimage church to see the thirteenth-century *Gnadenbild* (miraculous image) of the Madonna and Child, gilded and enthroned. The Kapuzinerkirche is an eighteenth-century pilgrimage church. The priory church of St Walburga is a Gothic hall church which incorporates the late Romanesque tower from an earlier building. The altars are well worth seeing and include a fifteenth-century canopied one in the south aisle and a side altar (dated around 1560) representing the life of Our Lady. The contents of the Heimatmuseum include references to salt mining and pilgrimages while the Missionsmuseum has collections from areas visited by Franciscan missionaries.

While here, at the northern limit of the Sauerland, it is an easy journey of a few minutes to visit Soest 9 miles (14km) to the east along *Bundesstrasse* (Federal road) B1 or along the parallel *Autobahn* 44. **Soest** has a rather fine medieval town centre and is another place in which the visitor could well spend some interesting hours. The old Rathaus (1713-18) is well worth seeing. Also not to be missed is the church of St Maria zur Wiese and the three lofty aisles which make it one of the most beautiful hall churches in Germany. The building is mainly from the fourteenth century; there are fine windows from the end of that period and amongst these is the curiosity of the *Westphalian Last Supper* in which Jesus and his disciples are depicted as in a Westphalian tavern partaking of a meal with boar's head, ham and beer. The Madonna of Werl was once in this church. Parts of its Romanesque predecessor are incorporated in the church of Maria zur Höhe (around 1225) which is noted for its particularly fine wall paintings. Wall paintings are also a feature of the Protestant parish church of St Peter (twelfth to thirteenth century) and of the twelfth-century Nikolaikapelle. The cathedral is the collegiate church of St Patroklus: the present building corresponds in all essentials to the twelfth-century original, the opportunity having been taken to remove certain later disfiguring alterations in the course of repairs to damage sustained in World War II. The massive tower is considered to be the finest Romanesque tower in Germany. Nearly all the Romanesque wall paintings were destroyed in the war as was most of the original glass. The most important feature of the furnishings is the tall 7ft (2m) tall triumphal cross.

The old ring wall is largely intact and the massive Osterhofentor houses one of several museums concerned with local history and culture. The biggest inner town fair in West Germany takes place in the shadow of the cathedral from the first Wednesday in November after Allerheiligen (All Saints Day) until the following Sunday and this is followed in December by the annual Christmas fair. About another 10 miles (16km) eastwards along the B1 is **Erwitte** an un-spoiled little town where a royal court was established by Heinrich I in 935. However the long two-storey moated *Burg* was only built in the seventeenth century; it was re-built in 1934 and is now owned by the town.

Also worth seeing are the sixteenth to eighteenth-century half-timbered houses around the Marktplatz, the former Rathaus (1716) and the former residence (1716) of the Droste family, which became the Marienhospital in 1859. The imposing thirteenth-century tower of St Laurentius' Catholic parish church vies in its impressiveness with that of St Patroklus in Soest while the interior decoration in-cludes nine near life-size wooden apostles (1763), the *Madonna of the Seven Swords* and a thirteenth-century wooden crucifix.

Only about 5½ miles (9km) south of Soest along the B229 the community of **Möhnesee** is made up of fifteen little villages. The name is taken from that of the major man-made lake of 4sq miles (10km²) created by the damming of the river Möhne. This was the scene of the successful but costly war-time air attack by the British 'dam-busters' of 617 Squadron, RAF. Several other reservoirs in the Sauerland were also subjected to similar raids but it is the Möhne episode which has been most publicised in war stories and films. The raid resulted in the death of nearly 1,300 people, many of them foreign workers pressed into the service of German industry. All this is now part of local history and the souvenir kiosks at the lakes have books telling the stories of the raids and postcards with graphic pictures of the breached dams based on official photographs taken at the time. Today the Möhnesee is at the heart of one of the most popular outdoor holiday areas in Westphalia, the accent being on water-based activities of course. Steamers ply from April until Octo-ber and there are many rowing and sailing boats for hire. There is a 220 bed youth hostel and many camp sites and car parks ring the water. There is a lot of holiday accommodation here including a high proportion of *Ferienwohnungen*.

The parish church in **Körbecke**, the biggest village in the group, has fine baroque furnishings while the Heilig-Geist-Kapelle (chapel of the Holy Ghost, dated around 1140) in **Druggelte** is a small,

Möhnesee from the dam wall

vaulted, twelve-sided rotunda with lavish architectural ornamentation. Körbecke has a museum with a permanent exhibition of the works of local artists.

Here, in the Arnsberg Forest Nature Park, the B229 continues for 6 miles (10km) or so beyond the Möhne to **Arnsberg**. A great loop of the river Ruhr encloses much of the town including the charming old part with its many splendid timbered buildings and ruined *Schloss*. Do not miss the historic Maximiliansbrunnen (a fountain) of 1779. Only the priory church of St Laurentius remains of the Premonstratensian abbey of Wedinghausen which was founded here in 1173 and dissolved in 1803. The tower area is from the twelfth century, the early Gothic choir was consecrated in 1253 and building continued into the sixteenth century to create the church seen today. Of interest within are the early baroque high altar in marble and alabaster, the tomb of Friedrich von Fürstenberg (around 1680), the double high tomb of Count Heinrich and his wife Ermengard (fourteenth century), the pulpit and the pews (around 1740).

Near the priory church is the Hirschberg Gate of 1753 while the Altes Rathaus (1710) is also worthy of inspection. The imposing Glockenturm (Bell Tower), an old gateway, dominates this upper end of the old town and in its shadow the Stadtkapelle justifies a few minutes of the visitor's time. The Landberger Hof (1605) now houses the Sauerlandmuseum. Arnsberg is a very good shopping centre;

Historic iron postbox near the Glockenturm, Arnsberg

there is plenty of accommodation of all types and prices are fairly modest considering the popularity of the area.

About 3 miles (5km) north-west of Arnsberg at **Hüsten** is the Deutsches Vogelbauermuseum (Birdcage Museum) which traces the history of the keeping of birds as pets over the last five centuries; not only birdcages but paintings, etchings and literature. In addition to the comprehensive facilities at Arnsberg, the town of **Neheim-Hüsten** has its own attractions including a rather rare nine hole golf course. The Wasserschloss of Herdringen is considered to be the most significant neo-Gothic palace in Westphalia.

Six miles (10km) south-west of Arnsberg the eastern side of the Sorpesee mentioned earlier is reached. The central resort here is **Sundern** in the Röhrtal and it is surrounded by a host of large and small villages in a fine holiday area. Much of the community is within the Homert Nature Park, a wonderfully picturesque country-side with a wealth of facilities. Each village has its own particular attractions. For example, **Langscheid** is a *Luftkurort*, that is to say it is a health resort where the air (*Luft*) is considered to be especially beneficial; **Wildewiese** is noted for its winter sports activity with eight ski-tows and a floodlit slope; there are indoor pools in Sundern, Hagen (not to be confused with the city already described) and Langscheid, the latter having a sauna and massage facilities; Sundern has a tennis hall and there are courts in a number of other places.

To the east and south-east there is an area of great tranquility with the remarkable name of Altes Testament (Old Testament) which comprises the villages of **Hellefeld**, **Altenhellefeld** and **Grevenstein** right at the centre of the imaginary clock-face. There is quite a lot of farmhouse and self-catering accommodation here as well as more formal quarters in hotels and *Gasthöfe*. Well-tended parks and gardens provide for the visitor who does not wish to indulge in the more strenuous rambling along the many waymarked paths in the neighbourhood. This is a place for a pleasant stay at any time and all leisure activities are catered for according to season. There is a ski-tow for winter visitors.

To the north-east the old town of **Meschede** is another which is at the centre of a group of holiday resorts in an extremely popular location in the heart of the Sauerland. There is an enormous choice of accommodation scattered over a large area. Meschede itself is on the river Ruhr between the Homert and Arnsberg Forest Nature Parks. A fine example of modern church architecture is the church of the Königsmünster Abbey just north of the town centre. The monks are responsible for a large *Gymnasium* (grammar school) which provides a fine education for pupils of all denominations. South of the town the landscape and activity is dominated by the Henne-talsperre with its large man-made lake on which there are cruises from April to October. Rowing boats and pedalos can be hired and there is a windsurfing school. There is a camp site close to the lake and the bungalow village 'Hennesee' has twenty houses available for short-term letting. There is also a large youth hostel.

North of Meschede a picturesque secondary road leads to **Hirschberg** about 6 miles (9km) away. The Catholic church here has an altar worth stopping to see. Two miles (3km) from the village there is a forest nature trail and a woodland play area, together with a keep fit circuit. The forests around Hirschberg are particularly well provided with car parks making it very easy to get access to the splendid network of footpaths. At Hirschberg a visit can be made to the caves, the Bilsteinhöhle, which are in a *Wildgehege* (a forest enclosure for red deer, wild boars and other animals). The town of **Warstein** 3 miles (5km) east of Hirschberg is surrounded by forests with well-marked footpaths and provision is made for skiing in winter. There is a *Hallenbad* and a heated *Freibad* to serve the many visitors to this centre which is well provided with accommodation including a lot for self-caterers and prices are generally moderate.

The town museum of Warstein in Haus Kupferhammer is by no means the conventional small town collection of local relics. The house was the home of one Wilhelm Bergenthal (1805-93), the indus-trialist who was primarily responsible for the growth of the metal-working industry in Warstein and many other neighbouring places. The house was part of the Kupferhammer (copper works or foundry) property from which it derived its name. Bergenthal was a privy

Rüthen town hall

councillor with diverse industrial interests and he also sought the furtherance of agriculture and the public well-being in general. The competition from the rapidly growing Ruhr industrial area soon resulted in a decline in Warstein.

After his death, Bergenthal's grandson — also Wilhelm — took over the dwindling undertaking and this, and the family itself, finally died out with the death of his wife Ottilie in 1951. She had arranged that her home and the surrounding park should fall to the town to be used as a museum and cultural centre. It tells not only of the history of the family and the industry but also has many works of art including the so-called *Muttergottes von Warstein*, a sandstone Gothic madonna from the fourteenth century. From time to time concerts take place in the museum.

Still in the Arnsberg Forest Nature Park **Kallenhardt**, 3 miles (5km) east of Warstein, has a fifteenth-century Rathaus, a baroque style church from 1722, the Wasserschloss Körtlinghausen and caves called the Hohler Stein a little way to the south. Here too, there is no shortage of parking places in the forest. A picturesque but somewhat twisty road goes 4 miles (6km) northwards to **Rüthen** just outside the Arnsberg forest and close to the north-eastern boundary of the Sauerland. With its many outlying villages Rüthen is a scattered community. The town itself is a rather charming old place with ancient fortifications including the town wall which is a mile (2km) long. There is a baroque town hall with a splendid external double staircase, a number of timbered buildings and two churches worthy of inspection. The leisure area Bibertal has ample parking, a nature trail, play areas, minigolf, a heated outdoor pool and a youth hostel.

Eastwards from Meschede on the B7, upstream along the river Ruhr in about 6 miles (10km), is the resort of Bestwig, but a stop should be made on the way to see the church and the little timbered Rathaus in Eversberg. **Bestwig,** and the numerous villages which contribute to its population, lies in the *Feriengebiet* (holiday area) Ruhr-Valme-Elpetal and offers its guests a wide variety of activities and interests. In addition to all the more usual attractions there are organised rambling events and tours on horse-back to local beauty spots. Accommodation is mainly in the *Gasthof* and pension categories with an ample selection of self-catering houses and flats, some of them on farms. Three or four miles (5 or 6km) to the south the Erzbergbau-Museum (Mining Museum) at **Ramsbeck** is well worth a visit but do not economise by paying only to visit the museum; make sure that the visit includes a tour of the vast underground workings. The visitor will be asked to don protective overalls and a 'hard hat' and will then take his or her seat in the diminutive carriages of the train which used to convey the miners to the workings to labour at the extraction of zinc, silver and lead, a journey of about 12 minutes in almost total darkness. In the heart of the mountain the visitor is taken on a comprehensive tour of the installations which were in production until just a few years ago. Inside the mine the visitor is actually far beneath one of the many family leisure parks which have sprung up in recent years. This one is called Fort Fun Abenteurland (Adventure Land) and it has the almost obligatory 'Western' town and modern mechanical contrivances galore as well as a genuine old roundabout. The giant *Rutschbahn* (chute or summer bob-run) is 2,493ft (760m) long and a favourite pastime for all age groups. From April until October the replica of a 'Wild West' railway is in operation.

Back in the Ruhr valley, leave Bestwig on the B7 but soon turn off to visit **Olsberg**, the principal resort in a scattered community located in an area of great charm. Olsberg is a year-round *Kneippkurort*, that is to say, it is a health resort at which treatment is available in accordance with the principles of the famous Sebastian Kneipp. Of course, a health problem is not necessary for enjoyment of the many splendid facilities. There are indoor and outdoor pools — as well as special bathing facilities for those taking the *Kur* — and a concert hall.

In the summer months, concerts also take place in the *Kurpark*. Some 186 miles (300km) of waymarked paths are accessible. Schloss Gevelinghausen is now a fifty-bed hotel and restaurant. To the south of the town, **Assingshausen** (4 miles, 6km) has the interesting ancient granary, the Riesenspeicher (1556), another timbered building to delight the photographer. Almost adjoining to the east is **Bruchhausen**, famous for its rocky out-crops called the Bruchhauser Steine on the Istenberg, reminding one slightly of the 'tors' on England's Dartmoor. Bruchhausen also claims the distinction of being an access point to the (2,765ft, 843m) Langenberg, the highest point in the Sauerland. This is a favourite winter sports area and there is a camp site which is open all year round.

Back on the B7, **Brilon** is by far the biggest place in the extensive group of habitations of which it is the centre. Of interest in the town are the sixteenth-century *Marktbrunnen* (fountain) and the baroque façade of the Rathaus. The unusual turreted tower of the Propsteikirche St Peter and Andrew dominates the skyline behind the Rathaus. The church has some fine stained glass windows. Brilon is a very lively *Luftkurort* with every amenity one could wish for. Those who are here for health reasons can enjoy modest exercise on 31 miles (50km) of easy footpaths but another 279 miles (450km) of waymarked paths provides for those desiring more ambitious activity. There is winter as well as summer recreation here with provision for floodlit skiing. There is a large youth hostel and the extensive catalogue of accommodation would make it appear unlikely that any person wishing to stay here would be disappointed. There is, however, a very heavy demand in the summer holiday months and again during the winter sports season so advance booking at those times is strongly recommended.

Space considerations preclude mention of the many more delightful little places along the final 17 miles (27km) of the B7 into **Marsberg** almost at the eastern extremity of the Sauerland in a sort of peninsular that sticks out rather like the head of a tortoise from the main body. The town actually comprises Niedermarsberg and Obermarsberg, both of which claim the title *Ferienort* — holiday place. The former lies in the valley of the river Diemel and is the 'modern' town with swimming pools, a sports hall, a riverside promenade, a music pavilion, the Heimatmuseum and so on. Obermarsberg is a historic town, once the Saxon fortress of Eresburg which was overthrown by Karl der Grosse in 772. The collegiate church of St Peter and St Paul was completed about 1410 on the remains of a thirteenth-century church which had been destroyed by lightning and fire. The crypt beneath the chancel with its dominant octagonal middle pillar is of special interest. Interior decoration and the organ are baroque, an unusual feature in this region. The small

Nicolai Chapel is first mentioned in the records in 1247 and is one of the most significant and charming early Gothic buildings in Westphalia. Inside there are tall round pillars topped by early Gothic leafwork capitals. Particularly to be noted are the surviving old windows and the Romanesque south portal.

Other things of interest in this part of the town are the Roland Column (1737), an old gateway and the Benediktusbogen with two towers and a sixteenth-century pillory. There are conducted tours round the old town: details from the information office at Bülberg 2. The Diemelsee about $7\frac{1}{2}$ miles (12km) to the south-west is another man-made lake which is popular with anglers as is the river Diemel itself. Trout and pike are amongst the fish to be caught here: information and fishing permits can be obtained from the *Verkehrsbüro*.

If there is a need for a place to go on a wet day, note should be taken of the proximity of the city of **Kassel** to this end of the Sauerland. From Marsberg the B7 goes right into Kassel but by using the A44 the motorist could reach the city in about 30 minutes. It is a fine place and there are many sights of interest: museums include that devoted to the Grimm Brothers and one with the theme of wallpaper. There are many notable churches and other buildings to see and the railway enthusiast might enjoy a historic steam train trip between Kassel and Naumburg ($20\frac{1}{2}$ miles, 33km) in the Hessen Courier.

However, back to the Sauerland where the south-eastern corner will now be explored. If elsewhere the areas have been dominated by the lakes and their associated water activities, here the accent is on the mountains and, in particular, on their influence upon the winter sports scene. Indeed, in many of the resorts in this area, it is the winter which is the peak season with summer coming only a close second. There are, of course, the indigenous agricultural and forestry activities, but this is an area given over almost exclusively to the needs of those who come for relaxation in the beautiful countryside.

Willingen is a health resort with *Kneipp* — a type of treatment using the properties of water — and other facilities and is a winter sports centre. The climate is considered beneficial for sufferers of heart and circulatory conditions or with breathing and nervous disorders. For those unable to do more there are many level footpaths but the more active visitors are not forgotten with many high-level paths, indoor and outdoor tennis courts, an ice rink, riding stables and so on. There is a Wald- und Heimatmuseum and there are conducted tours of the Christine slate quarries. A vast amount of accommodation of all kinds is provided and no less than sixteen of the hotels have their own indoor pools. Visitors will always find a public swimming pool within easy distance, especially in the summer when the open-air facilities are available.

Medebach, right on this south-eastern fringe of the Sauerland, is yet another of those places encircled by its satellite villages, most of them very small. One of the latter, **Küstelberg**, has been a winner in the Federal Republic's 'Beautiful Village' competition many times. The re-furbished church has a huge, modern stained glass window and outside a spring marks the Sauerland watershed. From here the streams flowing westwards eventually contribute to the river Rhine while those heading east find their way to the Weser. Everywhere are marked paths, those near the villages being generously provided with seats. Here too, the rambler will frequently come across that peculiarly German installation, the *Tretbecken*. There is no English word equivalent but this is a shallow basin or pool, usually fed by a natural stream, in which the passer-by may paddle to cool his or her feet. It is ideal after a warm and strenuous ramble although it often appears that the *Tretbecken* are even more popular with elderly ladies here for their health — indeed, some places claim that theirs are *Kneipp Tretbecken*, the worthy Sebastian having been convinced of the therapeutic qualities of water.

Nine miles (14km) west of Medebach **Winterberg** is at the centre of the biggest group of village resorts in the whole Sauerland. It is a health resort at the foot of the 2,758ft (841m) Kahler Asten and claims to be the highest 'town' in West Germany. In fairness it must be noted that the same claim is made by several other places including Oberstdorf in Bavaria which, at 2,765ft (843m), lies higher than the summit of the Kahler Asten! It is entirely appropriate that the name of Winterberg should be primarily associated with winter sports but it is a delightful place at any time of year. In common with most Sauerland resorts there is no defined 'high season' here although there are acute peaks of activity in winter when skiing conditions are good and during the summer school holidays.

At all seasons the splendid vantage point of the Kahler Asten is a great attraction and another easy excursion is that to the source of the river Ruhr a few kilometres north of the town. Here, as elsewhere in the area, efforts are made to keep tracks clear for cross-country skiers and winter walkers.

The B236 runs south-east from Winterberg to **Hallenberg**, a distance of 9 miles (14km). From June to September the open-air theatre here is a great attraction with productions for children and adults. The picturesque old centre of Hallenberg is one of those places really worth visiting with its part-slated, timbered houses and

Oberkirchen

the fountain of 1756 in the market place. A pilgrimage chapel dates from the eleventh century and the parish church of St Heribert from the seventeenth century; both of them justify a visit as does the church in the village of **Hesborn** about 4 miles (6km) to the north which has altars from the former Kloster Glindfeld (a monastery). The church tower was built in 1127. Just to the west of Hesborn the 2,486ft (758m) Bollerberg has a tower which commands an extensive view of the countryside.

In a westerly direction from Winterberg, the B236 passes through a number of charming villages; Langwiese, Hoheleye, Albrechtsplatz (watch out for signs to the *Wildgehege*) and Ober-kirchen on the little river Lenne. **Oberkirchen** is another previous winner of the 'Beautiful Village' competition. A little road to the south leads to **Grafschaft** (1 mile, 2km) where the former monastery is an extensive baroque complex (1729), now a hospital run by the nuns of the Benedictine Order. The small and mostly modern church of St George is attractive. Since Medebach the territory explored has been in the Rothaargebirge Nature Park which extends over the Sauerland boundary to cover a large part of the neighbouring Sieg-erland. The walker will find many historic remains in this old south-ern frontier land of the Saxons.

The B236 follows the Lenne to **Schmallenberg**, a bigger place than most in this area. It is a *Luftkurort* and unashamedly does all it can to provide every amenity and attraction for its many visitors. The large swimming pool complex includes a *Wellenbad*, sauna, sunbathing terrace, restaurant and café. The enormous network of footpaths radiating from the town make it easy to ascend to the viewing tower on the top of the Wilzenberg (2,158ft, 658m) or to several other worthwhile hilltops to survey the countryside below.

Neighbouring **Fredeburg** is a *Kneippkurort* and apart from the special facilities available to those taking the *Kur* it has a huge range of activity possibilities for the general holidaymaker. Some of the *Tretbecken* in the forest have an additional basin in which the arms may be cooled as well as the feet! There is a roller-skating rink, several bowling alleys, and adventure playgrounds, while concerts and folk evenings are regular events. In winter there are all types of skiing and instruction for those, including children, who still have to learn.

Visitors to Schmallenberg and Fredeburg should not fail to visit the little churches in nearby Berghausen and Wormbach. St Cyriacus in **Berghausen** is a Romanesque building from the end of the twelfth century. The date 1861 on the tower relates to major repairs carried out in that year. The church is notable for its fine ceiling and wall paintings dating from the early thirteenth century. These were cleaned and restored during renovations in 1961 when intruding baroque embellishments were removed, better to reveal the paintings. The old high altar completely concealed the marvellous paintings in the apse and was given to the church in Schönholthausen while two side altars were presented to the Jesuit church in Paderborn. A mile away (2km), the Romanesque church in **Wormbach** is considered to be the oldest church in the Sauerland. As was formerly the case in Berghausen, the baroque high altar conceals whatever may be of interest in the apse. The Wormbach organ recitals are a regular feature of the summer programme in this area. Four miles (6km) north-west of Fredeburg the tiny village of **Nierentrop** is of interest for its old rural bakehouse, disused now but still in good condition at the time of writing. There are numerous skiing possibilities at **Rimberg, Osterwald** and **Bödefeld** all of which lie to the north of Fredeburg and can be reached in a few minutes by car.

North-west in this segment is **Eslohe**, a *Luftkurort* in the Homert Nature Park with the holiday resort of **Reiste** within its orbit. This is a good central place with ready access to fine forest landscapes and to several lakes including the Sorpetalsperre and the Hennetalsperre already mentioned.

Lennestadt, taking the name from its river, is an administrative unit rather than a town in its own right. It was created in 1969 by the combination of eight closely related communities and, of course, a number of small villages. Of these constituent parts, **Saalhausen** to the east is a *Luftkurort,* Elspe to the north has a history going back more than a thousand years and **Bilstein** to the west stands at the foot of the historic *Burg* of the same name. The castle is now a youth hostel but is open to visitors. At **Oberhundem,** to the south-east, is another modern leisure complex, the Panorama Park Sauerland. There are mechanical amusements and extensive areas of fine countryside with enclosures for bison, deer, wild boar, elk and other animals. There is the inevitable 'Wild West' stockade, unusual power-driven bumper boats and a very long dry bob-run.

A rather different entertainment is provided by the Karl-May-Festival at **Elspe**. Here stories by the famous 'Western' writer are brought vividly to life. Almost daily from mid-June until September the battles between Red Indians and white men are re-enacted.

The visitor may bypass Olpe if this town has been visited earlier and complete his or her tour in the southernmost tip of the Sauerland at **Wenden**, a place of some interest and a peacefully situated holiday centre with surrounding villages. In Wenden the church of St Severinus should be inspected and the pilgrimage chapel in **Dörnschlade** is also worth a visit. Industrial archaeology in unusual form is to be found at the Wendenerhütte, the old iron-smelting furnace from 1728 which was fired by wood. In the village of **Römershagen** there is the source of the river Bigge which flows northwards to feed the huge reservoir which takes its name.

Sauerland is not a land with a large number of cultural monuments; there is nothing here to compare with the extravagent baroque churches of Bavaria but, all the same, a number of churches and chapels justify a visit if one is nearby. There is a certain amount of industrial archaeology but the outstanding civil engineering of the great reservoirs is likely to be of more interest to most of today's visitors, not only for the technical achievement but for the recreational facilities which these man-made lakes provide.

Natural attractions abound in the many caves, rivers, mountains and valleys. Lovers of outdoor life will certainly find plenty to occupy themselves. Visitors with young families will praise the leisure facilities, the swimming pools, the animal enclosures, the pleasure centres and so on.

Visitors are recommended to arm themselves with the special map of the area, the 'Aral' *Tourenkarte Sauerland-Bergisches Land* (1:200,000), obtainable from Aral filling stations. Not only is it detailed but on the reverse is a comprehensive summary of places of interest.

Further Information
— The Sauerland —

Boating and Sailing

At many of the large artificial lakes boats or windsurfing equipment may be hired. The principal locations are Biggesee, Diemelsee, Harkortsee (Hagen) — May to mid-October; Hengsteysee (Hagen) — Easter to mid-October; Hennesee, Listersee (Meinerzhagen), Möhnesee, Seilersee (Iserlohn) and Sorpesee.

There are pleasure cruises on: Biggesee — Easter until end October; Diemelsee — May to end October for groups of ten or more; Harkortsee (Hagen) — Easter to September; Hengsteysee (Hagen) — April to September; Hennesee — April to October; Möhnesee — April to October; Sorpesee — May to September. Outside the main holiday season sailings may be suspended during poor weather.

Caves

There are a number of caves that may be visited — but not for potholing. The principal ones open to the public are listed below.

Attendorn
Attahöhle
Finnentroper Strasse
☎ (02722) 3041
Open: summer 9am-5pm, winter 10am-4pm.

Balve
Balver Höhle
☎ (02375) 6380 or 2269
Open: April to October, Tuesday to Thursday 10am-4pm, Saturday 10am-3pm, Sunday 11am-4pm.

Balve-Volkringhausen
Reckenhöhle
☎ (02379) 209
Open: March to November, daily 9am-4pm.

Ennepetal
Klüterthöhle
Höhlenstrasse 20
☎ (023331) 7865
Open: all year.
Recognised cure establishment for asthma sufferers etc.

Iserlohn-Letmathe
Dechenhöhle
☎ (02374) 71421
Open: April to October, 9am-5pm, November to March, 10am-4pm.
DB station Dechenhöhle. Restaurant.

Warstein
Bilsteinhöhle
☎ (02902) 2731
On the road to Hirschberg.
Open: daily April to November, 9am-5pm, December to March, weekdays 10am-12noon, 2-4pm, Sunday and holidays 9am-4pm.
In addition to the caves, free adventure playground and *Wildpark* with deer, wild boars, etc. Restaurant. Free parking.

Cycling and Cycle Hire

Addresses from local tourist information offices. Cycles may also be hired from the DB railway station in Willingen. Cyclists arriving by train pay only half the normal hire charge.

Museums and Other Places of Interest

The following list, arranged in alphabetical order by town, does not include museums with very limited or irregular opening hours.

Altena
Museum Grafschaft Mark, Märkisches Schmiedemuseum, Deutsches Drahtmuseum, Jugendherbergsmuseum, Wandermuseum

public but admission charge and also car parking charge. Access to 2,765ft (843m) Langenberg, the Sauerland's highest mountain.

Sports and Leisure Centres

Iserlohn
Eissporthalle Seilersee
Seeuferstrasse
Closed in July.
Skating rink, restaurant.

Lüdenscheid
Freizeitbad
Pool with waves, warm pools, sauna, solarium, keep fit room, bowling alleys, covered tennis and squash courts. Cafeteria.

Menden-Lendringsen
Freizeitzentrum Biebertal
Minigolf, go-carts, keep fit path, table tennis, roller-skating, children's play area, heated open-air pool. Café.

Willingen
Eissporthalle
☎ (05632) 6019
Closed May and June.
Ice rink. Café and restaurant.

Tenniscenter Hochsauerland in Hoppecketal
☎ (05632) 6666
Tennis hall and open-air courts, shop, restaurant.

Tennispark 'Der Sauerland Stern'
Kneippweg
☎ (05632) 69481
Tennis hall and open-air courts, three squash courts. Restaurant.

Winterberg
Eissporthalle
Ice rink. Space for 1200 spectators. Cafeteria.

Asten-Center
Im Mühlengrund 25
☎ (02981) 1634
Tennis hall, bowling alleys. Restaurant.

In addition to those mentioned above there are more than eighty public swimming pools, indoors and outdoors. Most of the latter are heated. Many hotels have their own *Hallenbad*, sometimes available to non-residents on payment of a fee.

Tourist Information Offices

Landesverkehrsverband Westfalen
Südwall 6
4600 Dortmund 1
☎ (0231) 527506/7
(The main office for the Federal State of Westphalia).

Touristikzentrale Sauerland
Postfach 1460
5790 Brilon
☎ (02961) 91229
(The main office for the Sauerland in general and for Hochsauerland, the south-eastern segment, in particular).

Kreisverkehrsverband Südsauerland
Seminarstrasse 22
Postfach 1545
5960 Olpe
☎ (02761) 6822
(For the south-western corner around Olpe).

Märkischer Kreis, Amt für Fremdenverkehr
Heedfelder Strasse 45
Postfach 2080
5880 Lüdenscheid
☎ (02351) 671873
(For Märkisches Sauerland, the northwestern corner excluding Hagen and environs).

Hagen
Mittelstrasse
Pavillon
5800 Hagen
☎ (02331) 13573
(For the city of Hagen and immediate vicinity).

Kreis Soest
Hoher Weg 1-3
4770 Soest
☎ (02921) 302851/3

(For north Sauerland with Soest at the centre).

In addition to the principal offices listed, each place has its own *Verkehrsamt* to which inquiries may be addressed.

Zoos and Wildlife Parks

Arnsberg-Vosswinkel
Wildwald Vosswinkel
5760 Arnsberg
☎ (02932) 25195 or 23005
On B7 12 miles (20km) north-west of Arnsberg.
Open: daily until dusk.
Deer, foxes, wild boars, raccoons, etc.

Brilon
Brummerhagen
Two miles (45km) north-west near B516.
Open: daily.
Wild boars.

Madfeld
Nine miles east (14km) near B7.
Deer.

Ennepetal
Erholungspark Hülsenbeckertal
5828 Ennepetal
Open: daily.
Fallow deer, exotic birds, ornamental fish.
Small animals enclosure.

Eslohe-Wenholthausen
Auf dem Eibel
Four miles (6km) north of Eslohe.
Open: daily.
Red deer, fallow deer, wild boars.

Finnentrop-Weuspert
Weuspert
Four miles (7km) north-east of Finnentrop.
Open: daily.
Deer, fallow deer, wild boars.

Hagen
Wehringhauser Bachtal
Open: daily.
Deer.

Haspe
Three miles (5km) west of Hagen.
Open: daily.
Wild boars.

Fleyer Wald
North of Hagen.
Open: daily.
Wild boars, fallow deer.

Lennestadt-Kirchveischede
Heinrich Brill
Five miles (8km) west of Altenhundem on B55.
Open: daily.
Deer.

Möhnesee-Völlinghausen
Am Wildpark
About 2 (4km) miles from Völling-hausen at east end of the Möhnesee.
Open: daily.
Sika-deer, fallow deer, birds.

Warstein
Bei der Tropfsteinhöhle
Near the caves on road to Hirschberg.
Open: daily.
Deer, fallow deer, wild boars. Admission and parking free. Restaurant.

Willingen
Am Ettelsberg
3542 Willingen
☎ (05632) 6810 or 69198
Two miles (3km) south-west of Willingen.
Open: daily 9am-6pm.
Deer, fallow deer. Fairytale park.

The above list should not be regarded as exhaustive. *Wildgehege* are not necessarily always in exactly the same location and a call at the local tourist information office to check might save a fruitless search.

4 • The Rhineland

E ver since Victorian times the Rhineland, defined as the stretch of river between Cologne and Mainz with its tributaries, has been popular with British and American travellers. The historic towns and romantic scenery that lie on this stretch of the Rhine still attract vast numbers of tourists and this is the only area of Germany that can be said to be on the map of the large package-tour companies. The Rhineland is not off the beaten track, but even in the height of summer it is possible to find charming wine villages just off the river and up its tributaries, that are visited only by the discerning few.

It is, of course, a very beautiful track, whether one travels by boat, car, or train. The most attractive stretch for a boat journey is from Koblenz to Bingen and a boat, of course, enables you to look at the castles that crown the hills on either bank as you pass. There are roads and railways on both sides of the river which offer views of the opposite bank; most trains travel along the west bank, but by a careful study of time tables it is possible to find a train that will take you back on the other side. Attractive towns to stay at are **Boppard**, with a line of hotels along the river, a little local museum and a branch railway up to the Hunsrück hills; **Oberwesel**, with two Gothic churches and an old castle above the town that houses both a charming hotel and a youth hostel, and **Bacharach**, nestling from both road and railway behind its old town walls with a youth hostel in the castle above. All these places will be packed with visitors at summer holiday times, but out of season you can have them to yourself.

Wine

These villages rely almost solely upon the cultivation of grapes for the production of wine. A journey through them, tasting the local wines as you go, can be a lesson in the appreciation of German wine. A little knowledge of the method of wine production and of the considerations that influence the quality of the wine produced, will greatly enhance the enjoyment of your journey.

First, a potted guide to German wines. The considerations that affect the quality of wine are: the grape, the soil on which it grows, and the climatic situation. These three influences come together in certain regions of Germany to produce wines that have characteristics which are unsurpassed anywhere else in the world: fresh, fruity, spicy, low in alcohol and subtle in fragrance.

The main vines grown in German vineyards are Riesling, Silvaner, Müller-Thurgau, and Traminer. These all have white grapes producing white wine. Riesling tends to produce the lightest, most delicate wine of these. Silvaner wines tend to be more mellow and fruity, at the best full-bodied and vigorous. Müller-Thurgau was developed in Switzerland, by a Dr Müller in the canton of Thurgau, 100 years ago. It is said to be a cross between Riesling and Silvaner, but experts now doubt this and nobody knows exactly how it was created; anyhow, it has proved very successful as it grows well on all kinds of soil. Traminer, with its variant Gewürztraminer (Spicy Traminer), is grown only in small quantities. It produces a very distinct type of wine that is somewhat spicy and distinctly aromatic; it is not suitable to drink with a meal, but excellent as an aperitif or for the dessert. Germany does not produce a great deal of red wine, and cannot claim comparison with the best French wines in that respect, but a few areas do produce perfectly good red wines from the Spätburgunder grapes (known as Pinot Noir in France). A fair quantity of standard red table wine is made from Portugieser grapes (which have nothing to do with Portugal). *Weissherbst* — that is rosé wine — is made from Spätburgunder grapes which have been pressed immediately after gathering so that only a little of the colour of the blue grapes is taken up into the juice. If red wine is being made, the grapes are left to ferment in a 'mash' for several days, during which the colour of the skins fully enters the fermenting juice. *Weissherbst* wine made from Portugieser grapes has to be so declared, or called Portugieser Rosé. There are, of course, other varieties and cross-breeds, with research into wines going on all the time, but these are the main types of wine to remember.

The vine has deep roots that can go down for 20ft (6m) or more, and the soil from which it draws its sustenance has a strong influence on the grapes it produces. The best soil is stony, light to work, quickly warming, retaining its heat, and dry. In general, these are soils unsuitable for other types of cultivation. Good soil may contain slate, volcanic rock, limestone, Keuper red marl (lime and clay), chalk, gravel, and many other types of rock.

A vineyard should be in a position facing south, where it can

Enkirch, in the Rhineland

An old wine press in
Rüdesheim, the
Rhineland

Linz am Rhein

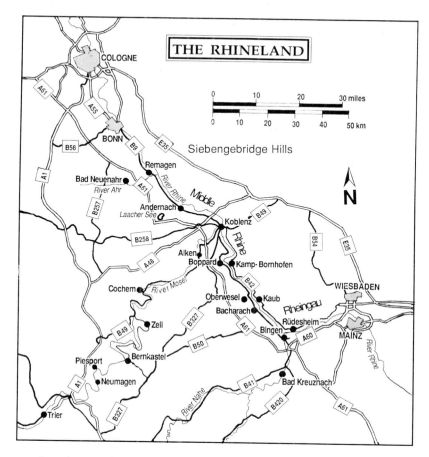

THE RHINELAND

receive the maximum amount of sunlight, be sheltered from cold winds, and often benefit from reflecting sunlight from adjoining water. These features are often to be found on steep hillsides, which make cultivation laborious and the construction of terraces essential, and are found in abundance in the Rhineland.

In Germany the grapes are normally picked between mid-September and the end of October. Some growers will leave a few vines unpicked at first, waiting for the grapes to ripen further and to produce a sweeter wine; this is called *Spätlese*. If the *Spätlese* harvest is limited to carefully selected, fully ripe bunches of grapes, the wine may be described as *Auslese*. Wine made from over-ripe berries individually picked, and daubed with the greatly valued noble mould, are described as *Beerenauslese*, and if these selected grapes have shrivelled on the vine to resemble dry raisins, the wine is

Trockenbeerenauslese. These last two types can only be produced in rare and exceptionally favourable weather conditions, and you are unlikely to ever meet them. If you happen to, a single bottle will cost almost as much as a moderately decent second-hand motor car!

The production of wine in Germany is controlled by very stringent laws, and the label on the bottle provides a classification of quality as follows: *Deutscher Tafelwein* is table wine made from grapes grown in any region of Germany, possibly with two or more mixed together; it can be a perfectly decent wine, but will not have the characteristics of any special region. *Qualitätswein* is a wine of good quality from a specific named region. *Qualitätswein mit Prädikat* is specially selected quality wine to which no extraneous sugar has been added. In addition, the information on the label includes the name of the wine-growing region from which the wine comes, the date of the vintage, the area (*Bereich*) in which the vineyard lies, the individual site (*Lage*) of the vineyard, and the type of grape from which the wine has been made. For instance a moderately priced bottle of wine, with the following words on the label:

MOSEL - SAAR - RUWER
1983 Wiltinger Schwarzberg
Riesling Kabinett
Qualitätswein mit Prädikat
A.P. Nr. 2 907 409 20 86

indicates that the wine came from the Mosel-Saar-Ruwer wine region, that it was made in 1983 from Riesling grapes, and grown on the Schwarzberg site in the area of Wiltingen, a village on the river Saar. It has been judged by a panel of experts as of superior quality, with the official test number (*A.P.*) quoted, and is completely natural wine without any added sugar (*Kabinett*). The label may additionally carry, in much larger letters, the name of the bottler or the wholesaler and a fancy coat of arms, but these are of far less importance.

There are, of course, many well known German wines whose labels do not carry all this information. Wines labelled *Bernkastler Riesling*, for instance, merely indicate that they are made from Riesling grapes grown anywhere in the Bernkastel area, perhaps several miles from the famous vineyards of that town. Then there are the proprietory brands, like Liebfraumilch, Goldener Oktober, Blue Nun, and so on. These are produced by blending wines from different areas to produce a standard type of wine that the blenders know is acceptable to many drinkers. They are perfectly respectable, but the true lover of wine likes to identify what he or she is drinking with a specific area and site. Therefore if he or she has ever visited that site the pleasure of drinking is greatly enhanced.

Harvest time in the vineyards of the Mosel

The Rhine

Armed with this knowledge, the exploration of the wine villages of the Rhineland can begin. A car is the only practical means of transport, unless walking is preferred. One can walk from Bingen to Bonn. Most of the way is along the well-marked Rheinhoenweg on the west side of the river crossing to the Siebengebirge on the east for the final stretch. This is a good route scenically but misses the best wine areas.

Opposite Bingen, on the right bank of the river, is the most famous region of all German wine production, the Rheingau. The Rieslings produced here are one of the greatest white wines of the world. The most famous vineyard is at Johannisberg Castle, where the discovery of the value of the 'noble mould' was made in the eighteenth century. At that time the vineyard was under the ownership of the abbey of Fulda, and the Benedictine monks at Johannisberg had to obtain the permission of their mother house before starting the harvest. The story is as follows: when the grapes seemed ripe they despatched a mounted courier, carrying a sample grape with him, to Fulda 100 miles (161km) away. They waited and waited for his return, but he did not come. Rumour has it that he was delayed by an amorous encounter! At last he returned, some weeks later, with the necessary permission, but meanwhile the grapes had become covered with mould! The monks thought the wine had been ruined but, to their amazement, it turned out to be the best and sweetest they had ever known. The first *Beerenauslese* had been produced!

Some other villages in the Rheingau worth visiting both for their wine and their attractions are **Oestrich**, with an old crane on the river that must have loaded many barrels of wine on to barges in its day; **Lorch**, with a famous fifteenth-century altar in its parish church of St Martin; **Rauenthal**, with a fine view of the Rhine valley and a four-teenth-century sculpture of the Virgin and Child, holding out his hand for a grape, in the parish church; **Kiedrich**, with a church choir that continues a 600 year tradition of Gregorian choral singing in the unique Germanic tradition associated with Mainz, and which chants Latin liturgical hymns associated with wine and the labour of wine-growing at Sunday mass and **Ebersbach**; a former abbey with the famous site of Steinberg, which has a museum of antique wine-presses and vats, the Kloster Eberbach Museum. The village of **Rüdesheim**, on the river, is a popular stop for tourists and its narrow street is lined with wine taverns. It is not, perhaps, the place for the leisurely contemplation of a fine vintage, but it is heart-warming to see good wine being enjoyed as a popular drink rather than for some imaginary snob appeal. Just round the bend of the river, the Höllen-berg valley above Assmannshausen is renowned for its Spätburgun-der red wines, one of the very few red wines made in the Rhineland.

Moving north, the visitor arrives at the region of the Middle Rhine, which stretches on both sides of the river nearly as far as Bonn. This is the most beautiful scenic stretch of the Rhine, but the wines here are not considered as of outstanding quality, though they pro-vide good refreshing drink for the local inhabitants and the tourists. Most of the production is Riesling, but there are small pockets of red wine production at Patersberg, above St Goarshausen, and at Unkel. This stretch of river ends at the Siebengebirge hills. Here a site on the Drachenfels rock produces a red *Drachenblut* wine that is treasured more for its romantic name (Dragon's Blood) than for its true quality, and the Domlay vineyard at Rhöndorf overlooks the graveyard in which Konrad Adenauer, the first chancellor of the Frederal Repub-lic, is buried. Like all true Rhinelanders, Adenauer was no mean connoisseur of wine. Lying to the west of Andernach on the other side of the river is the Laacher See, with the abbey of Maria Laach near it. This is not vineyard country, but the abbey is interesting as it is still an active monastic community. The church dates from the eleventh century, but the monastery is chiefly noted for the artistic

The Rhine from the Drachenfels

movement that developed here in the 1920s, aimed at replacing the sentimental style of religious art, then generally popular, with something more worthy.

Motorists who want to avoid the worst of the traffic beside the river in this region can escape to the hill roads. On the west, between the river and the *Autobahn*, is the Rheingoldstrasse from Bacharach to Boppard and on the east, the Loreley-Burgenstrasse from Kaub to Kamp-Bornhofen. Travellers on these roads will pass through many pleasant and modest wine-growing villages and be rewarded with magnificent views of the Rhine valley.

The Ahr and Nahe

The Rhine receives three tributaries on its left bank, all of which are lined by good vineyards. The most northerly is the Ahr, which runs through an extremely narrow valley flanked by almost precipitous hillsides to join the Rhine near Remagen. Because of the steep slopes, the vines have to be trained on separate unconnected stakes, rather than on wires as is usual elsewhere. Most of the small vine-growers are joined in co-operatives for the making and marketing of their wine. The main town of the valley, **Bad Neuenahr**, has only a few sites and is better noted for its Apollinaris mineral spring. Wine villages stretch for some 15 miles (24km) above it. Most of the wine produced here is Portugieser and Spätburgunder red, and the valley is known as 'the German red wine paradise'. Despite some claims to the contrary, the quality of the wine is not really outstanding, but the beauty of the valley provides ample compensation for the traveller.

The most southerly tributary is the Nahe, which joins the Rhine near Bingen. The production is almost entirely of white Silvaner, Müller-Thurgau and Riesling wines, and because of the different types of soil the quality and characteristics vary a great deal from place to place. Some Nahe wines are very similar to those of the Rhine, and others closer to the Mosel. The best known sites are at Schlossböckelheim, which were cleared for vine planting as recently as the beginning of this century by convict labour. Some of the soil here is of weathered porphyry, and two huge red porphyry rocks are a prominent landmark at Bad Münster, providing a stunning near-vertical precipice and Germany's steepest cliff face. Not far off is the castle of Ebernburg, the most famous of the area. The Kauzenberg Castle, at **Bad Kreuznach**, has a pleasant restaurant and terrace overlooking the river and a clutch of Riesling vineyards on red sandstone soil. Bad Kreuznach itself is an important spa with radium brine baths. The Germans are great frequenters of spas, and the German Health Service provides for treatment at many of them. British visitors to Germany can make use of medical and hospital services without charge, provided they carry the necessary documentation (DHSS form E111), but this does not cover treatment at spas, for which foreigners normally require a doctor's certificate.

The Mosel

The most famous of the Rhine tributaries is, of course, the Mosel (as it is spelt in German with the stress on the first syllable), which joins the Rhine at Koblenz. This is a valley of great beauty, less dramatic in its scenery than the Rhine but with a charm of its own; the river winds between low hills whose southern slopes are clothed with vines. The water is clear and clean. Half-timbered villages and medieval churches line the banks and the air is mild and soft. Boats provide a regular summer service and road and railway run beside it. Though not so heavily visited as the Rhine, this too attracts large crowds in the summer and can hardly be described as off the beaten track, but the discerning traveller can join the pleasures of wine-sampling with those of admiring beautiful landscapes and relaxing in the welcoming inns of unspoilt villages.

Mosel wines come, in fact, from the Mosel and its two tributaries, the Saar and the Ruwer. They are exclusively white — Riesling and Müller-Thurgau—and the vines grow mostly on slate. The wines are on the whole lighter, somewhat less alcoholic, less full-bodied, and rather more airy and fragrant than those of other regions. They can be distinguished, apart from the labels, by their green bottles; Rhine wines come in brown bottles.

Travelling up the river from Koblenz the village of **Winnigen**, which holds a particularly splendid wine festival at vintage time, and the splendid castles at Alken and Eltz are passed. Between these two you can strike a few miles south-east to Schloss Ehrenburg near Brodenbach, one of the less known but probably most attractive of all the German castles. It was built in the twelfth century by the archbishop of Trier on Roman foundations, and is superbly situated in a remote and romantic spot with distant views of the Eifel hills. The valley in which it lies was a safe area for Jews in the Middle Ages, under the protection of the Metternich family (which still owns the Johannisberg vineyard). The castle ruins now house a small restaurant and has simple, inexpensive accommodation in a youth hostel. Returning to the Mosel the visitor comes to **Cochem**, the largest town of the valley, in a beautiful situation but usually very crowded in the summer. It is, however, worth staying at **Cond** on the opposite bank for the sight of the floodlit fairytale castle of Cochem seeming to float in the night sky; like most of the best castles in Germany this is actually a creation of the nineteenth-century Romantic movement. **Beilstein**, at the foot of the Burg Metternich, is a tiny medieval village; at **Ediger**, high up on the hillside, is a little chapel with a sixteenth-century stone carving of Christ treading the wine press as alluded to in the Book of Revelations. The vineyards beyond Bremm are the most precipituous in all Germany, and perhaps in the world. In this Lower Mosel area, the soil is reddish greywecke slate, which has to be carefully conserved to prevent it slipping down the hillside and exposing the roots of the vines; as in the Ahr valley, the vines here are individually staked.

At **Neef** the Frauenberg site produces some very fine Rieslings, and the financial return is sufficient for the owner to be able to afford the services of a helicopter to spray his vines — something quite beyond the resources of most vineyard owners who must look at the machine with envy as they toil laboriously up to their lofty sites. As **Alf** is approached, the ruin of Burg Arras provides one of the most picturesque sights of the valley, and from here the reddish slate gives way to the bluish argillaceous slate of the Middle Mosel. **Zell**, with its handsome castle, produces a wine labelled as Schwarze Katz, popular rather because of the plastic black cat attached to its top than for any special quality of the contents. Similar to this, as an example of marketing technique, is the Nacktarsch (Bare Bottom) wine produced at Kröv, whose label depicts a father spanking his young son.

Slate-hung houses at Enkirch

The wine connoisseur will stop rather at the attractive village of **Enkirch** with its much esteemed sites, or at **Traben-Trarbach**, with its predominantly Protestant community (unusual here) and yet another ruined castle.

The finest viticultural stretch of the valley, with the famous sites at Bernkastel and Piesport, is now entered. At **Bernkastel** the far famed Doktor vineyard owes its name to the legend that a four-teenth-century archbishop of Trier was restored to health after drinking a copious draught of its wine; this site, just above the town's roofs, measures only about 3 acres, which is too small for individual classification under German wine law, but because of its reputation it has been allowed to retain its name. At **Piesport** the most famous site is the Goldtröpfchen, from which the wines were served at the banquet after the coronation of Queen Elizabeth II. Moving up the valley we come to **Neumagen** the site of the discovery of some important Roman antiquities, which may be seen in the Lan-desmuseum at Trier; and Trittenheim, from whose bridge a road leads up to a restaurant whose terrace commands one of the finest views of the Mosel valley.

A little further the river Ruwer flows into the Mosel and a few miles beyond this the Saar comes down. The lower reaches of both these rivers are lined with vineyards whose wine can be of excellent quality but tends to be somewhat more acid and prickly than that of the Mosel. Much of the less superior quality goes to the making of

Sekt, a sparkling wine, not to be compared with true champagne but very welcome on a hot afternoon or in the interval at the opera.

Trier

Between the tributaries of the rivers Ruwer and Saar lies Trier, a city of great interest and the oldest in Germany. It is certainly the best preserved Roman city north of the Alps, and in some ways conveys the atmosphere of Roman civilisation even better than Rome, as its buildings have been cleaned from later additions. There are three buildings in particular that repay careful study.

The Porta Nigra, the massive town gate, greets you as you enter the city. It is worth visiting the adjoining Städtisches Museum to study the pictures and plans in it that demonstrate the remarkable history of this imposing structure. It was built in the second century to keep out the Germanic hordes, but apparently never completely finished; in the eleventh century a Syrian monk shut himself up in a cell inside it to live as a hermit. He acquired a reputation for sanctity and, in his honour, the structure was transformed into a double church; an upper and a lower one. Romanesque and Gothic features were added, and from seventeenth- and eighteenth-century prints it is impossible to discern its original purpose. When the French army entered Trier at the end of the eighteenth century, Napoleon demonstrated his interest in archaeology by demolishing most of these later additions, and in the mid-nineteenth century, when the city became part of Prussia, the authorities showed their good taste by continuing the work and restoring the Roman gate to the condition seen today.

Even more impressive is the basilica or Aula Palatina, built by Constantine the Great in about 310 as part of his palace. The remainder of the palace has been replaced by a charming eighteenth-century rococo building, with a formal garden in front of it but — again under the archaeological good taste of the Prussian rulers — the basilica has been restored to its original architectural form and now serves as a Protestant church. One feels that the simplicity and austerity of a Lutheran church, with its plain brick walls, is well fitted to what one imagines to have been Roman *gravitas*, and it is a bit of a shock to discover from reconstructions in the nearby Landesmuseum that the walls were originally plastered and brightly decorated. The Landesmuseum, incidentally, contains extremely important collections illustrating Roman life in Trier, including much evidence of the vineyards that they established on the Mosel and the wine trade that was carried on.

The *Dom*, or cathedral, is another fascinating building, though this time because of its additions rather than in spite of them. There is a core of original Roman work of the time of Constantine, which can be recognised on the exterior by the alternate courses of brick and red sandstone; this has been extended to east and west at various periods between the eleventh and eighteenth century, but largely in the Romanesque style, so that the whole exhibits an impressive unity in which it is difficult to distinguish where the work of one century ends and another begins.

Adjoining this is another church, the Liebfrauenkirche. Two churches, side by side, were part of Constantine's original plan, and it seems that this one was a catechumen church, for the use of converts to Christianity while under instruction. Only after baptism were they allowed into the bishop's church next door. This church is now a sober thirteenth-century Gothic building, and in fact the earliest Gothic church in Germany. Its ground plan represents a twelve-petal rose, the mystic flower as a symbol of the Virgin Mary, and, with a central altar in the modern liturgical fashion and some good post-war stained glass to replace what was lost through bombing, the building has a deeply spiritual and reposeful atmosphere.

After these splendid architectural monuments of past civilisations, the last building you would expect to find in Trier is the birthplace of Karl Marx at Brückenstrasse 10, with a small museum to illustrate the immense influence of this man's writings upon the twentieth century. Finally, in the cellar of the Rathaus — almost all town halls in Germany have excellent restaurants in their cellars — you can drink the wines of many of the places you have passed through on your journey up the Mosel.

Cologne, Mainz and Bonn

The two historic towns of Cologne and Mainz lie at either end of this stretch of the Rhine. **Mainz** now has a rather sleepy air, with a good Romanesque cathedral although with later accretions. A visit to this city should be urged if you have a strong feeling for the art of printing. It was here, in about 1440, that a goldsmith called Johannes Gutenberg invented the art of printing from movable type. Incredibly, the first book that he printed was the complete Bible, and even more fascinating is that it remains to this day one of the most beautiful books ever printed, with close-spaced typography, solid inking and firm presswork. This book, the forty-two-line Bible, was published in 1456. He printed another edition of the Bible with thirty-six lines to the page and a popular encyclopedia. All these books can be seen in the Gutenberg Museum of the Art of Printing. Of course they can be seen in other great libraries around the world, but if there is any feeling for the magic of place it is a moving experience to gaze on them here, where it all began.

From Mainz the art of printing spread, first through Germany and then round the world. It was the greatest German contribution to civilisation. Nothing that has come since can compare with its influence upon our society. After this burst of creativity, Mainz gently retired into a quiet provincial city.

Cologne, on the other hand, has continued to grow and flourish as a busy modern city with an historic past. You cannot ignore the cathedral, even if it is very decidedly *on* the beaten track. It stands just outside the railway station and its twin spires rear high above everything else. No sky-scrapers or office blocks have been allowed to challenge this supremacy here. The interior is a superb work of pure fourteenth-century Gothic, possibly a little cold in feeling but immensely impressive. Beside its overwhelming impact the individual works of art pale to insignificance. However, study the golden reliquary of the bones of the Magi — the Dreikönigenschrein — behind the high altar. It is more than likely that not many take the authenticity of these skeletons very seriously nowadays, but the sarcophagus of about 1200 is a great work of Romanesque art, only to be compared perhaps with the reliquary for the body of Charlemagne in Aachen Cathedral (now shown in the treasury) which may perhaps be seen on the way home.

When you leave the cathedral, look back up at the twin spires of delicate lattice-work stone. Work came to a halt in about 1550, with only stumps for spires, when money and religious fervour ran out. It was not until the middle of the nineteenth century that the influence of the German Romantic Movement and the new pride in a united Germany inspired Germans to complete the building. The original builders' plans were discovered in Paris and Darmstadt, and were followed in every detail; it is now impossible to tell where sixteenth-century work ends and the work of about 1850 begins.

There are many other churches in Cologne, but the most interesting of these are Romanesque rather than Gothic in style. If you would like to make a little architectural tour that would be, to some extent, off the beaten track, visit a group of these Romanesque churches which are all within walking distance of the centre and which comprise a unique artistic treasure of the city. Fine though the cathedral is, there are other Gothic cathedrals in France and England that can match it, but there is nothing anywhere in the world to match the Romanesque churches of Cologne, so here is a selection.

Gross St Martin, near the river, is situated between the Hohenzollernbrücke and the Deutzer Brücke and easily recognised by its high tower. It is indeed an impressive start to the tour. St Maria in Lyskirchen, near the river between the Deutzer Brücke and the Severinsbrücke, was originally the boatmens' church, and has interesting murals. St George, a little further from the river, is the only intact early Romanesque pillar basilica in the Rhineland, with a noble west section. St Maria im Kapitol, back in the direction of the cathedral, has a famous and extraordinary trefoil chancel and unique wooden carved doors. St Cäcilien, near the Neumarkt, now houses the superb ecclesiastical art treasures of the Schnütgen Museum. St Aposteln, in the Neumarkt, is where compline is chanted every day before the evening mass and, if your legs are tired by now, a rest can be taken in a sympathetic atmosphere. St Andreas, near the cathedral, is at present (1988) under repair but will be well worth visiting when it is re-opened. St Kunibert, near the river and on the far side of the railway station, is the last of the great Romanesque churches of Cologne and was consecrated in 1247, the year before the laying of the foundation stone of the cathedral which marked the coming of a new style of architecture.

There are, of course, several other fine Romanesque churches only a little further out from the centre and, if you are interested in church architecture, a number of post-war churches in the suburbs that illustrate, and influenced, the development of the fusion of architecture and liturgy which has marked recent decades. The tourist office, facing the cathedral, can give information about these.

Cologne suffered terribly from air raids during the war, as photographs in many of these now restored churches demonstrate. The cathedral, fortunately, survived almost intact. One rare happy consequence of the bombing was the discovery of a wonderful Roman mosaic beside the cathedral during the building of an air raid shelter. This Dionysos mosaic, which once graced the floor of a Roman villa, is now the centre piece of the Römisch-Germanisches Museum which has been built round it, and which houses excellent displays of Roman life in Germany.

Among other museums and art galleries, the Wallraf-Richartz-Museum, with a fine collection of Rhenish and other paintings, is outstanding. The same building houses an American Pop Art collection on the upper floor. A museum that has not yet got into the guide books, and is due to open in 1989, is the Circus Museum in the Roncalli Bau at Neuratherweg 7. The Roncalli Circus was founded by André Heller and Bernhard Paul in 1976 as a kind of 'art circus', with traditional circus skills presented with something of the style of the best contemporary theatre. It has proved enormously popular in Germany, playing for long seasons in most of the big cities. Over the years the directors have assembled a large collection of posters and other memorabilia to illustrate the history of the circus. This should make a fascinating display.

Cologne can, of course, boast a famous opera house and any number of other theatres. However there is one theatre that is hardly known to foreign visitors but is 'Cologne to the core'. This is the Hänneschen Puppet Theatre. In the year 1802 a tailor from Bonn called Johann Christoph Winters founded a puppet theatre for the benefit of the working class audiences who were now settling in the big town of Cologne. He created a tradition that is still carried on today. The chief character in all the plays is a local boy called Hänneschen (Little Hans) who has been joined by a whole cast of local types: his girlfriend, Bärbelchen; his grandmother, Mariezebell; his grandfather, Besteva; a big-nosed peasant, slow and stupid, Tünnes; a city slicker, Schäl, and so on. These stock characters appear in a whole range of plays reflecting the life of this Rhineland city. The puppets themselves are of a type that is not found anywhere else, and nobody knows just how they originated; they are stick puppets, that is full length figures supported by a long wooden rod reaching to the ground. One arm is usually controlled by an extra wire. The operators move the figures from below, and succeed in imparting a great range of lively movements.

The plays are spoken in a local dialect and it is unlikely that you will understand a word of it, but the vigour of the performance and the atmosphere of the little theatre are well worth experiencing. You will find the theatre in the Eisenmarkt, one of the courts between the Heumarkt and the river.

If you are staying anytime in Cologne and tire of the streets, there are parks and green belts all round the city, especially the Rhine Park on the right bank and the Stadtwald in Lindenthal. There is a story about these: Immediately after the British army had occupied Cologne at the end of the war, the authorities looked round for a reliable non-Nazi to act as mayor under the British administration. The choice fell upon a former mayor, Konrad Adenauer, who had just been released from a concentration camp. In the first bitterly cold winter after the war, when fuel was in short supply, the British military governor ordered the mayor to have the trees in the city's parks cut down so as to provide fuel. Adenauer refused. He said that the citizens of Cologne could put up with the cold for one more year, but it would take a hundred years to replace the parks. For this refusal he was sacked for incompetence. He went on to become the first chancellor of the Federal Republic, to preside over Germany's 'economic miracle', and to become one of the founding fathers of the European Community. The trees are still there!

Between Cologne and Mainz is the town of **Bonn**, a quiet university city that was suddenly catapulted into the international limelight when it was chosen as the temporary capital of the Federal Republic of Germany in 1949. The temporary status has become permanent.

If you paused in Mainz because of your interest in printing, you may pause in Bonn for the love of music, as it was here that Beethoven was born. A visit can be made to his birthplace, a comfortable middle-class house with an interesting collection of relics. It was from this house that his father, a singer in the electoral choir, declined into alcoholism and the family sank into poverty, creating perhaps the emotional tension in the adolescent and musically gifted boy who erupted into a genius. The fine Beethovenhalle offers some of the best concerts in Germany.

In Bonn there is, of course, the building housing the Bundestag, the Federal parliament, and you can attend debates if you have an interest in politics. The suburb of Bad Godesberg — which escaped the ravages of World War II — retains the atmosphere of a prosperous nineteenth-century residential area, which housed some 200 millionaires by 1914. It now accommodates the embassies of almost every nation on earth. This has ensured that these fine old mansions have been kept in use and are well looked after.

A feature of popular life all down the Rhine, from the Ruhr to Mainz, is the pre-Lent Carnival. Every town has a number of carnival clubs, representing different trades and professions, and at the witching hour of 11 minutes past 11 on the eleventh day of the eleventh month (11 November) they elect a prince from among their members, who will preside over the festivities. After the New Year, celebrations begin in earnest with numerous balls, culminating in the week before Lent with street processions and fancy dress. Sunday is the day for children to dress up and parade, and Monday (Rosenmontag) is the big day for processions through the streets with highly elaborate floats. On Tuesday one recuperates, and then Ash Wednesday follows with, in theory at least, fasting till Easter.

All classes share in these celebrations, and the streets are crowded. Hotels hire out windows and grandstands are erected for spectators. This is in no sense off the beaten track, but it is a time of the year when few tourists are around and for foreign visitors it is indeed something quite new. You will be welcome to join in the fun, provided you respect the fundamental Rhineland decencies that lie behind the merrymaking.

Further Information
— The Rhineland —

Firework Displays

The Rhine in Flames
Between Bingen and Rüdesheim on the first Saturday in July.
Between Koblenz and Braubach on the second weekend in August.
Between St Goar and St Goarhausen on the third weekend in September.

Museums

Cologne
Wallraf-Richartz-Museum (Art Gallery)
Wallrafplatz
Open: daily 10am-5pm. Tuesday and Friday 10am-10pm.

Ludwig Museum (contemporary art)
Above the Wallraf-Richartz-Museum.
Same opening times as stated above.

Schnütigen-Museum (ecclesiastical art)
In Cäcilien Church
Cäcilienstrasse
Open: daily 10am-5pm, Wednesday also 8am-10pm.

Römisch-Germanisches Museum
(Roman settlements in Germany)
Beside the Dom (cathedral)
Open: daily.

Stadtmuseum
Zeughausstrasse
Open: daily.
History of Cologne.

Rautenstrauch-Joest Museum of
    Ethnology (Völkerkundemuseum)
Ubierring 45
Open: daily 10am-5pm, also Tuesday 7pm-10pm.

Museum for East Asian Art
Kattenburg 24
Open: Monday to Friday by appointment.

Archiepiscopal Diocesan Museum
Gereonstrasse 48
Open: Monday to Friday 10am-12noon and 2-4pm.

Engine Museum
Klöckner-Humboldt-Deutz AG
Deutz-Mülheimer Strasse 11
Open: Monday to Friday 9am-5pm.

Trier
Landesmuseum (Roman antiquities)
Ostallee 44

Bischöfliches Museum (ecclesiastical
    art)
Banthusstrasse 6

Städtisches Museum (history of city)
Simeonstift

Karl-Marx-Haus (birthplace of Marx)
Brückenstrasse 10

Tourist Information Offices

Assmannshausen
see Rüdesheim

Bacharach
Verkehrsamt
Oberstrasse 1
6533 Bacharach
☎ (067) 43 1297

Bingen
Verkehrsamt
Rheinkai 21
6530 Bingen
☎ (06721) 14269

Boppard
Verkehrsamt
Karmeliter Strasse 2
5407 Boppard 1
☎ (06742) 103

Cologne
Verkehrsamt der Stadt Köln
Am Dom
Köln
☎ (0221) 2213345

Kaub
Verkehrsamt
5425 Kaub
☎ (067) 74 222

Kamp-Bornhofen
Verkehrsamt
Rheinuferstrasse 34
5424 Kamp-Bornhofen
☎ (067) 73 360

Koblenz
Fremdenverkehrsamt
Verkehrspavillon Gegenüber dem Hbf
5400 Koblenz
☎ (0261) 31304

Lorch
Verkehrsamt
Rathaus
Postfach 1109
6223 Lorch 1
☎ (067) 26 317

Mosel
Mosel Valley
Verkehrsamt
Endertplatz
D 5590 Cochem
☎ 0 26 71/3971/3972

Oberwesel
Verkehrsamt
6532 Oberwesel
☎ (067) 44 8131

Patersberg
Fremdenverkehrsverein
5421 Patersberg
☎ (067) 71 464

Rhine
Rhine Valley
5407 Boppard 1
☎ 007 42/103-17/18/19

Rüdesheim
Verkehrsamt
Rheinstrasse 16
6220 Rüdesheim
☎ (067) 22 2962

Trier
Verkehrsamt
An der Porta Nigra
D 5500 Trier
☎ 4 80 71/718 448

Wine Festivals

Assmanshausen
Ascension Day (Mimmelfahrtstag)

June
Lorch (third weekend).

August
Rüdesheim (third weekend).

September
Kaub (first weekend).
Bingen (first and second weekend).
Oberwesel (second weekend).
Rhens (second weekend).
St Goarshausen (second and third
    weekends).
St Goar (third weekend).
Boppard, Koblenz-Lay, St
Goarshausen (last weekend).

October
Boppard, Bacharach, Braubach, Kaub
(first weekend).
St Goarshausen (third weekend).
Rüdesheim and neighbouring sites.

Similar festivals, though not quite so
tourist-orientated, are held at all the
wine-producing villages in the Rhineland during October.

5 • The Saar Valley

The river Mosel, especially between Koblenz on the Rhine and Trier, is a fairly well-trodden tourist route and features in the itinerary of many 'package' holiday deals. Even the person who has not visited this famous valley of vineyards will probably be familiar with the names of many wine-producing areas such as Traben-Trarbach, Bernkastel and Piesport. The other two rivers of the Mosel-Saar-Ruwer wine-growing trio are comparatively little known and in this chapter we explore the larger of the two — the Saar.

This tributary of the Mosel comes over the border from France at Saargemünd and joins the Mosel some 56 miles (90km) to the north close to the Luxembourg border and just west of the ancient city of Trier. The traveller from Britain, whether by road or rail, will probably reach this area via Luxembourg since that is the most direct route. The motorist can choose a short sea crossing to Calais and drive east to join the continental motorway network near Dunkirk, proceeding then via Lille, Namur and Luxembourg. The night services on the longer crossings from Hull, Felixstowe or Harwich to Rotterdam or Zeebrugge allow ample time to reach any part of the Saar valley without another overnight stop.

The distance from Calais to Trier is around 290 miles (467km) and from the Dutch and Belgian ports a little less. Either way, the routes are predominantly motorway or fast dual carriageway. For the rail traveller a very direct route is that via Dover and Ostende, then through Brussels, Luxembourg and Trier. From there, trains run south to Saarbrücken calling at many of the places mentioned in this chapter. The railway enthusiast changing trains at Brussels Nord could spend an interesting half-hour in the excellent free railway museum in the station there.

The main international airports suitable for this area are Brussels or Frankfurt and possibly Cologne and Luxembourg from each of which the journey can readily be completed by train or hire car. The airport at Saarbrücken has connections from Frankfurt as well as from Düsseldorf, Munich and Berlin. The Saar valley is eminently suitable for the visitor reliant upon public transport but there are, of course, advantages in having a personal motor vehicle.

At its north end, the Saar does not yet have the international water traffic of the Mosel but this will no doubt develop with the completion of the full canalisation which is being undertaken. Southwards from the industrial area around Saarbrücken the river is already extensively used, for just over the border at Saargemünd it gives access to the French canal system by means of which large freight vessels can reach places like Strasbourg or Paris.

There are many similarities between the Saar and the Mosel, particularly at the north end where extensive vineyards are much in evidence. Closer acquaintance will reveal delightful towns and villages engaged in the wine industry, ruined castles, many traces of Roman occupation and countless hostelries serving good food and the fine wines of the region. The steep slopes either side of the river are the dominant feature of the landscape and as one travels south from Konz — the actual meeting place of the Saar and Mosel — the vineyards gradually give way to forested areas. The rambler and cyclist will find many well-marked touring routes, some of which lead to fine vantage points high above the river. At first the bordering hilltops rarely exceed 820ft (250m) but soon reach up to around twice this height. Even at the south end where industrial activity often dominates the river banks it is only necessary to go a kilometre or two to escape the industrial fringe and be again in charming rural surroundings.

There is a lot of visitor accommodation in the area described in this chapter and the northern part is especially strong in self-catering facilities, both in bungalow villages and in individual private houses. It should be noted that while the north end of the valley is in the Federal State of Rheinland-Pfalz, from Mettlach southwards it is in Saarland. When writing to the principal state information offices, it is necessary to select the correct one. See the list of addresses later in the Further Information section. The self-catering houses and flats are comfortable, clean and well-equipped and offer very good value for money. Bed linen is nearly always provided but check when booking, also about any 'extras' although amounts for these are likely to be small. In private houses the hosts are usually delighted to welcome English speaking visitors. There are hundreds of small hotels, inns and pensions with modest prices but the bigger hotels in Saarlouis and Saarbrücken feature higher in the price-scale.

There are countless opportunities for walking in the countryside with waymarked footpaths everywhere and there are three impor-

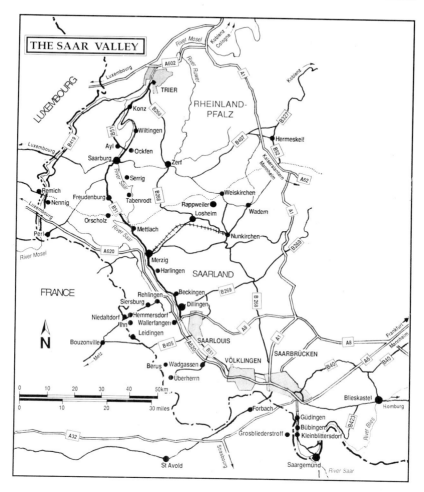

tant long distance paths. The European Long Distance Path from the Atlantic to the Bohemian Forest (Czechoslovakia) — waymark blue St Andrew's Cross — crosses the river Mosel from Luxembourg at Perl and reaches the Saar at the great Saarschleife, turns northward to roughly parallel the river which it crosses at Saarburg before resuming an easterly course.

The Grossier Saarrundweg — waymark black SR on white — is a circular route of some 32 miles (60km) with its approximate centre at Saarburg. The Saarland — Rundwanderweg is also a circular route. It is about 167 miles (270km) long starting and finishing at Saarbrücken and is confined to the State of Saarland. Optional exten-

The great loop in the river Saar near Orscholz

can add about 62 miles (100km). The waymark is a 10cm square sign with vertical red and white bars.

Maps for these major routes are readily available in book shops as are those for the more modest rambles. The shorter walks include various 'trails' and the visitor may see signs such as 'Naturlehrpfad' (Nature Trail), 'Waldlehrpfad' (Forest Nature Trail) and 'Weinlehrpfad' (Vineyard Nature Trail). Keep fit paths will be found near principal towns and holiday centres with the signs 'Trimm Dich' or 'Sportpfad'; the paths are laid out with sixteen or twenty stations at which simple exercises are to be carried out using the equipment provided. There is no charge for using the facilities.

The first place actually in the Saar valley is **Konz** where there is an interesting open-air museum to be visited. A chapel from 1730, timbered houses and many rooms with domestic and agricultural exhibits may be seen. Cycles may be hired at the railway station in Konz. The Saartalstrasse (Saar valley road) and the railway closely follow the river as it winds southwards between the enclosing hills. The wine lover constantly comes upon villages with names familiar from wine bottle labels — Wawern, Wiltingen, Ayl and Ockfen for example. Most of the villages have a car park suitable for the start of a circular walk of a few kilometres through the vineyards and woods. For the more serious walker, a marked route (black G3 on white) starts at the south end of Konz off the road to Wiltingen and climbs rather steeply up into the vineyards. After about 3 miles (5km) through the vines the route enters a wood and just before the village of Oberemmel turns sharply westwards to drop down to the Saar at Wiltingen. Waymarks SR on this latter section refer to the Grosser Saarrundweg, as it makes its tour through the Saar valley recreation area. From Wiltingen, G3 climbs again into the vineyards but soon enters a wood from which it emerges 2 or 3 miles (3-5km) later into the extensive vineyards of Ockfen, reached in another 2 miles (3km) or so. From here, the route remains in the valley until it enters Saarburg, 14 miles (22km) from Konz. The very detailed map, *Erholungsgebiet* (Recreation Area) *Saartal* (1:25,000) is a useful asset and the walker will readily identify routes in keeping with his or her capabilities; G3 is typical of this northern part of the valley.

Saarburg is a charming little town overlooked by its castle ruin — an attractive viewpoint with a pleasant, but slightly expensive, restaurant nearby. The castle was built by Count Siegfried of Luxembourg in 964. He appreciated not only the picturesque charm of the landscape but the strategic importance of this rocky eminence and a town quickly grew up around the foot of the stronghold. After crossing the river, the direct route from the station enters the town by means of a tunnel driven through a spur of the castle rock. On emerging from the tunnel, a short walk to the right (away from the town centre) leads to the lower station of the chair-lift up to the Ferienzentrum Warsberg (a holiday and leisure centre) and an extensive self-catering complex with many purpose-built bungalows. There is also a lot of self-catering accommodation in and around the town itself as well as a comprehensive range of hotels and guest houses, a youth hostel and a large well-appointed camp site. Leisure activities of every kind are provided for; walking on many kilometres of waymarked paths, cycling along recommended quiet routes (inquire at the tourist information office in the town centre about cycle hire and itineraries), canoeing on the Saar, riding and swimming. There is a fine heated outdoor pool and an indoor one is planned. Considering the quality of the fare provided, prices will be found to be remarkably modest at several attractive restaurants in the town centre and the wine served may well have come from a vineyard only a few minutes away.

A remarkable sight in the town centre is the waterfall of the river Leukbach as it tumbles down past old water-mills to join the Saar in the valley. Over the centuries, flooding of the Saar has been a problem and in the Altstadt, beside the river, may be seen high water marks on several houses. Balconies used to be attached to the houses

*The Leukbach
waterfall, Saarburg*

at first floor level so that the occupants could be rescued by boat in the event of a sudden rise in the water level. Although the balconies have been dismantled, their positions can still be seen; it is assumed that the river canalisation has removed danger of flooding in the future. The river improvement scheme has also been of advantage to the little motor-ship *Stadt Saarburg* which now operates cruises up and down the river. Prospectus of the year's programme is available from the *Verkehrsamt*.

In the Altstadt the old Glockengiesserei (bell foundry) may be visited where bells of all sizes are for sale; an unusual idea for a souvenir, perhaps. Parking in the town centre is difficult; use the large free car park a few minutes walk away near the swimming pool. In Saarburg, as in all the other towns and villages nearby, a highlight of the year is the annual wine festival. Actual dates can be obtained from the local information offices.

An interesting excursion could be made eastwards from Saarburg, 24 miles (38km) along the B407 to Hermeskeil. After passing through Zerf, 7 miles (11km) from Saarburg, the road runs roughly parallel with the upper reaches of the Ruwer, the third of the famous wine-growing rivers. **Hermeskeil** is worth visiting anyway (there is a youth hostel here) but the object of the journey here is to visit two interesting museums. The first is the Dampflok-Museum at the station, where railway enthusiasts can see some of the last steam locomotives to have worked in this area, as well as many other railway technical rarities. The other museum, 2 miles (3km) away in **Abtei**, specialises in air transport. The Flugaustellung has a comprehensive display of civil and military aircraft, models, technical equipment and so on. There is a café in a full-size Concorde replica.

Three miles (5km) south of Saarburg the community of **Kastel-Staadt** west of the Saar is the goal for an excursion to a remarkable reminder of the Roman occupation of the area, the so-called *Klause*. Begun in the year 54, this was once an important complex centred on the palace of the Roman generals. Of particular interest is the use made of the rock to provide guardrooms and other apartments for the soldiers. Staadt is on the river bank and it is a fairly stiff climb of about half a mile (1km, waymark G7) to the *Klause* perched on the cliff 328ft (100m) above the river. Kastel is already at the upper level and it is a short walk from the car park to the *Klause*. The cemetery nearby, for Germans who fell in World War II, may also be of interest not least for its wonderful situation overlooking the Saar valley. The area is easily reached on foot from Saarburg by following waymarks G7 along the river or through forests and vineyards along a route marked by a blue St Andrew's cross on a white ground. The latter is along the old Roman road and is part of the European long-distance path from the Atlantic to the Bohemian Forest in Czechoslovakia.

There are few vineyards now on the shady west slopes of the valley, but across the river the attractive large village of **Serrig** has extensive plantations. Here, as elsewhere along these famous wine rivers, the growers often offer accommodation in their homes. Sometimes the accommodation is let on a self-catering basis but the guest may be treated to private *Weinproben* (wine tastings) with the family. Details of this and all other accommodation is available from the tourist information offices.

There is no lack of ruined hilltop castles but a visit should be paid to one of the more impressive ones which is prominent above **Freudenberg**, less than 4km south-west of Kastel. Continuing southwards from here, return to the river at one of its most spectacular and romantic places, the Saarschleife, a great hairpin bend in the river best seen from the west side near Orscholz. There is a free car park near the prime viewing location at **Cloef** and a forest and bird nature trail goes down towards the river through a little valley called the Steinbachtal. Adjacent to the car park is the Märchenpark Orscholz, a fairytale park with small animals.

Down on the river, the little town of **Mettlach** on the east bank has quite a number of sights of interest. Excavations around the former Benedictine abbey have revealed that there must have been a cruciform church here from about the year 700. Several later buildings occupied the site and an old tower from about 1000 has survived. It is not really a tower in the usual sense of the word but rather a chapel with a large dome, probably modelled on the Palatinate chapel in Aachen. Many of the important furnishings from this building, including a famous reliquary in the form of a triptych from about 1230, are now to be found in the Catholic parish church of St Luitwin. This church was only built around the turn of the century. It is an impressive and colourful building with rich mosaics. The decorations remind one of Italy and the terracotta Stations of the Cross, made and presented by the well known local ceramics firm of Villeroy and Boch, are copies of an Italian series.

The visual presentation *Keravision* and the museum of Villeroy and Boch now occupy the former monastery buildings which have a baroque façade 367ft (112m) long. Admission to the presentation and museum is free and 1 to 1½ hours should be allowed for the visit. The *Keramic-Symposium* is a display of modern ceramic 'sculpture' which has been in the adjacent park since 1974. Note the fountain designed by K.F. Schinkel at the park entrance. Ceramics are also the principal theme of the museum in the nearby Schloss Ziegelberg.

A mile (2km) west of Mettlach the ruins of Burg Montclair occupy two cliff sites above the Saar with splendid views. There was a fortress here from about the year 1000 but the present ruin is that of a second rebuilding which took place in the period 1428-39. It finally fell into disrepair in the sixteenth century. Christian Kretschmar, who had been responsible for rebuilding the monastery in Mettlach in 1728, also built the Pagodenburg at St Gangolf 2 miles (3km) southwest of the town in 1745. It is an octagonal rotunda with five domes. Also worth seeing is the eighteenth-century former tithe house of the Mettlach abbey; the building with residential and service rooms is to be found at Besseringen, a mile (2km) south-east of Mettlach.

Four miles (7km) south of Mettlach along the B51 is Merzig and after this the road closely follows the east bank of the river for the remaining 40 miles (65km) to Saargemünd. It is parallelled on the west bank by the new *Autobahn* A620 which has come in from

The town hall, Merzig

Luxembourg in the west. **Merzig** is a pleasant small town and, like Saarburg and Mettlach, makes a good base from which to explore the river and the surrounding countryside. From the second half of the fourteenth century until 1778, Merzig was the principal town in the Lorraine-Trier condominium of Merzig-Saargau. The people of Germany, France and Luxembourg have for centuries been used to moving freely about the area and today's frontiers have made little difference to this pattern so that there is a constant coming and going which the near common language of the border territory helps to encourage. Nevertheless, the foreign visitor should remember that the frontiers do exist and carry his or her passport.

The former collegiate church of St Peter in Merzig was originally built in the twelfth century but modifications continued until well into the nineteenth century. The quite striking exterior is dominated by the massive west tower. Inside are very pointed arches similar to those often found in Lorraine. The lavish furnishings include a larger than life crucifix from about 1300 on the altar and various figures in the choir. Most of these are from the baroque period but some were added in the nineteenth century. The town hall was built between 1647 and 1650 as a hunting lodge for the elector of Trier. Later alterations affected the open-air staircase and the main doorway but it is a building worthy of inspection. The nearby Staadt-Marx'sche

Bürgerhaus, a citizen's fine house of about a hundred years later, was the work of Christian Kretschmar (1728-71), one of the two most significant baroque architects in this area and already mentioned for his work in the Mettlach area. The comfortable restaurant in the Stadthalle (Civic Hall) has a terrace overlooking an attractive park. Accommodation in Merzig is rather limited and mainly in the small hotel and pension categories. For the motorist, the *Verkehrsamt* has prepared the itineraries for 3 day tours and the free leaflet describing these may be had on request.

Before leaving the vicinity of Merzig, visit the unique *Wolfsfreigehege* just north of the town, the biggest wolf enclosure in Germany. There are really several enclosures, each housing a different kind of wolf, including the rare white arctic variety. As with most *Freigehege*, there is no charge for admission.

An excursion could be made to **Losheim** and then to **Nunkirchen**, travelling some 12 miles (20km) along the historic steam railway, the Saar-Hochwald-Dampfbahn. The rescue of this line from extinction came about in a strange way. In 1981 a small group of friends in Losheim got together to form a model railway club with the object of building a large HO scale layout. They were able to acquire a few items of redundant railway equipment which was put in store. Eventually they were given the old station building at Brotdorf to use as a club house and in 1982 they were allowed to take over the neighbouring redundant line for use as a museum railway. Operations became possible when like-minded enthusiasts from Luxembourg placed an old steam locomotive at the disposal of the Losheim club. In 1983 a locomotive was given by a local mining company. Since then, passenger services have operated each year on specified dates, usually on national holidays or in connection with local events.

A quite different interest requires a journey of a little over 12 miles (20km) in the opposite direction to the village of **Nennig** in the valley of the Mosel. In the year 1852, a farmer discovered the remains of a Roman villa which was eventually revealed as a splendid building 410ft (125m) long. The banqueting hall has a mosaic floor measuring 33 by 52ft (10 by 15m), the largest Roman mosaic yet discovered north of the Alps. At Nennig, a visit could also be made to Schloss Berg, a palace of which the oldest parts date from the twelfth century. Additional buildings were added in the fourteenth to sixteenth centuries and damage from World War II has since been made good.

About 5 miles (8km) north-east of Losheim, the health resort of **Weiskirchen** is the principal settlement in a group of idyllic villages — the others being Konfeld, Rappweiler, Thailen and Weierweiler —

in a very little known area in the so-called Schwarzwälder Hoch-
wald; no connection though with the better known Schwarzwald
further south. **Weiskirchen** is at an altitude of about 1,312ft (400m)
and the surrounding hills go up to 2,296ft (700m). The extensive
medical facilities here owe their existence largely to the healthy
woodland air and the generally mild climate which the area enjoys.
The ordinary holidaymaker though, will be more interested in the
possibilities of a base with access to some really charming scenery
but at the same time within easy reach of many places of interest.
Rappweiler has a 185 acre *Wildfreigehege* where the creatures to be
seen include boars, deer, bison and many varieties of birds. There is
a rustic restaurant here and during fine weather, meals may be taken
on the covered terrace with a view of the forest. The other resorts in
the group all have attractive camping and caravan sites and there is
a youth hostel in Weiskirchen. More conventional accommodation
will be found in the many hotels, pensions and private houses. There
is some self-catering accommodation in the area but farm quarters
are not easy to find; local information offices will furnish detailed
lists upon request. Needless to say, there are many well-marked
footpaths in the woods and Weiskirchen has indoor and outdoor
swimming pools and all the usual resort facilities — minigolf, outdoor chess, table tennis, band concerts and other entertainments.

However, this is essentially an area for open-air activities and
lovers of water sports find that the leisure centre at the *Stausee*
(reservoir) near Losheim offers boating, windsurfing, angling and
bathing amongst its facilities. There is a camp site here and some
Ferienhäuser (self-catering holiday homes) as well. The places mentioned are representative of a whole host of attractive little towns and
villages within quite a small area.

Back close to the river and about 2 miles (3km) south of Merzig the
little village of Harlingen boasts a chapel by Kretschmar. Another 3
miles (5km) or so and **Beckingen** is backed by a pleasant area of
woodland, on the fringe of which are several car parks giving access
to easy round walks of varying length. It will take the motorist but
a few minutes to reach **Dillingen** where the acknowledged industrial activity is conveniently separated from the residential and
business area of the town, with its spacious *Fussgängerzone* (pedestrian precinct). In the district called Pachten close to the Saar, a
number of significant Roman buildings have been revealed. The
remains of the biggest Roman civil settlement in the Saarland, a
cemetery and a fortress, may be seen. Call at the *Kulturamt* (cultural
office) in the Dillingen Rathaus, to obtain details of viewing arrange-

ments. Dillingen is also one of those places with a regular *Flohmarkt* (Flea Market) which takes place from March to September, usually on the third Saturday in each month.

There are a number of places of interest between the river and the French border. On the west bank, a short distance to the north there is a *Schloss* of 1624 in **Rehlingen**; the building probably stands on the site of the twelfth-century customs post of the dukes of Lorraine. A couple of kilometres to the south-east along a minor road through a *Naturschutzgebiet* (conservation area), is the ruined castle of Siersburg on a hilltop (1,010ft, 308m) with broad views over the valley and up and down the Saar; the original object of this stronghold was to keep watch on the river traffic. In this often disputed territory, the Siersburg was, for a long time, a bone of contention between the dukes of Lorraine and the bishops of Trier. The castle gave its name to the neighbouring village of **Siersburg** at the south end of which is **Itzbach**, home of a *Schloss* of 1740 which also owes its existence to the one-time Lothringian feudal lords. Like the *Schloss* in Rehlingen, this one is more like a superior farmhouse or manor house rather than the usual visualisation of a palace. A little more imposing is the recently renovated *Schloss* (1670) in **Grosshemmersdorf**. This village is about 2 miles (4km) west of Siersburg on the north bank of the little river Nied and gives a picture of a typical little old-Lothringian settlement. Once again the history of the *Schloss* reflects the influence of Lorraine with its ambitions and feudal traditions.

This is popular camping and caravanning country and there are many sites, especially around the Siersburg; there is another in **Hemmersdorf**, the part of this village south of the river Nied. A mile or two to the south-east, the village of **Niedaltdorf** is close to the present French border and is noteworthy for its *Tropfsteinhöhle* which may be visited. Just to the south in the village of **Ihn** there are Roman period excavations, and 4 miles (6km) to the east is another remarkable monument in the Roman copper mine which has survived virtually intact from its foundation by one Emilianus in the third century until the present day. The copper mined here was taken to the foundry in the Roman settlement in Dillingen already mentioned. Of more interest than the copper in recent times is the colouring agent azurite which it is said was used by the famous artist Albrecht Dürer in his painting. The mine may be visited by giving prior notice.

Wallerfangen is on the west bank of the Saar, from which it is separated by the A620; now a suburb of the city of Saarlouis, it is actually a much older place. In 1850 a treasure trove of tools and

The courthouse, Saarlouis

ornaments from the Bronze Age was discovered here and further exploration revealed that the area was settled also in Celtic and Roman times. Wallerfangen became the principal place in the domain of Franconian counts, but later appeared in the possession of Lothringian dukes and was probably elevated to the status of a 'free' town by Duke Friedrich III (1251-1303). Thereafter it was fortified by the construction of castles, walls and town gates and from the late Middle Ages became the headquarters of the officials dealing with the German speaking part of the duchy. The town suffered in the Thirty Years War when it was occupied by the French and the Swedes and was largely destroyed in 1635 during the counter attacks of the emperor's forces. The prehistoric finds of the Wallerfangen area may be seen in an exhibition in the *Rathaus* during normal business hours. The restaurant Epe (Bernard Epe is the name of the restaurant owner) has been awarded a coveted Michelin star and gourmets turn here with confidence for a memorable meal. Note, however, that this establishment is closed on Saturdays and for about 3 weeks between July and August. Many restaurants in this area specialise in French cuisine.

In 1680, Louis XIV, the Sun King, founded the modern city which was named after him and was acknowledged to be the political and strategic successor to Wallerfangen. **Saarlouis** remained a French stronghold until the fall of Napoleon in 1815 after which it came under Prussian rule until 1889. The original fortifications were the concept of the distinguished French military architect and engineer Sebastien Vauban of whom there are still many reminders. It is not surprising that in this town with its military tradition, two of its citizens became famous soldiers. Michael Ney, marshall of France, was called by Napoleon 'the bravest of the brave' and he is remembered in Saarlouis with a monument on the so-called Vauban island (in an old arm of the Saar) and by a tablet on his birthplace at Bierstrasse 11. General von Lettow-Vorbeck (born 1870) was the defender of German East Africa in World War I and had the honorary freedom of the city conferred upon him in 1956. His birthplace at 10 Silberherzstrasse has a memorial tablet and a street and a bridge have been named after him. Also on the Saar island is the interesting and striking little statue of the French soldier Lacroix; he somehow missed the retreat of his compatriots in 1815 — some say that he was asleep! — and remained at his post until the Prussians arrived. Saarlouis was very badly mauled in the course of the allied advance at the end of World War II, but is now a clean airy town around the Grosser Markt, the huge square which serves as a car park, except on market days. The visitor arriving by train must walk for about 20 minutes to reach the town. In so doing the heavy industry near the railway is left behind and after crossing the bridge over the canalised Saar, a route may be taken through the fine Stadtpark to the bank of the disused arm of the river. There is a woodland nature trail and the park also accommodates indoor and outdoor swimming pools and a fine camp site, noted for its international patronage. With war damage made good, the Altstadt is an area of some charm within the extensive pedestrian zone. The old military headquarters is now the main post office, facing the Grosser Markt, and there is a postal museum under the same roof. The town museum and library are found in former barracks in Alte Brauerei Strasse; the new Rathaus has Gobelins which were the gift to the town of Louis XIV. The *Glockenspiel* in the town hall tower plays at 8 and 11am, 6 and 9pm.

There is enough in Saarlouis to occupy the visitor for quite a long time but another excursion must be made to the west. Leaving via Metzer Strasse (B405), **Felsberg** is reached in approximately 2 miles (4km) and about half a mile beyond this village there is a car park in which a stop may be made in order to undertake the modest climb to the Teufelsburg castle ruins (1,161ft, 354m) for all-round views over the countryside. There has apparently been a fortress here since at least 1179 when it was in the possession of an obscure knightly line, the Herren von Felsberg. Another mile or two brings the visitor to **Düren** where a former *Schloss* (1760) is now a rather superior farming complex. In the Middle Ages most of the land around here belonged to the abbey at Lungfelden, near St Avold, which gradually bought

The chapel of St Oranna near Berus

out the property of the minor aristocracy. The Düren *Schloss* was built by one of the last of these, the French Franz von Bély.

Now close to the border, although there is nothing of particular interest there, it is worth going on to see the novel situation at **Leidingen** where the frontier runs right through Neutraler Strasse, so that the properties on one side are German and on the other French. Needless to say, border formalities are non-existent. Turn south-eastwards following the border as closely as possible to Berus. Just before reaching the village of Berus the ancient chapel of St Oranna should be visited. It is built in the early and late Gothic style and there are certainly parts dating from the thirteenth century, although much of the structure has been rebuilt much more recently. This has been a place of pilgrimage since the Middle Ages and the saint, or her memory, is credited with healing powers, especially in the realm of head and earache. The colourful windows were created as recently as 1950 by the Alsatian artist Tristan Ruhlmann, who illustrated ancient legends in this modern art form. The south side of the chapel has a large crucifixion group from the baroque period. The tomb of St Oranna is in the parish church in **Berus** which has other treasures also, including a high baroque altar and a Marienaltar (altar to the Virgin Mary) from about 1600.

On the outskirts of Berus is the startling and rather ugly Europäer-Denkmal, a monument dedicated to great post-war Europeans. It stands on historic ground and long disputed territory, with the reminders of successive battles all around and a population which, over the years, has had to allow itself to be called German, French, Lothringian, Prussian or Bavarian. Even the Russians have been here and Marlborough passed through with his armies, or would have done had not the then newly fortified Saarlouis halted his progress for a while. Here, where once in the confusion of war a whole village was destroyed, this new monument has been erected to commemmorate the reconciliation and new friendship between the French and German peoples, bringing up to date as it were, the centuries old message of peace which has gone out over the Saar, Lorraine and the Mosel lands from nearby St Oranna. Remembered are those who overcame their experiences and prejudices to lay the foundation stones of the new post-war Europe, in particular Robert Schumann of France (first president of the European parliament), Konrad Adenauer (Federal German Chancellor from 1949 until 1963), de Gasperi from Italy and Josef Bech from Luxembourg. Do not leave Berus without a brief look round the substantial remains of some of the fortifications of the past.

Leave southwards through Überherrn and then turn east to follow a broad valley of many little water courses back to the Saar. In **Wadgassen** stop at the former Premonstratensian abbey whose history goes back to at least 902. It was in its heyday in the thirteenth and fourteenth centuries and until the end of the latter was the last resting place of the counts of Saarbrücken. It suffered badly in the Thirty Years War, especially through the laying waste of its farms and the de-population of the countryside, but made a recovery in the eighteenth century when a lot of building was undertaken. At the beginning of the revolution, the abbey was occupied and plundered by French troops. The monks fled and the church eventually became a ruin while the remaining rooms of the abbey were given over to secular use in the construction of a crystal factory, now a gallery of the firm Villeroy and Boch.

The detours to places of interest in the countryside serve to conceal the fact that since Dillingen, the Saar has had a very industrialised aspect although it must be said that pleasant scenery is never very far away. From the river, or riverside paths, the scene is of an incongruous mixture of agriculture and heavy industry with steelworks predominating. Continuing upstream past Völklingen the hills can be seen behind the chimneys and cooling towers; within a mile or two there are numerous car parks giving access to walking and cycling routes, fine viewpoints, huts belonging to the various

Roadside wine sales in the Mosel Valley

Ediger-Eller, in the Rhineland

Bremm, in the Rhineland

The river Saar from the old bridge at Saarbrücken

rambling organisations, playing areas and even a *Wildpark*, an enclosure for deer or wild boars in Köllerbachtal.

But entry into the capital of the Federal State of the Saarland should be no longer delayed. The reader may find it strange that a city with a high population should feature in a book purporting to lead him or her off the beaten track. Yet few foreign visitors find their way to **Saarbrücken**, for in this corner of West Germany it is not on the direct route to any of the more well known tourist goals. Most people are hard pressed to think of a single fact about the city or even to pinpoint its precise location. As an important industrial centre it suffered grievous damage during World War II, in some parts the destruction being as much as 90 per cent, so it is hardly surprising that there is not a comprehensive picture today of its always stormy history. Nevertheless, much of interest has survived. Originally a Roman settlement stood at the intersection of the Lombardy road and the road from Metz to Mainz but by the end of the tenth century this junction had moved downstream as far as the trading post of St Johann. Saarbrücken was still separate at that time and both towns were granted charters in 1321. The Thirty Years War and other conflicts inflicted damage on all the Saar towns and it was not until the end of the eighteenth century that they were again able to enjoy a period of peace and prosperity. In 1909, Saarbrücken and St Johann united and together with St Arnual and the industrial area of

Malstatt-Burbach, formed the basis of the modern city. In 1947 a university was founded and in 1957, after a short period as the capital of an autonomous region, Saarbrücken became the capital of the new German Federal State called Saarland.

Saarbrücken, nudging the French border, rightly regards itself as a cosmopolitan city and the influence of the neighbouring country is seen everywhere, not least in many of the restaurants. Indeed, the word *Salü*, which will be encountered frequently, has a French origin and can be used as a general greeting like the Bavarian *Grüss Gott*. This little word has been adopted in the city's slogan *Salü Saarbrücken* which is also the name of one of the little pleasure vessels which ply upstream to Saargemünd and into the French waterway system. The city is a member of a tri-partite partnership, the others being Nantes in France and Tbilisi in Georgia (USSR). The uncertainties about the role of Saarbrücken after the last war were finally resolved as a result of a referendum in 1955 and once France recognised the Saarland as part of the German Federal Republic, the way was clear to develop a peaceful and friendly relationship between the two countries. This new era is nowhere better symbolised than in the magnificent Deutsch-Französischer-Garten (Franco-German-Garden) which was opened in 1960 having been created as a joint effort between the two countries, the state of Saarland and the city of Saarbrücken.

The 123 acre (49 hectare) park has something for everybody. From the main north entrance, a miniature train takes the visitor round the large lake to be dropped off wherever the fancy takes him or her. From the south end of the lake there is a chair-lift for an effortless ride up to the eastern end of the park. There is boating on the lake which is also the location of the largest water organ in Europe. Young and old will enjoy the Land of the Lilliputians, models of famous buildings from all over the world built to a scale of 1:33 and set out in an area of some $5\frac{1}{2}$ acres ($2\frac{1}{4}$ hectares). Many people visit the garden just for the lovely array of flowers and trees which is to be found here. There are several eating places or one may picnic on the lawns at will.

Many historic buildings in the city have been carefully restored after the ravages of war. After the burning down of the Protestant Ludwigskirche in an air raid in 1944, there was much debate as to whether it should be rebuilt to the original plans of 1762-75 or in a modern style. The church, designed by the municipal architect F.J. Stengel, was considered to be the most important church in the Saar, and so it is fortunate that the final decision was to restore it to its original form and this is the building which faces the Ludwigsplatz. Stengel was also responsible for the Catholic parish church in St

Johann (1754-58) and for the Altes Rathaus (1758-60) on Schlossplatz. An earlier work of his was the *Schloss* (1738-48) which gives its name to the square. In 1793 it was looted and burned but was rebuilt to the architect's plans in 1810. Near the Schlossplatz and just over the Alte Brücke (Old Bridge) from the modern town, is the Protestant Schloss-kirche and town parish church, a fifteenth-century building which is the funerary chapel of the princes of Nassau-Saarbrücken. Damage caused by fire in 1677 and by air raids during World War II was made good on each occasion but most of the original furnishings were lost. The new windows by G. Meistermann should be noted.

Not to be missed is the Protestant parish church in **Bischmisheim** about 4 miles (6km) east of the centre. This is an octagonal, symmet-rical rotunda designed in 1822 by the Berlin architect K.F. Schinkel. It is based on the palatinate chapel in Aachen with a tent-like pyra-mid roof and a lantern over the octagon. It is a typical Protestant preaching church with the altar, pulpit and organ in line one above the other.

From the Schlossplatz area, the Alte Brücke (1546-8), which was modified in the eighteenth century, leads over the Saar to the Staats-theater, built in 1937-8. The square which the theatre faces is now called Tbilisser Platz, acknowledging Saarbrücken's partnership with the Georgian city. Musicals and drama are staged by the resi-dent company. The little Saarländisches Landestheater confines it-self to 'straight' theatre. There are numerous museums and art gal-leries in the city and the tourist information office will gladly for-ward literature (largely in English) giving details of all places of interest. In addition to the international park already mentioned, the Saarbrücken zoo about 2 miles (4km) east of the city centre is a popular goal. It can readily be reached by bus and there is ample parking space. Be warned that it can be very busy indeed on Sundays and holidays when a thousand additional parking spaces are made available near the south entrance.

The holidaymaker may look askance at a big city as a base and there are certainly many smaller and more peaceful places within a short distance. But for the person dependent on public transport there are advantages in being at the focal point of rail and road services and as an international metropolis, Saarbrücken is able to offer a good range of hotel accommodation. There is ample provision for leisure activity with several indoor and outdoor swimming pools, many children's play areas, numerous tennis courts and so on.

The river Saar flows for some 5 miles (8km) through the Saarland capital and its inner suburbs and as the city is left to continue the journey southwards, the Saarland radio mast is seen on the Hallberg (840ft, 256m) where there is a good viewpoint and a rather romantic palace, the Schloss Hallberg. Most of the industrial activity is now left behind and in 4 or 5 miles (6 or 8km) **Güdingen** is reached, with its race course occupying an attractive site beside the river. For the next 6 miles (10km) the Saar itself forms the boundary between Germany and France. **Bübingen** almost adjoins Güdingen and is the last place within the administrative domain of Saarbrücken. There is little evidence of the national frontier and there is constant movement between the two countries. Passport and customs officials content themselves with an occasional random check. Between Kleinblittersdorf in Germany and Grossblittersdorf in France there is a footbridge built jointly by the two communities and known as the Bridge of Friendship. The French, however, call their town Grosbliederstroff; most of the towns and villages along here have French and German versions of their names creating a situation which can sometimes be confusing for the foreign visitor. A little further to the south the 430ft (131m) long railway bridge between Hanweiler and Saargemünd is another example of international co-operation. Along these last few kilometres of the Saar and to the west the coal mines and other necessary eyesores of the French industrial region across the river, with the continuous movements of buckets along overhead cableways may be seen. The German side of the river cannot lay claim to any outstanding scenic attractions either, but there are two surprises. The villages of Auersmacher and Sitterswald have both been gold medal winners in the Federal Republic's 'Beautiful Village' competition and are well worth visiting.

So far as West Germany is concerned, this is the end — or rather the beginning — of the river Saar which, here at Saargemünd (Sarreguemines in French), comes up to the border from France where it has been called the Sarre. This too is where another long river, the Blies, adds its waters to the Saar and itself takes over the frontier watch for a while. It is surprising that it is the Blies and not the name-giving Saar which has the greater length in Saarland although the latter is, of course, the longer river in total.

Although the Saar journey is over, the visitor could be excused for cheating a little and following the Blies upstream to the rather charming baroque town of **Blieskastel**, a former royal seat and a present day spa, run according to the theories of the renowned Sebastian Kneipp. The historic buildings here include the Schlosskirche (1778-81) built for the imperial Countess Marianne von der Leyen by Stengel's pupil Reheis. Also worth visiting are the Orangerie (1669), officers' and officials' houses on the Schlossberg (from 1765) and the Rathaus (1775). An adequate range of guest accommodation and many leisure facilities, including swimming pools, would appear to make this an ideal centre for the visitor wishing to explore the area yet not stay in Saarbrücken itself. In any case, the capital is only 14 miles (23km) away.

Further Information
— The Saar Valley —

Buildings and Gardens

Mettlach
Abbey Park
Open: during daylight.
Home of the Mettlacher Keramik-Symposium.
Admission and car parking free.
Close to town centre with restaurants, etc.

Burg Montclair
☎ (06864) 1774
Open: Saturday, Sunday, and holidays 8am-6pm. Other days by prior arrangement.
Impressive ruin overlooking the Saarschleife.

Saarbrücken
Botanischer Garten der Universität des
    Saarlandes
Im Stadtwald
6600 Saarbrücken
☎ (0681) 3022405
Open: Monday to Thursday 8am-4pm, Friday 8am-12noon. Greenhouses closed 12noon-1pm.
Guided tours by prior arrangement.

Deutsch-Französischer-Garten (DFG)
Metzer Strasse
6600 Saarbrücken
☎ (0681) 53437
Open: all year.
Splendid gardens and lake. Water-organ, miniature train, chair-lift, etc in summer. Admission free in winter. Restaurants.

Caves

Niedaltdorfer Tropfsteinhöhle
Neunkircher Strasse 10
6639 Rehlingen-Niedaltdorf
☎ (06833) 444
Open: daily 10am-12noon, 2-6pm.
Prior telephone call appreciated.
Splendid underground spectacle with caverns and passages and many stalactites and stalagmites.

Cycling and Rambling

Tourist information offices supply brochures with suggested itineraries and details of 'packages' which include maps, accommodation and sometimes the transport of heavy luggage. The 'packages' of 2 to 5 nights arranged by the Saarburg office include bed and breakfast, evening meals, packed lunches, cycle hire and a wine tasting.
Details and bookings:
Verkehrsamt
5510 Saarburg
☎ (06581) 81215 or 6

Cycles may be hired from: Jakobstrasse 21, Trier: Verkehrsamt, or railway station, Konz: Verkehrsamt, Saarburg: Losheim Stausee leisure centre and also in Saarholzbach.

Rambling 'packages' of 3 to 6 nights are arranged by the Saarburg tourist office and the prices include bed, breakfast and evening meal, packed lunches and transport to the starting point of each day's walk. Details and bookings from the address and telephone number above.

Museums

Hermeskeil
Dampflok-Museum
Am Bahnhof
5508 Hermeskeil
☎ (06851) 6260 or Reisebüro Vignal
(06851) 5585
Open: Saturday & Sunday 10am-7pm.
Groups can be accommodated on other
days by arrangement.
Steam locomotives and other historic
railway equipment.

Flugaustellung
5508 Hermeskeil-Abtei
☎ (06503) 7693
Two miles (3km) north of Hermeskeil
on B327.
Open: April to October daily 9am-6pm.
The history of air travel; military and
civil planes, models and technical
equipment. Café in Concorde. Reduced
admission charge for children. Free
parking.

Konz
Volkskunde- und Freilichtmuseum
Roscheiderhof 1a
5503 Konz
Open: March to November, Monday to
Friday 9am-4.30pm, Saturday, Sunday
and holidays 10am-5pm.
Groups and bus parties should make
prior arrangements. Artisans' tools,
agricultural exhibits. Many furnished
rooms, timbered houses and chapel
(1730).

Merzig
Heimatmuseum
Fellenbergschlösschen
6640 Merzig
☎ (06861) 80 or 130
Open: Sunday and holidays 2-6pm.
Groups at other times by prior ar-
rangement. Local history including
Roman finds.

Mettlach
Villeroy and Boch Keravision
In der alten Abtei
6642 Mettlach
☎ (06864) 81251

Open: Monday to Friday 8am-12.30pm,
2-5pm, Saturday 9am-1pm.
History and products of the famous
ceramics firm. Admission free. Free car
parking in adjacent abbey park.

Keramikmuseum
Schloss Ziegelberg
6642 Mettlach
☎ (06864) 81294
Open: Tuesday to Saturday 9am-
12.30pm, 2-5.30pm, Sunday 10.30-
12.30pm, 2-6pm. Closed weekends
December to February.
Exhibition of the products of Villeroy
and Boch, etc. Reduced admission for
students, children, etc.

Nennig
Roman Mosaic Floor
6641 Nennig
☎ (06866) 279
Open: April to September, Tuesday to
Sunday 8.30-11.30am, 1-5.30pm,
October, November and January to
March, Tuesday to Sunday 9-11.30am,
1-4pm.
Finest Roman mosaic floor north of
Alps. Reduced admission charge for
children, students, clubs, etc. Groups
should telephone in advance. Free car
park.

Saarbrücken
Abenteuermuseum
Im alten Rathaus
Am Schloss
6600 Saarbrücken
☎ (0681) 51747
Open: Tuesday and Wednesday 9am-
1pm, Thursday and Friday 3-7pm,
some Saturdays 10am-2pm.
Adventure experiences from Asia,
Africa, South America and New
Guinea based on the travels of Heinz
Rox-Schulz since 1950. Facilities for
groups, including film show by ar-
rangement.

Landesmuseum für Vor- und
    Frühgeschichte
Am Ludwigsplatz 15
6600 Saarbrücken
☎ (0681) 5947

Open: Tuesday to Friday 10am-4pm,
Saturday 10am-1pm, Sunday 10am-
6pm.
Pre- and early history. Admission free.

Saarberg Geological Museum
Saarbergwerke AG
Hauptabteilung Ausbildung
Postfach 1030
Trierer Strasse 4
6600 Saarbrücken
☎ (0681) 4054098 or 4053544
Open: Monday to Friday 10am-5pm,
first Sunday in month 9am-1pm.
Closed holidays. Geological history of
the earth and especially the Saarland.
Mineralogy. Admission free.

Stadtgalerie, Kulturcafé
St Johanner Markt
6600 Saarbrücken
☎ (0681) 3001751
Open: Tuesday to Sunday 11am-7pm.
Admission free.

A free brochure is available giving
details of the above and other museums and galleries in Saarbrücken.
Contact one of the following:
Info-Pavillon
Ecke Trierer Strasse/Faktoreistrasse
(opposite Hauptbahnhof)
6600 Saarbrücken
☎ (0681) 3098222 or 36515
Open: Monday to Friday 7.30am-8pm,
Saturday 7.30am-4pm.

Amt für Touristik
Rathaus St Johann
6600 Saarbrücken.

Saarlouis
Neues Rathaus
Grünebaumstrasse
6630 Saarlouis
☎ (06831) 443263 or 443228
Open: during normal business hours.
Gobelins from Louis XIV and baroque
furniture (not always available for
viewing but inquire at main entrance).
Carillon plays from tower at 8 and
11am, 6 and 9pm.

Postmuseum
Grosser Markt
6630 Saarlouis

Located on upper floor of main post
office building. History of postal
facilities and transport in the area.
Some exhibits may be seen any time
office open to public. Main collection
seen by arrangement. Write in advance
or call at administrative office on south
side of building.

Städtische Museum
Alte Brauerei Strasse
6630 Saarlouis
☎ (06831) 193265
Open: Tuesday and Thursday 9am-
12noon, 3-6pm, Sunday 3-6pm.
Valuable treasures from the history of
Saarlouis and surrounding area.
Admission free.

Trier
For information on places of interest in
Trier write to:
Verkehrsamt
Simonstift
Postfach 3830
5500 Trier

Wallerfangen
Vorgeschichtliche Funde in
    Wallerfangen
Rathaus
6634 Wallerfangen
Open: during business hours.
Valuable collection of prehistoric finds.

Römisches Bergwerk St Barbara
Schloss-strasse 98
6634 Wallerfangen
(office of Landkreis Saarlouis)
☎ (06831) 444410
Open: for inspection on prior notifica-
tion to Landkreis office. Roman copper
mine in remarkable state of
preservation.

Museum Railway
Merzig-Wadern-Nunkirchen
(Saar-Hochwald-Museumsbahn)
Museums-Eisenbahn-Club-Losheim
(MECL)
Tulpenstrasse 6
6646 Losheim
☎ (06872) 3592

Information also from:
Verkehrsverein
Postfach 1169
6696 Losheim
☎ (06872) 6169
and
Café Erbacher
6640 Merzig
☎ (06861) 2809
Twelve mile (20km) long line. Steam or
historic diesel passenger trains operate
on selected dates about once each
month March to beginning of October,
often on Sunday but also on Easter
Monday and Ascension Day. Traditional St Nikolaus (early December)
and New Year (early January) journeys. Annual model railway exhibition
in November. Actual details of services
and exhibition from Verkehrsverein.

Public Transport

The principal public transport service
through the Saar valley is provided by
Deutsche Bundesbahn (German
Federal Railway) with about twenty
trains daily (fewer Saturday and
Sunday) between Trier and
Saarbrücken calling at intermediate
stations. Overall journey time 1hr10-
1hr 20min. There are also services
between Saarbrücken and the French
frontier stations of Saargemünd (Sarre-
gemuines) and Forbach, between
Dillingen and Niedaltdorf and between Völklingen and Überherrn, most
of the latter being operated by DB
buses. Handy pocket time-tables are
available free from the station inquiry
offices in Trier and Saarbrücken.

There are numerous bus services
in and around Saarlouis, Völklingen
and Saarbrücken and there are also
many services based on the railway
stations at Saarburg and Merzig. From
about Easter until the third week in
October there are sight-seeing bus
tours of the city of Saarbrücken every
Saturday afternoon.

Tourist Information Offices

Rheinland-Pfalz
Fremdenverkehrsverband Rheinland-
Pfalz
Postfach 1420
Löhrstrasse 103-105
5400 Koblenz
☎ (0261) 31079

Verkehrsamt
Postfach 100
Graf-Siegfried-Strasse 32
5510 Saarburg
☎ (06581) 81348 or 2027

Saarland
Fremdenverkehrsverband Saarland
Postfach 242
Am Stiefel 2
6600 Saarbrücken 3
☎ (0681) 35376

Verkehrsverein Saarbrücken
Rathaus St Johann
6600 Saarbrücken
☎ (0681) 96222

Fremdenverkehrsverein
Poststrasse 12
6640 Merzig
☎ (06861) 73874

Amt für Öffentlichkeitsarbeit
Kaiser-Wilhelm-Strasse 6
6630 Saarlouis
☎ (06831) 4441

Zoos and Wildlife Parks

Ballweiler
Wildpark
South of village which is 4 miles (6km)
south-west of Blieskastel.

Differten
Wildgehege
South of road between Wadgassen and
Überherrn.

Karlsbrunn
Wildgehege on the Steinberg
In southernmost tip of Saarland, west
of Forbach.

Ludweiler
Wildgehege in the Scheidwald
Four miles (6km) south-west of
Völklingen.

Merzig
Wolfsfreigehege
Two miles (3km) north of town.
Admission and car parking free.
Restaurant near entrance.

Neunkirchen
Zoo
Twelve miles (20km) north-east of
Saarbrücken.

Orscholz (Cloef)
Märchenpark
☎ (06865) 434 or 505
Close to viewing area for Saarschleife.
Open: daily April to mid-October 9am-
7pm, mid-October to March 2-5pm.
Fairytale park with small animals.
Reduced admission charge in winter.
Free car park.

Rappweiler
Wildfreigehege
A mile (2km) south-west of
Weiskirchen.
Open: daily 9am-8pm or dusk if
earlier.
185 acres forest enclosure with deer,
boars, bison and birds. Reduced
admission charge for children, groups,

etc. Restaurant open all year. Free car
park.

Saarbrücken
Zoologischer Garten
Graf-Stauffenbergstrasse
6600 Saarbrücken
☎ (0681) 812494
Open: in summer 8.30am-6pm, in
winter 8.30am-dusk.
37 acres of park with animals of 250
different species, Africa-house with
nocturnal creatures, tropiquarium, etc.
Reduced admission charge for groups
of more than twenty. Restaurants.

Wildgehege am Homburg
Two miles (3km) north of city centre
on road to Dudweiler.

Saarwellingen
Wildpark in the Dorschter Wald
A mile (2km) north-east of town. (B405
north-east from Saarlouis.)

Völklingen
Wildpark in Köllerbachtal
Two miles (3km) north of town centre.

There are also other forest enclosures
(*Gehege*) for wild boars, deer, etc
usually accessible at all times without
charge. Contact local information
offices for precise locations.

6 • The Palatinate Forest Nature Park

M ost of the territory to be explored in this chapter lies within the boundaries of the Palatinate Forest (Pfälzer Wald) Nature Park along the east edge of which the German Wine Road (Deutsche Weinstrasse) runs from north to south. The nature park covers an area of 443,050 acres of which 71 per cent is wooded, making it the biggest uninterrupted forest in the Federal Republic. Some 186 miles (300km) of footpaths are cared for by the Pfälzerwald-Verein (PWV) with many shelters and parking places for ready access to the favourite viewpoints. Whereas the area is in general sparsely populated, the named road comprises a chain of closely spaced towns and villages, nearly every one being concerned, to a greater or lesser degree, with the production of wine. It is hardly surprising since this is part of Germany's biggest wine-growing area. This region enjoys warm and sunny summer months, and by the time the southern end of the Weinstrasse is reached it is one of the warmest parts of Germany.

By whatever means of transport, this area is easy to reach. Air travellers arriving at Frankfurt could reach Neustadt, fairly central on the Weinstrasse, by train in about $1\frac{1}{2}$ hours. Rail travellers from Britain will find it quickest to travel via Cologne and Frankfurt although there are several less direct alternatives which could be used. The motorist from Britain may choose whichever of the ferry crossings to the continent is most convenient for him or her, and join the continental motorway network to cross into Germany at Aachen. From there the route is at first eastwards in the direction of Cologne on *Autobahn* A4 and this is left near Kerpen after about 25 miles (40km) to join A61 going south-east. This splendid motorway is followed for some 118 miles (190km) to Alzey, from where Bundesstrasse (Federal Road) B271 goes southwards, shortly to become the Weinstrasse. It could hardly be easier. If it is not desired to join the named road at its start, the *Autobahn* can be followed for up to a further 31 miles (50km) then left to turn west to the planned destination.

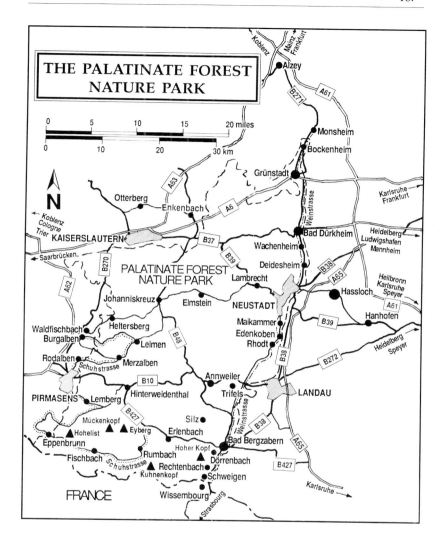

Starting at the north end of the 'wine road' the first village is **Monsheim**, 10 miles (16km) from Alzey and fairly typical of the places where the grape dominates life. There are no special attractions here, but watch out all along the route for roadside stalls selling locally grown fruit and vegetables — a bonus for the self-caterer, for prices are very reasonable. Needless to say, wine is also readily available and occasionally *Weinproben* is invited. In the small towns and villages not specially geared to the tourist trade there is always a certain amount of modest accommodation available and this may well appeal to the reader of this volume rather than what is on offer in the more well known resorts. From **Bockenheim** 2 miles (3km) further on (where there is a vineyard nature trail), the Weinstrasse marks the eastern fringe of the designated nature park of the Pfälzer Wald and the traveller is not obliged to adhere strictly to the named road but can indulge at whim in attractive detours up to 25 miles (40km) to the west to enjoy the forest scenery or visit other places of interest.

Grünstadt, a little town 4 miles (6km) south of Bockenheim, is the former home of the counts of Leiningen and is today the economic and cultural centre of a vineyard district called Unterhaardt. Amongst the sights are the baroque Rathaus (1750-55), the charming baroque portal of the former royal court (1716) and the Gothic Martinskirche (1494-1520). The town has both a *Freibad* and a *Hallenbad* and on the hill above the pools the *Stadtpark* (town park), with a large free car park and tennis courts, provides fine views over the countryside and could be the starting place for local walks.

From Grünstadt, the motorist might well join the A6 for a speedy 15 miles (24km) westwards to the Enkenbach exit and turn north to **Enkenbach** where the former Premonstratensian monastery church of St Norbert is well worth a visit. It is now the Catholic parish church and is an essentially Romanesque building which was added to the then existing monastery complex in the thirteenth century. The porch is regarded as one of the most beautiful Romanesque constructions in Germany. In this little town the Protestant parish church has a fine organ and there are some interesting old houses in the Hauptstrasse. It would be worthwhile going a further 7 miles (12km) west to see the Cistercian monastery church (1181-1254) in **Otterberg**. There is a lovely rose window here and it is of interest to note that this building has been shared by Catholic and Protestant congregations since 1707. The stately Rathaus is also worthy of inspection. It was built by Walloon refugees in 1753 and is one of the most picturesque town halls in the Palatinate.

From here it is only a few kilometres into the city of **Kaiserslautern** where there are many sights of interest and a fine shopping area with a number of good restaurants. The 'Kaiser' in the name probably goes back to Emperor Frederick Barbarossa who built a fortified castle above the river Lauter in 1152; it was blown up by the French in 1703 during the War of the Spanish Succession. Churches include the former Premonstratensian church of St Martin and St Maria built for the monastery in early Gothic style 1250-90 and the former Minorite church (1300), now the Catholic parish church of St

Martin. Nineteenth- and twentieth-century art is exhibited in the Pfalzgalerie at Museumplatz 1, and there is a local history collection in the Theodor-Zink-Museum at Steinstrasse 48. There are indoor and outdoor pools and there is a bathing beach on the tiny lake at **Gelterswoog**, 4 miles (7km) to the south-west. Another heated outdoor pool is to be found in the little village of **Trippstadt** about 6 miles (10km) south of Kaiserslautern. The baroque palace (1766) here is now the home of the State Forestry School but it is for the rambling possibilities in this most beautiful part of the Pfälzer Wald that people come here. The Karlstal is a particularly picturesque valley and a favourite goal for walkers.

From the centre of Kaiserslautern the B37 is a pleasant road eastwards through the forest to reach **Bad Dürkheim**, back on the Weinstrasse, in 20 miles (33km). Dürkheim describes itself as the spa between the forest and the vineyards and was famous in Roman times for the same reasons as it is today, the forests, the wine and the thermal springs. It enjoys a mild climate and is a favourite centre for people wishing to undertake forest walks or to enjoy the good food and wine of the area. The *Kur*, the medical aspect of the spa, is not taken too seriously here but there is ample opportunity for bathing in either the *Thermalbad* (pool with water from the natural thermal springs), which maintains a temperature of 32˚C (90˚F) or in the leisure bathing complex called the Salinarium. Dürkheim also has the attraction of the only casino in the area covered in this chapter. The Dürkheimer Wurstmarkt (Sausage Market), despite its name, claims to be the biggest wine festival in the world and takes place on the second and third weekends in September.

The three-aisled former palace church of St Johannes is now the Protestant parish church. It dates largely from the fourteenth century but has a neo-Gothic tower added in 1865-6. The church is notable for its various tombs, including that of Count Ernich IX and his wife. The nearby Kästenberg has the remains of a Celtic ring, the so-called Heidenmauer (Heathen Wall), and on the east edge of this same hill there are rock drawings indicating the existence of a Roman quarry here. In the town, local history is recorded in the Heimatmuseum while the natural history of the area is dealt with comprehensively in the Pfalzmuseum für Naturkunde. The Kloster Limburg nearby is the remains of a former Benedictine monastery founded by Emperor Konrad II in about 1025 and now constitutes one of the most grandiose church ruins in Germany. Concerts and open-air theatrical productions take place here in summer. **Kallstadt**, to the north of Dürkheim, is a particularly attractive village straddling the Weinstrasse.

Wachenheim is only 2 miles (3km) south of Bad Dürkheim on the B271. The former *Schloss* is the headquarters of a wine firm specialising in *Sekt*, the German version of champagne. A peep into the well-preserved courtyard is worthwhile. Four miles (7km) to the south-west on the road to Lambrecht is the 395 acre Hochwildpark Kurpfalz, an area of great beauty in which many animals including deer, bears, boars and wolves live in natural surroundings. There are many pleasant paths through the woods with viewing platforms here and there from which the animals in their large enclosures may be observed.

In another 3 miles (5km) along the 'Wine Road', the charming old town of **Deidesheim** is reached. This is a place which deserves more than a casual glance in passing. The over-riding influence here is the wine and much of the history and legend has to do with this desirable product of the area. For example, the inn Zur Kanne dates from the twelfth century and possesses a book in which Alexander von Humboldt made an entry on the subject. It still serves good wine and the Michelin guide has found the food worthy of mention too. In the Marktplatz (Market Square) the Catholic parish church is an important late Gothic building (1464-80), rebuilt in 1689. It is a basilica with a nave and two aisles and contains notable busts of the apostles and prophets from about 1480. The crucifix at the high altar is from about 1510. Also in the Marktplatz the historic Rathaus has a striking exterior staircase (1734) and the Museum für Weinkultur, telling the story of wine over the centuries with a varied collection of drinking vessels, literature and works of art on the subject. The Spitalkirche is a chapel of 1496 with adjoining sixteenth- to eighteenth-century hospital buildings; the chapel of St Michael, a late Gothic building of 1662, was restored in 1951 following war damage. The museum of modern ceramics at Stadtmauergasse 17 is also worth seeing.

Neustadt an der Weinstrasse (to distinguish it from many other towns with the same name) is by far the biggest place on this named route and is a centre of commerce and culture. One of the most important buildings in the Palatinate is the former Liebfrauen collegiate church here in Neustadt. It is mainly fourteenth century but the lower storeys of the south tower were inherited from an older building; under the baroque dome is the tower watchman's accommodation which was in use until a few years ago. Inside, the sculptural ornamentation includes monkeys and grotesque figures. The Casimirianum in Ludwigstrasse was founded in 1597 as a university for those members of the Reformed Church who had to leave the Lutheran Heidelberg University. It is a three-storey building with an

Deidesheim

attractive staircase tower and a fine Renaissance doorway. The Rathaus shares the market place with many houses which have fine courtyards. Numbers 4 and 11 Marktplatz, 4 Rathausgasse and 55 and 91 Hauptstrasse are all worth seeking out.

The Heimat- und Weinmuseum features local history as well as the history of wine. Two miles (4km) south of the town, above the suburb of Oberhambach is the eleventh-century castle called Kästenburg, the Hambach Schloss; its fame and interest derives from a student demonstration in 1832 in favour of the unification of Germany and the federation of Europe. The people of the Pfalz gave the castle to Crown Prince Maximilian of Bavaria as a gift and he had it rebuilt from 1846 in the style of a Venetian-Gothic palazzo. Major restoration work was carried out to celebrate, in 1982, the 150th anniversary of the events of 1832. Parts of the old building were incorporated in a new one which is now used for concerts and exhibitions, with fine views from the terrace café.

Those family groups who enjoy the modern style leisure park should take time for a visit to Holiday Park between Hassloch and Hanhofen about 7 miles (12km) east of Neustadt, where they will find entertainment and fun to keep them going all day. There are mechanical 'rides' of various descriptions, aquatic displays, a dolphinarium and much more. There is another *Weinmuseum* in the Holiday Park with a collection of wine artefacts and demonstrations

Hambach Schloss

of vineyard management. In this direction too, is the noble city of Speyer with its imposing cathedral and other places of interest. Although it is actually outside the scope of this chapter, it can be recommended as a possible excursion goal for it lies only some 12 miles (20km) from Neustadt.

Railway enthusiasts will enjoy a visit to the railway museum near the Hauptbahnhof (main railway station) in Neustadt where they will see several notable historic steam locomotives and some thirty other vehicles. From time to time some of these are operated on the line which runs west from Neustadt to Elmstein, a distance of about 11 miles (18km). Between these places a stop could be made at **Lambrecht** to visit the Deutsches Schaustellermuseum (literally Showman's Museum) where a miniature representation of a *Kerwe* or *Kirmes* (old church fair) can be found.

The main road south from Neustadt is the B38 and although it continues for a while to mark the nature park boundary, the Weinstrasse now follows a less important road to the west to take in several wine producing communities such as Maikammer, St Martin, Edenkoben and Rhodt. There is access to numerous picturesque roads leading westwards into the hilly area known as the Haardt where the visitor will find the sources of many little rivers from which the waters eventually flow into the Rhine. There is a chair-lift, the Rietburgbahn, a mile west of Edenkoben which takes one quickly to the Rietburg castle ruin, at 1,804ft (550m) with another splendid viewpoint. There is a *Wildpark* at the top where the restaurant is open daily from Easter to October. In the Schloss Villa Ludwigshöhe near the foot of the Rietburgbahn, there is a collection of the works of the artist Max Slevogt and the rooms have wall and ceiling paintings and other works of art. This little palace was erected to celebrate the 90th birthday of Prinzregent Luitpold of Bavaria in 1911 — the Palatinate was formerly part of Bavaria. In **Edenkoben** there is a wine and nature trail to be followed and the exhibits in the Heimatmuseum are again strongly influenced by the wine industry. The area around **Maikammer** is particularly attractive in the spring when peach and almond trees blossom in the orchards.

The B38 continues into **Landau in der Pfalz** (to distinguish it from its namesake in Bavaria), a town which straddles the nature park boundary. Three-quarters of the medieval town was burned down in 1689 when Vauban, the architect who designed fortifications for Louis XIV was working here. However, a certain number of Vauban's works have survived, including the French and German gates. The Protestant parish church is the former collegiate church Unserer Lieben Frau which was built in the fourteenth century to serve an Augustinian canonry founded in 1276. It is a large, long building and the tower in 1458 had an octagonal belfry built on to the lower square storeys to create a somewhat unusual feature. In the course of restoration work in 1897-8, groin vaulting was added to the chancel and nave. The Catholic parish church of Heiliges Kreuz (Holy Cross) adjoins the Augustinian monastery. The church (1405-13) was damaged during World War II but was re-built to the original plans. Inside there is a font from 1506 and the famous *Landau Madonna*, a wood carving from the seventeenth century, which has been in this church since 1893. The east section of the monastery buildings (1740-50) was destroyed in the war and has not been replaced. French influence can be seen in some seventeenth- and eighteenth-century houses and number 17 Martin-Luther-Strasse, 9 Kaufhausgasse and 1 Max-Josephs-Platz should be specially noted. Number 50 Marktstrasse (1827) was originally the garrison headquarters and is now the town hall. The Heimatmuseum in Villa Streccius has sections for early and prehistory, cultural history, folk art, military affairs and fortification systems.

The B10 leads westwards from Landau into the heart of the nature park. It soon crosses the Weinstrasse and in 9 miles (15km) reaches **Annweiler**. The outstanding attraction in this area is the imperial Burg of Trifels 4 miles (6km) to the east, so it is likely that, in the course of the journey from Landau, it has been seen. This fortress was a stronghold of the reigning monarchs from as early as 1081. From 1124 until 1274 the imperial treasure was kept in the shallow oriel chapel on the east side of the castle and Norman treasure was also stored here in 1195. The castle served to protect the important highway from Metz to the Rhine and although it never fell to its enemies, it could not resist a natural disaster and much of it was destroyed by lightning in 1662. Its impregnable position resulted in it being used to hold distinguished prisoners, including the English king, Richard the Lionheart, who languished here in 1193-4. During the Thirty Years War it was used as a refuge by the populace.

Since 1935 efforts have been made to restore parts of the building to its original condition and large sections have been completely rebuilt. The castle stands on a sandstone outcrop above the forest and can be seen from afar. From it there is a magnificent view in every direction and the visitor to the area should not fail to include this historic site in his or her itinerary. Exploration of the many rooms and towers will occupy the visitor for quite a while and there is a display of replicas of the Bavarian crown jewels — the originals are in Vienna. In Annweiler the displays in the Heimatmuseum understandably are influenced by the story of Trifels but there are also exhibits concerning the development of the tanning and textile industries.

Eleven miles (18km) beyond Annweiler turn southwards at Hinterweidenthal onto the B427, a pretty road which reaches **Dahn** in 4 miles (7km). The Museum für Naturkunde, Handwerk und Waffentechnik combines displays illustrating the natural history of the area with creatures of the forests and rivers, tools used by the ancient trades and the weapons of the two world wars. The Burgmuseum has assembled finds from several of the castle ruins in the neighbourhood and there is a fine heated *Freibad*. A little way south of Dahn, leave the B427 and turn right towards Wieslautern to discover another of Germany's named roads, the Schuhstrasse. This leads to a string of interesting places, many of which are concerned with Germany's shoe manufacturing trade although an apparent paucity of retail outlets is rather surprising.

After passing through Wieslautern the road gradually assumes a westerly direction and a brief pause may be made in **Rumbach** to see the old frescoes in the Christuskirche. The route is now through the

Sunflower crop near Landau

most hilly part of the nature park with summits like Kuhnenkopf 1,742ft (531m) on the left and Grosse Eyberg 1,683ft (513m), Grosse Mückenkopf 1,591ft (485m) and Hohelist 1,562ft (476m) on the right. The French frontier is but a few kilometres to the south. The attractive road continues through Fischbach to Eppenbrunn and the traveller will note the numerous possibilities for leaving his or her vehicle and rambling into the woods beside little streams or climbing up to one of the hilltops for rewarding views and perhaps a ruined castle. **Eppenbrunn** is an attractive little resort and would make an excellent base for an unsophisticated sojourn in this lovely countryside. In fairness the same might be said of almost every little place around here.

The Schuhstrasse leads on to **Lemberg** with its almost obligatory ruined castle and a forest nature trail and then into **Pirmasens** the shoe metropolis of Germany. This town on the fringe of the nature park is host each year to several international fairs concerned with the footwear trade and the leather industry. It is also a favourite venue for conferences of all kinds and there is an almost continuous programme of events of one kind and another. Unfortunately, there is little here of genuine historic interest since the town was almost completely destroyed during World War II. The late baroque Rathaus (1717-47) was one of the buildings which failed to survive but during 1959-63 it was rebuilt to the historic plans and is now a dignified building gracing the main square. It houses a museum of pre- and early history, the Heimatmuseum, the shoe museum and a gallery with the works of local artist Heinrich Bürkel (1802-69).

Pirmasens is well fitted to cater for its many fair and conference guests but it is not perhaps the ideal place for the general holiday-maker although the museum and gallery complex in the old town hall justifies a visit. The splendid and extensive pedestrian precinct sets an example which could well be followed by many British cities. Its centrepiece is a large artificial cascade which tumbles down the hillside opposite the restored Rathaus. At its head, the large rebuilt church stands behind a statue of its patron Pirminius who died in 753 and from whom the town takes its name. The rather charming *Schusterdenkmal* (Shoemaker's Statue) in the pedestrian precinct is a tribute to the trade from which the town derives its prosperity.

The Schuhstrasse now leads northwards into the countryside again, to **Rodalben** with its notable rock formations just 4 miles (6km) from the centre of Pirmasens and then east along a pretty road to **Merzalben** for the castle, Burg Grafenstein, and the Luitpoldturm which, when climbed, has panoramic views. After this the named road swings in a great anti-clockwise loop through Leimen and the valley of the little river Schwarzbach to its termination in **Waldfisch-bach-Burgalben** where the palace Grafensteiner Schloss is worth a brief halt. The ruins of the castle Heidelsburg in the Schwarzbachtal and the place of pilgrimage, Maria Rosenberg, just to the south of Waldfischbach are favourite excursion goals.

The traveller must turn east to get back to the Weinstrasse but rather than retrace the way to Leimen it is suggested that a slightly more northerly route be taken via Heltersberg to Johanniskreuz, from where the B48 runs south-eastwards back to Annweiler and on to Bad Bergzabern. The whole of the route from Waldfischbach to Annweiler is picturesque and passes through an area with very few habitations of any significance. About 6 miles (10km) beyond Annweiler the Weinstrasse comes in from the north and the B48 now assumes custody of the named road as well as being the boundary of the nature park. The ruins of Madenburg Castle nearby are quite extensive; it was one of the ring of hilltop castles which surrounded the Trifels.

In another 5 miles (8km) the spa of **Bad Bergzabern** is reached. This watering place is little known to English speaking tourists although quite popular with the French from Alsace for the border is only 5$\frac{1}{2}$ miles (9km) to the south. Bergzabern is an ideal centre for exploring this southern end of the Wine Road and the nature park,

Gasthof zum Engel,
Bad Bergzabern

for it is the focal point of a useful road network and it is good also for excursions into France with the historic city of Strasbourg only some 43 miles (70km) away.

Bergzabern is in the sunniest tip of the Palatinate and the extensive vineyards come right to the outskirts of the town. Indeed, it is pleasant to wander through the quiet *Kurpark* with its thermal swimming pool, large boating lake and minigolf course and linger to listen to a concert over a cup of coffee followed by a walk up through the vines to the cool woods beyond. On the southern fringe of the town there are fine modern indoor and unheated outdoor swimming pools although the former does not appear to open during the warm summer months. Much of the centre of this small town is a pedestrian zone and there is an extensive car parking area near the outwardly picturesque *Schloss*. This palace was the former seat of the dukes of Zweibrücken and the oldest of the four sections around the square courtyard dates from 1530. The others were added 1561-79 and the present domes and baroque windows were added during a rebuilding in 1725-30. The three-storey Gasthof zum Engel (1556-79) was once the official residence of the dukes and is said to be the finest Renaissance building in the Palatinate. Its three gables are adorned with scrolls and obelisks and there is a lavishly decorated oriel at each corner and a fine courtyard gate. With its two staircase towers, it is the most beautiful of the several fine houses in the town. Not to be overlooked are the fourteenth-century Market Church, rebuilt in 1772 and restored in 1896, the Protestant Schlosskirche (1720-30) and the Rathaus (1705). The Heimatmuseum exhibits the history and crafts of the area.

About 7 miles (12km) west of the town along the B427, **Erlenbach** is where the Burgmuseum der Raubritterburg Berwartstein recalls the days when robber knights occupied many of the hilltop castles. Emperor Frederick I presented Berwartstein to the Bishop of Speyer in 1152 and although it has been largely in ruins since 1591, parts of it are still occupied. It is one of many rock fortresses found in this area and the upper castle has rooms and passageways hewn from the living rock. Nearby to the south, another ruined *Burg* called Kleinfrankreich has a distinctive round tower dating from about 1480. For those with children, a popular excursion from Bad Bergzabern is that to the extensive Wild- und Wanderpark near Silz about 5 miles (8km) to the north-west. Many varieties of animals roam freely over the park which has a network of footpaths for modest rambles.

Climbing out of Bergzabern along the Weinstrasse — now the B38 — towards the French border, a minor road to the right leads to the village of Dörrenbach less than a mile from the main road. Described as 'das Dornröschen der Pfalz' (the Sleeping Beauty of the Palatinate) this lovely old village is a real treasure. Since the road does not go beyond the end of the valley in which it lies, there is no through traffic so there is little to disturb the peace. Fine old timbered houses line the narrow main street and include the Rathaus, a charming Renaissance building with elaborate carved window frames dating from 1590. There are several inns and restaurants serving excellent meals and the local wines. The village church serves both the Catholic and Protestant congregations. It is what is known as a *Wehrkirche*, that is to say, it was fortified to protect it and its churchyard against vagabonds, thieves and other marauders. Its stout walls and towers still stand as evidence of those earlier less peaceful days. Many of the newer houses on the fringe of the village offer guest accommodation in private rooms or holiday flats. At the end of the village, tracks lead directly and steeply into the forest where the lofty but unsightly tower on the Stäffelsberg commands fine views back towards Bad Bergzabern. A little further into the forest and one can discover the remains of the Westwall, the defensive fortifications popularly known as the Siegfried Line with which the Germans hoped to discourage invasion from the west in World War II. These defences were, in the end, no more successful than the French Maginot Line

Marienberg Castle, Würzburg, with the bridge over the Main in the foreground

genius to go round the sculpture room in the museum deciding which pieces are by him and which by 'his workshop' before reading the labels. You are unlikely to go far wrong.

On the other side of a small lateral valley lies the Käpelle, a pilgrimage church designed by Neumann, approached up the hillside by a row of carved Stations of the Cross. On a hot day it can be a tiring climb, but it is worth the effort to inspect the delightful interior of this church, whose frescoes and stucco work represent the highest expression of rococo art. After this, if a further climb can be faced, push on higher still to the Frankenwarte, from which you can enjoy a superb view across the valley of the Main to the city of Würzburg. At the top you will discover that a bus could have taken you all the way from the city!

There is much more to see and admire in Würzburg, and many pleasant restaurants and Weinstuben to linger in. One visit that should not be missed is to the country palace of **Veitshöchheim**, a few miles down stream, which can be reached by boat. The garden is the attraction here, with baroque sculptures of milkmaids and shepherdesses tumbling all over the place and a delightful open-air theatre, with the wings and back-scene of the stage in well-clipped box hedges. The statues here are actually replicas; the originals are in the Marienberg Museum. This kind of garden architecture seems to go best with courtly eighteenth-century life and is perhaps not best appreciated on a Sunday afternoon in summer when the grounds are crowded with the twentieth-century citizens of the Federal Republic enjoying themselves. You may be more in tune with the atmosphere of the age, in which gardens like this were created, if you can pay your visit on a hazy morning in early summer or an afternoon in late autumn when the mist from the river lends a touch of magic and poetry to the alleys, vistas and gesturing figures who inhabit them. Balthasar Neumann, the designer of so many splendid buildings in Franconia seems, indeed, to have surrendered to the appeal of this atmosphere when he chose to propose marriage to his sweetheart in a swannery!

The hills around Würzburg are covered with the vines of the Stein and Leiste vineyards, which are Franconian wines. These are hardly known outside Germany, but for some drinkers they are the most enjoyable of all the German wines. In character, thanks to the shell-lime and Keuper soils on which the vines grow, they are full-bodied, pithy and vigorous. Over half of the wine produced is made from Silvaner grapes, which give a dry and somewhat earthy taste. To many connoisseurs this is preferable to the slightly sweet wines from Riesling grapes that are produced in other areas of Germany. But any one who prefers a slightly less dry Franconian wine (what the Germans call *halb-trocken*) can choose one made from Müller-Thurgau grapes, which constitute almost all the remaining volume of Franconian wine production. Both varieties are sold in bottles of a distinctive shape, called *Bocksbeutels*, which are reserved by German law to the wines of Franconia.

Almost all Franconian wines are white, but there is a small area south of Aschaffenburg, based on the beautiful medieval towns of

Roman remains near
Kastel in the Saar Valley

Dörrenbach town hall, in the
Palatinate Forest Nature Park

Siebeldingen near Landau, in the Palatinate Forest Nature Park

Deidesheim, in the Palatinate Forest Nature Park

Miltenberg and Klingenberg, which produce very decent red wines from Spätburgunder grapes. Travelling upstream from Miltenberg on a wine drinking pilgrimage — what better pilgrimage to undertake in Franconia? — one comes to **Homburg** (another town of this name, near Frankfurt, gave its name to the hat), whose vineyards produce some of the greatest wines of Franconia, including some exceptional Rieslings. At the point where the Main turns south on another of its great loops the river Saale joins it from the north. This small tributary is flanked by good vineyards, especially at Hammelburg, lying below the old castle of Saaleck. Resuming the course of the Main, the visitor arrives at the attractive old town of Karlstadt with its medieval town walls, before reaching Würzburg.

A few miles beyond Würzburg is the large village of **Randersacker**, whose vineyards produce some of the finest wines of the district. In the past this was a favourite retreat for the prince bishops of Würzburg who owned and developed its vineyards. These were later inherited by the kings of Bavaria, and have now passed to the state domain, which owns large estates in the area and has done a great deal to preserve and improve the quality of Franconian wines. The *Weinprobier-Stuben* (wine-tasting inns) of Randersacker attract many citizens and students from Würzburg to taste the wines. There is nothing here now to remind the visitor of the 80-year quarrel with the neighbouring village of Eibelstadt over the right to a vineyard between them (which led to fixed battles with weapons), nor the sacking of the place during the Thirty Years War. On the hill above the town, where the *Autobahn* comes down towards the Main, there is a huge quarry from which the stone was dug that provided the building material not only for a large part of the castle at Würzburg but also for the Isar bridge in Munich, the town hall in Leipzig, and the Olympic Stadium in Berlin. An exploration of this labyrinth could provide an adventurous introduction to geology, especially for children.

Continue upstream, to the charming old village of **Frickenhausen**, with excellent vineyards on its southerly slopes. It lies between the old world towns of Ochsenfurt and Marktbreit. It is difficult to realise today, when visiting these well-preserved and prosperous communities with their fine churches, town halls, *Weinfests*, and spring and autumn festivals that the Swedish troops passed through them, plundering as they went, in the Thirty Years War, or that plague struck in the fifteenth and sixteenth centuries, leaving them deserted. A little further on, the walled and turreted town of **Sulzfeld** offers, as do many of these towns on the Main, a fine

Renaissance Rathaus, many old houses, a parish church enlarged in the seventeenth century, fishing, water sports, footpaths, wine-tasting, and a street *Weinfest* at the beginning of August.

After the Main has twisted once more to take a north-south course, one comes to **Kitzingen**, the largest town of this stretch of the river, the only place on the railway and a centre of the wine trade. A few arches of the old bridge stretch into the river, and the town can offer what claims to be the oldest *Weinkeller* (wine cellar) in Germany and a Fastnachts (Carnival) Museum in the old Falter Tower. Moving upstream the visitor arrives at the walled village of Dettelbach, and then to **Volkach**, one of the oldest towns of Franconia and the site of some famous vineyards. This is now something of a show place, a resort noted for its fruit and vegetables as well as for its historic buildings, where a town councillor in Renaissance costume may welcome you on special occasions. The gem of the place is the pilgrimage chapel of Maria im Weingarten, set on a small hill outside the walls and surrounded by a luxurious wreath of vineyards. It contains a famous statue of the *Madonna im Rosenkranz* by Tilman Riemenschneider.

A little distance away from the river valley is the Steigerwald, a range of low wooded hills, whose lime and clay soil produces wine of a distinctive quality. The most attractive place here is the little town of **Iphofen**, with imposing walls, a splendid Rathaus, a fine Gothic church, and the Zehntkeller (tithe barn) housing one of the most popular hostelries in Franconia. An unexpected discovery here is the Knauf-Museum, an old mansion housing casts of famous monuments from the oldest civilisations in history that have been assembled from museums throughout the world. Nearby is **Castell**, situated at the foot of a large baroque castle, with a *Schlossgarten*.

The church here is particularly interesting as it is a rare example of the rococo style in a protestant church. It might be thought that the florid characteristics of rococo architecture were ill-suited for the sober manner of Lutheran worship, but in this church, built by the local lord in 1783, the spirit of the age has triumphed, substituting only the pulpit for the high altar as the main focus of attention. Generally in Germany the religious loyalties of the people depended upon those of the local lord, as recognised by the Peace of Augsburg in 1555. The older church buildings reflect this decision to this day. In many areas of mid-Germany, between the north and the south, adjoining villages may have either a Catholic or a Lutheran church.

After leaving the wine villages of the valley behind the visitor soon arrives at **Bamberg**, an historical town of great interest, almost

The thirteenth-century Bamberg Rider *in Bamberg Cathedral*

unvisited by British and American tourists and, for a merciful
change, almost untouched by bombs. Among many buildings of
great beauty is the outstanding old town hall. The Gothic structure,
baroquised in the eighteenth century, stands like a ship on its own
little island in the river. A little further up the hill is the cathedral,
situated in what is claimed with justice to be the finest square in
Germany. The cathedral contains some of the best examples of

medieval sculpture in all Europe, among which the so-called *Bamberg Rider*, an ideal of knightly chivalry, is deservedly famous. Opposite is the Neue Residenz in full baroque style while further up the hill is St Michael's Church with fine Gothic, Romanesque and baroque features. There is a wonderful view of the old town from its terrace which makes the climb up well worth while. If one has seen and enjoyed Offenbach's opera, *The Tales of Hoffman*, then one will be glad to know that this was E.T.A. Hoffman's home town. His house is open to the public. If a visit to this attractive city coincides with a performance by the world-renowned Bamberg Symphony Orchestra it will be an added plus.

A few miles south of Bamberg is **Pommersfelden**; a baroque palace built for the Prince Bishop of Bamberg by Johann Dientzenhofer in 1711 with a grand staircase almost rivalling that at Würzburg. It also has a romantic grotto room, and amusing *trompe l'oeil* decorations. A similar distance to the north are two wonderful monastic churches. The earlier of these at **Banz** (1711), was designed by the same architect as at Pommersfelden, with walls, galleries and ceilings in sweeping curves, all under the control of a master conception.

On the other side of the valley, facing it and built in a spirit of unedifying competition that has not infrequently inspired architecture intended for the glory of God, is the even more remarkable church of **Vierzehnheiligen** (1744) and erected on a spot where a shepherd boy saw a vision of fourteen 'saintly helpers'. The architect here was Balthasar Neumann, the designer of the Residenz at Würzburg, but much of the decoration is somewhat later and in the full glory of rococo. The history of this building is a complicated story, but what it all builds up to is the erection of an extraordinary altar to the honour of these fourteen saints. This so-called Gnadenaltar (1762) seems more like the sort of fairy coach in which Cinderella might have gone to the ball than anything else and has been well described as one of the strangest and most brilliantly fantastic creations of late baroque. Whether this is a valid expression of religious art or not, it is certainly something to be seen, and this church still attracts thousands of devout pilgrims.

Only a few miles away, though not quite in the Main valley, is **Coburg**. This town has a special interest for British visitors as it was the home of Prince Albert, the husband and consort of Queen Victoria. This high-minded German prince, who was so deeply loved by his young wife, made a great contribution to the popular appreciation of art in England, with the titles of the Victoria and Albert Museum and the Albert Hall as reminders. Here we can see the surroundings that influenced him as he grew up: Schloss Ehrenburg, the princely palace in which classical, baroque, French Empire and Biedermeier styles all merge together within a nineteenth-century Gothic revival exterior; Veste, the old castle above the town, in which Martin Luther found a safe refuge in 1530 and in which his study can be seen; and the fine collection of prints and paintings housed there. Coburg may seem a sleepy provincial town today, encircled on three sides by the German Democratic Republic, but as so often there are treasures, pleasures and surprises to be discovered by the traveller who goes off the beaten track.

Finally, not far from the source of the Main, is **Bayreuth**. To most people Bayreuth means Wagner but long before Wagner was born it was the seat of a petty princeling who married a sister of Frederick the Great. She thus became the margravine who commissioned a number of splendid buildings in the town. The Markgräfliches Opernhaus (1745), in particular, was decorated by two of the Bibienas, the famous Italian theatre designers, and is even more magnificent than the Cuvilliés Theatre in Munich. Safety precautions limit the use of the building for theatrical performances, though it is sometimes used for concerts, but really it is enough just to stand and stare. This is probably the most glorious example of flamboyant theatre architecture in all Europe.

The Festspielhaus was built in 1872 solely for the production of Wagner's operas in a style intended to unite music, drama and design in a total art form — a *Gesamtkunst* — to be attended in an atmosphere of reverent absorbtion. It is still directed by his descendants for that purpose. During the summer festival, Wagnerites from all over the world flock here. For the rest of the year the theatre is closed, but at all seasons you can visit the house in which Wagner spent the last years of his tempestuous life and in whose garden he and Cosima lie buried.

Further Information
— Franconia —

Museums and Other Places of Interest

Bamberg
Cathedral
Open: summer 8am-6pm.
In winter, 9am-12noon and from 2-4pm.

E.T.A. Hoffmann House
Open: only in summer from 1 May to 31 October, Tuesday and Friday 5-6pm. Saturdays and Sundays 10am-12noon.

Bayreuth
Festspielhaus
Open: April to September 10-11.30am.

Markgräfliches Opernhaus
Open: April to August 9-11.30am and
October to March 10-11.30am.

Coburg
Schloss Ehrenburg
Open: daily 9am-12noon and 1-4pm
throughout the year, except Mondays.
Guided tours of palace 9, 10 and 11am
and 1.30, 2.30 and 3.30pm.
☎ (09561) 7767

Iphofen
Knauf-Museum
Open: April to October, Tuesday to
Sunday 2-6pm. Tuesday and Thursday
10am-12noon.
☎ (09323) 31 4 87

Kitzingen
Deutsches Fasnacht Museum
Open: April to November, Saturday
and Sunday, 2-5pm.
☎ (09321) 2 33 55

Würzburg
Residenz
Open: April to September, Tuesday to
Sunday, 9am-5pm. October to March,
Tuesday to Sunday, 10am-4pm.
☎ (0931) 5 27 43

Tourist Offices

Bamberg
Fremdenverkehrsamt
Hauptwachstrasse 16
Bamberg
☎ (0951) 26401 87370

Bayreuth
Fremdenverkehrsamt
Luitpoldplatz 9
858 Bayreuth
☎ (0921) 22011

Coburg
Fremdenverkehrsamt
Herrngasse 4
8630 Coburg
☎ 095 61 9 29 29

Würzburg
Fremdenverkehrsamt
Falkenhaus am Markt
8700 Würzburg
☎ (0931) 37335

Village Tourist Offices

8716 **Dettelbach**
☎ (09324) 808

8701 **Eibelstadt**
☎ (09303) 216

8701 **Frickenhausen**
☎ (09331) 2726

8783 **Hammelburg**
☎ (09732) 80249

8715 **Iphofen**
☎ (09323) 3095

8782 **Karlstadt**
☎ (09353) 8275

8710 **Kitzingen**
☎ (09321) 205

8713 **Marktbreit**
☎ (09332) 3418

8703 **Ochsenfurt**
☎ (09331) 5855

8701 **Randersacker**
☎ (0931) 708282

8711 **Sulzfeld**
☎ (09321) 5474

8702 **Veitschöchheim**
☎ 91051

8712 **Volkach**
☎ (0009381) 571

Information about wine seminars from:
Gebietsweinwerbung Frankenwein-
Frankenland
Postfach 58 48
8700 Würzburg
☎ (0931) 12093

8 • The Tauber Valley

The little river Tauber enters the mighty river Main (pronounced 'mine') at Wertheim in Baden-Württemberg and this chapter traces its course for some 62 miles (100km) south-eastwards to the outskirts of the famous and well known medieval town of Rothenburg. The north bank of the Main is in Bavaria, the largest of the German Federal States, and parts of the route to be followed are actually within its boundary. By whatever means the Tauber is followed, the way is most pleasant but it is undoubtedly seen at its very best by those who go on foot or bicycle along the waymarked route called Liebliches Taubertal — Beautiful Tauber Valley.

Firstly, one must make the journey to Wertheim. The air traveller would best arrive at Frankfurt and could complete the journey by train in about 2 hours. This would also be the route for the rail traveller. Having arrived at Wertheim, there is a somewhat limited train service through the valley but places as far as Möckmühl, Weikersheim and Niederstetten can be reached by this means. Unless it is intended to walk or cycle, however, the hire of a car is strongly recommended. The international car rental firms have offices at Frankfurt airport and at main railway stations and many private garages also have vehicles for hire.

The motorist travelling from the west with his or her own vehicle has no problem in reaching Frankfurt via the continental motorway network and should then follow *Autobahn* A3 (signs Würzburg) about 43½ miles (70km) to the exit for Wertheim. Alternatively, leave at the Weibersbrunn exit 18 miles (29km) earlier and take the opportunity of visiting the picturesque *Wasserschloss* (moated palace) at **Mespelbrunn** about 4 miles (6km) to the south. Originally erected in the fifteenth century, this lovely little palace in its pretty wooded surroundings is just made for the photographer. The Rittersaal (Knights' Hall) reached from the small courtyard is the principal room on the ground floor. The Gobelinensaal contains a famous Gobelin tapestry from 1564 and the Chinese salon and other rooms with interesting furnishings are also open to view. From the direc-

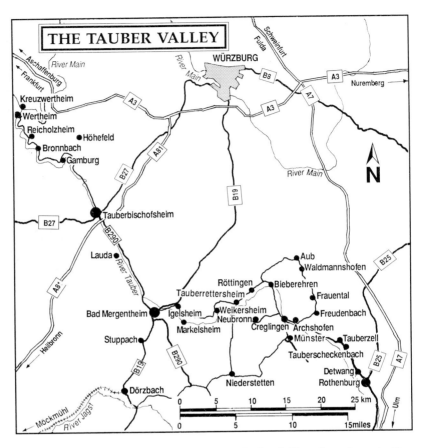

tion of the *Autobahn* there is a strange lack of direction signs to the palace and one has to go almost to the end of the attractive but straggly village of Mespelbrunn before reaching the left turn to the spacious car park.

Wertheim is now best reached along pleasant rural roads in about 18 miles (30km). This is a little town and embraces fifteen outlying villages. There is a lot of accommodation in all categories, including five camp sites, and there are a number of good restaurants. In the village of Bettingen, 6 miles (10km) to the east beside the Main, the peaceful but not inexpensive Schweizer Stuben earned a coveted Michelin star for its excellent cuisine. In common with most other German towns of this size, Wertheim has both indoor and outdoor swimming pools. Before starting in earnest on the journey up the Tauber, time should be taken to explore this historic town. Needless

Wertheim Castle

to say, this is best done on foot, indeed, this is the only way for most of the centre is a pedestrian zone. However, there are several car parks nearby.

The first settlement here was in the seventh century on the other side of the river Main in the part now called Kreuzwertheim. With the building of the fortified castle in the twelfth century, the centre moved to the south of the river. In 1631, during the Thirty Years War, the Swedes occupied the town and castle and as a result the latter was destroyed by the emperor's troops in 1634. It was never rebuilt but work has been carried out from time to time to prevent the ruins collapsing completely. The castle is seen at its most spectacular at night when it is floodlit. Several pleasant paths lead up from the town for rather splendid views over the river valleys.

The British visitor may well be astonished to come upon a red telephone box of the type so long familiar at home behind the market place. On it he or she will find a plaque recording that this was a gift of the people of Huntingdon and Godmanchester with which the community of Wertheim is twinned. The instrument within is of the standard German design, of course. The Rathaus has been created out of three former dwelling houses and has a staircase tower. Late Gothic fortified towers are vestiges of the old ring wall, and late Gothic is also the architectural style of the former Kilianskapelle (chapel of St Kilian), the basement of which served as an ossuary or charnal-house. The upper storey has ornate tracery and flying buttresses with finials and now houses the Heimatmuseum. It is just north of the Protestant parish church — late Gothic again — which has a number of features of interest including the little choir of the Heilig-Geist-Kapelle (chapel of the Holy Ghost) and the seventeenth-century tomb of Count Ludwig II of Löwenstein-Wertheim and his wife, popularly known as the 'bedstead' because of its canopy.

In addition to the Heimatmuseum there is the interesting Glasmuseum in Mühlenstrasse with a collection of historic glass and recording the development of glass manufacture from the earliest times. Between the Marktplatz and the parish church the interesting Engelsbrunnen (Angel Fountain) of 1574 is so named because of the two angels at the top holding the Wertheim coat of arms. All around are artistic timbered houses, mostly from the sixteenth century. On Wednesday and Saturday the market place is colourful with the stalls of the fruit, vegetable and flower vendors. The visitor will find many more interesting corners as he or she wanders around and the photographer will be more than pleased if lighting conditions allow him or her to make the most of the medieval townscape. A small thirteenth-century church is to be found in the part of Wertheim called Eichel close to the Main.

Boating and angling are favourite pastimes here; cruises may be made up and down the Main in the summer months and private boats may be moored in the yacht-harbour just inside the mouth of the Tauber. Special package holiday arrangements are on offer for anglers and their families for whom a programme is available from the tourist information office. Cyclists and ramblers too, have special provision made for them; cycles may be hired at the railway station and elsewhere.

On leaving Wertheim, the densely wooded slopes of this north end of the Tauber valley are quickly in evidence on either side, the woods often giving way to the more open aspect of extensive orchards or vineyards. This is a particularly attractive road in springtime when the fruit trees are in blossom and again in the autumn when the leaves are about to fall. The village of **Reichholzheim**, four miles (6km) from Wertheim, has a vintners' co-operative and is one of several places in the area where *Weinproben* may be enjoyed and up to sixty persons can be accommodated. Note the colourful coats of arms on the vintners' building. There is a camp site near the river.

In another 2 miles (3km) **Bronnbach** with its former Cistercian abbey church of St Maria is reached. This is now the Catholic parish

A modern fountain in
Tauberbischofsheim

church and is one of the most interesting early Cistercian churches in Germany with traces of Provençal and Burgundian influence. Although building began in 1157, the church was not consecrated until 1222; the baroque interior dates from the seventeenth and eighteenth centuries. Externally, the long cruciform three-aisled basilica has a ridge turret above the crossing as the only decoration. The lavish baroque altars with twisted columns are of artistic merit. Apart from peering through the wrought-iron grille, one must summon the custodian (bell-push nearby) in order to inspect the interior of the church. The abbey buildings are worth seeing too. The cloisters date from about 1230, the chapterhouse is twelfth century and has late Romanesque rib vaulting on four columns. The Josephsaal was created in 1727.

The picturesque road continues along the east bank of the river past the village of Hohefeld and in about 5 miles (8km) reaches **Gamburg** where there is an old stone bridge which enables one to cross to the twelfth-century castle on the west side. There is an old mill here as well and one may also see examples of *Bildstöcke* — posts

Tauberbischofsheim

at the wayside bearing a likeness of the Virgin or a saint. It would perhaps be an anti-climax to stop again before reaching Tauberbischofsheim 17 miles (27km) from Wertheim, although there are several attractive villages along the way.

Tauberbischofsheim is not a big place and nearly everything of interest is in the compact old town with its extensive pedestrian zone within a ring road, adjacent to which are several spacious car parks offering free parking as do most small towns. It is not worth the hassle of trying to find parking space in the narrow streets.

The history of Tauberbischofsheim goes back to the year 735 when the first German nunnery was founded here by St Lioba, a relative of St Bonifatius. Both of these saints have churches dedicated to them here, the Liobakirche at the end of the Marktplatz being that formerly associated with the *Kloster* — *Kloster* may be translated as monastery, nunnery, abbey, etc. It was considerably enlarged in the baroque style in 1735. The church of St Bonifatius is east of the town beyond the river Tauber and is a modern building. The Catholic parish church of St Martin is an impressive structure dominating the town centre. It was built between 1910 and 1914 and is considered to be one of the best examples of neo-Gothic architecture. The 226ft (69m) high tower and many of the valuable relics within are, however, from the previous church on the site. The bells are of various ages, the oldest having been cast about 1380 and the newest — the Liobaglocke — in 1953. The high altar was created in traditional style during the years 1915-32 by one Professor Thomas Buscher, one of five brothers, who were all sculptors. The pulpit from around 1700 came from the old church as did several side altars. The late Gothic Marienaltar is the pride of St Martin's and came from the School of Riemenschneider, if not from the great man himself. The Kreuzaltar nearby, for centuries housed two of the finest works of the artist Matthias Grünewald, *Christ on the Cross* and *Christ Carrying the Cross*. In 1882 these paintings were sold to the Kassel Gallery for 2,000 gold Marks but 6 years later at the behest of the church authorities were bought back for 7,000. This was not the end of the story for in 1900 they were sold again, this time to the Baden Art Gallery for 40,000 Marks. Today they are to be seen in the Hall of Art in Karlsruhe, their place in Tauberbischofsheim having been occupied by acceptable copies of the originals.

At the north end of the Marktplatz the Rathaus (1865) is another building in neo-Gothic style. The former *Schloss* of the electors of Mainz now houses the Tauberfränkisches Landschaftsmuseum, a treasure-chest of exhibits for those with an interest in the history of landscape, domestic life, dress and culture. The *Schloss* was originally built around 1250 but most of the present building is from the fifteenth and sixteenth centuries. Nearby are the remains of the one surviving watchtower from the thirteenth-century town fortifications. Originally there were twenty-one of them but the rest of these and the walls were finally demolished in 1812. The first weekend in July sees the medieval town centre, with its numerous picturesque timbered houses, hosting the annual Altstadtfest, a general merrymaking, dancing in the streets sort of festival facilitated by the spacious traffic-free areas. The second or third weekend in October is the time for the Martini-Messe (Festival of St Martin) in which some religious activity is combined with the annual Winzerfest (Vintage Festival), for since 1935 Tauberbischofsheim has again been a centre of the wine industry after some years of neglect.

It goes without saying that in and around Tauberbischofsheim there is ample accommodation and similarly ample opportunity for leisure activities including indoor and outdoor swimming. This is

A pause on the Liebliches Taubertal *cycle route*

one of the overnight stops on a 3-day cycle ramble between Wertheim and Rothenburg. Although the cycle route closely follows the river Tauber it is almost entirely along little-used rural roads, agricultural roads, etc, most of which although surfaced are barred to normal motor traffic. The cycle way is marked by a sign depicting a bicycle above the words *Liebliches Taubertal*, a tourist route which is equally available to walkers.

The motorist must now join Bundesstrasse B290 which he or she will note is designated the Romantische Strasse. This 'Romantic Road' is one of Germany's many named routes and runs from Würzburg in the north to the Alps close to the Austrian border 199 miles (320km) away to the south. After $10\frac{1}{2}$ miles (17km) one arrives at **Bad Mergentheim**, a very pleasant spa with many activities and sights of interest. Unlike some spas, Mergentheim is a place for the general holidaymaker just as much as for the person coming for health reasons. The leisure centre Solymar caters especially for those wishing to indulge in water activities; there is a *Wellenbad* (pool with artificial waves) which is open at all seasons and in the evenings, a mineral spring pool and a heated open-air pool. Those not wishing to participate can watch from the bar or restaurant. In the town centre, the massive Deutschordenschloss (a castle of the Teutonic Order) houses the museum of the order but is not otherwise of outstanding interest except for its now Protestant church with its gigantic ceiling frescoes by the Munich master Nikolaus Gottfried Stuber (1734). Awe-inspiring perhaps but not a particularly beautiful church. The Catholic *Münster* of St John was built in 1250-70 by the knights of St John of Jerusalem and taken over by the Teutonic Order in 1554. Churches though are not an outstanding feature of the Bad Mergentheim scene.

The fine Rathaus stands in the centre of the Marktplatz which is surrounded by many well-preserved ancient buildings. The 'historic' post-box on the Rathaus wall — there is another between here and the *Schloss* — is not, apparently, a genuine antique. According to the German Post Office authorities, these boxes have been manufactured to resemble the Württemberg town letter boxes of 1877 but are not an exact copy. They were purchased by the town council, presumably with the intention of adding a further historical touch to the pedestrian zone in the town centre. Just off the Marktplatz is the Auto-Mobil-Museum with an interesting collection which includes several old racing cars, saloons, motor-cycles and many pictures and souvenirs of famous international racing drivers. In addition to irregular concerts, theatrical productions and so on, Bad Mergentheim has a calendar of regular events which includes the departure of the Teutonic Order Company and the historic Rifle Corps (both in April) and the re-entry of the latter in October, a veteran car rally (May), the festival 'Around the Town Hall' (June), Catholic and Protestant church communities festival (June to July), citizens' and folk festivals (July and August) and a Christmas market in December. In nearby Markelsheim the wine festival is the first weekend after Whitsun and Herbsthausen has its *Bockbier* (strong Bavarian beer) festival the first weekend after Ascension Day. About 4 miles (6km) south of the town on the B19 in the parish church (1607) of the village of **Stuppach** is the so-called *Stuppach Madonna* by Matthias Grünewald, painted 1517-19 and one of the most important works of old German painting. Continuing on B19 for another 5 miles (8km) beyond Stuppach one comes to the village of **Dörzbach**, the eastern terminus of the Jagsttalbahn, a preserved narrow-gauge railway which runs along the valley of the river Jagst to Möckmühl. Also to the south of Bad Mergentheim but on the B290, is the excellent *Wildpark* with many animals in natural surroundings together with a comprehensive animal museum. Falcons and other birds of prey are allowed to fly freely twice daily between 1 May and the latter half of September, but if these demonstrations are missed, there is a continuous television presentation in the museum. Also twice daily one may see the feeding of the zoo's baby bears and thereafter of the

*Dörzbach station on
the Jagst Valley
Railway*

wolves which emerge from the dim recesses of their large wooded enclosure to devour enormous quantities of meat at astonishing speed. The wolves here constitute the largest pack in Europe. Both the *Madonna* and the *Wildpark* are well signed from the town centre.

The Romantische Strasse and the visitor's route now turn generally eastwards to follow the Tauber, leaving Mergentheim on the B19 (direction Würzburg) but shortly turning off right (sign-posted Rothenburg) past Igersheim and Markelsheim 'vineyard nature trail' along a broad valley with extensive vineyards right down to the roadside. About 6 miles (10km) further on the health resort of **Weikersheim** is reached and must be considered an essential stop for the visitor. This is the last place in the lower end of the Taubertal directly accessible by train. The outstanding sight here is the Renaissance *Schloss* with its brilliant interior. The most important room is the Rittersaal which reflects the hunting passion of Count Wolfgang von Hohenlohe for whom it was built. Many other furnished rooms are to be seen, but this can only be done on a conducted tour which is included in the admission price. The commentary is in German but

Weikersheim

an English language guide book is available.

The *Schlosspark* was laid out from 1709 onwards and is one of the finest baroque gardens in Germany. There are colourful flower beds, a pond, an orangery and many grotesque and amusing statues. From June to September concerts or operas are given in the *Schloss* or its courtyard by the Musical Youth of Germany. The nearby Haus der Musik (Music School) was opened in 1981. There is a pleasant town centre with many historic buildings and each year on Christmas Eve there is traditional carol singing in the illuminated Marktplatz in front of the town church. On New Year's Day a concert is followed by a festive supper; on the second Sunday in May (Mothers' Day) there is spring music in the Marktplatz. The first Sunday in September is dedicated to the Weikersheimer Kärwe, a traditional folk festival with an historic procession. In the Marktplatz the Tauberländer Dorfmuseum has a large collection devoted to the village culture of the Tauber area.

There is accommodation of all types in Weikersheim. Prices are generally moderate and especially good value is obtainable in the many private houses which have a few rooms set aside for guests. There is an indoor pool in the town and a heated outdoor one in very attractive surroundings in the village of Neubronn a few kilometres away. Also just outside the town above the village of **Laudenbach** is the Bergkirche, a pilgrimage church dating from 1412. This charming building impressed the poet Eduard Mörike so much that he dedicated a poem to it.

Leaving Weikersheim, a sign reveals that the road is entering Freistaat Bayern and the first Bavarian village is soon reached. Bavaria is an exception for it is the only one of the Federal States allowed to use the term *Freistaat* (Free State). **Tauberrettersheim** lies on the far bank of the Tauber and to reach it one must cross the bridge of 1733 built by Balthasar Neumann (1687-1753), the distinguished engineer and architect from Würzburg. On the bridge there is a statue of St Johann Nepomuk, the patron saint of bridges, who is often encountered in this area. Tauberrettersheim has its wine festival early in May and this is followed by Wine Week in **Röttingen**, a little town a few kilometres further along the road. For about 4 weeks in July and August the town is again a hive of activity for there is a theatre festival here which attracts its audience from a wide area. The baroque Rathaus presides over the small Marktplatz presenting a fairly unspoiled medieval scene and there is a small historical exhibition in the Rathaus lobby. The old town wall has seven towers and the new bridge over the Tauber is once again under the eye of Nepomuk. There is an archaeological trail and a rather surprising one with the theme of sundials which are found in considerable numbers around here.

Only a few minutes are needed to reach **Bieberehren** and the last of the vineyards. Turn off the main road here and cross the river to the foot of the Kreuzberg, a modest hill surmounted by a chapel to which the approach from the roadside — 274 steps — is flanked by the Stations of the Cross in a series of very detailed reliefs. From the chapel there is an extensive view eastwards over the valley. Back on the Romantische Strasse the visitor soon passes through the village of **Klingen** and upon crossing the Tauber re-enters Baden-Württemberg to arrive in a few more minutes in **Creglingen**, an attractive town lying mostly aside from the main road with ample free parking. This is a central location in the upper Taubertal and makes a fine base for exploring the area. This is one of the places where the *Verkehrsamt* is happy to arrange accommodation for visitors.

The principal attraction in the town is the Herrgottskirche (Church of the Lord God) which contains what is regarded as Tilman Riemenschneider's finest wood carving, the altar of the Virgin Mary. Riemenschneider (1460-1531) was a modest citizen of Würzburg who worked hard at his trade, producing altarpieces, sepulchres, reliefs and statues for churches and dignitaries. While running his business he also helped to run the city serving variously as council-

The carved wooden altar in the Herrgottskirche, Creglingen

lor, judge, tax-collector, head of local defence and finally *Bürgermeister* (mayor), the highest civic post. In 1525 his peace and prosperity
were shattered when the Peasants' Revolt against the ruling princes
erupted across Germany. Riemenschneider stood firm with other

councillors in refusing to send troops to quell the uprising but the revolt failed and he was imprisoned. Eventually released, he died 6 years later at the age of 71. Many of his works are now collected in a gallery in the Mainfränkisches Museum in Würzburg. No other artist has been able to portray with such feeling and accuracy the features of man: the title 'Master Carver of the Middle Ages' is certainly well-deserved.

The triptych in Creglingen was probably created in the period 1505-10 and was designed specifically for this little church. The wooden part surmounts the stone altar to give a total height of 36ft (11m) and it is about 13ft (4m) wide. The work depicts the Assumption of the Blessed Virgin and the various scenes are carved in the most intricate detail. The light limewood is unpainted giving a specially soft and warm effect and contrasting well with the reddish hue of the pinewood frame. The church itself dates from 1389; it became a place of pilgrimage and by 1500 sufficient funds were available to have the interior adorned with various art treasures including the altar already mentioned. In 1530 the church became a Protestant one and the Riemenschneider masterpiece was closed up and only re-opened in 1832. Across the road from the church is the unique Fingerhutmuseum, a collection of thimbles from all over the world and from Roman times until this day.

Creglingen's pleasant little heated *Freibad* is in the village of Freudenbach about 4 miles (6km) east and open-air bathing is also possible in the artificial lake near the camp site at Münster 2 miles (4km) to the south. Those staying in this area should not fail to obtain from the tourist office the *Urlaubspass* (visitor's passport) for which there is a nominal charge and which allows reduced entrance fees for museums, swimming pools, cycle hire, minigolf, tennis and so on in the towns of Creglingen, Weikersheim, Röttingen and Niederstetten, a resort about 6 miles (10km) south of Weikersheim. The *Schloss* in **Niederstetten** is the home of a hunting museum and of the Albert-Sammt-Zeppelin-Museum which has many exhibits, photographs, etc concerning the history of the Zeppelins. It is named after Albert Sammt, the last German airship captain, who died in 1982.

The popularity of cycling in the Taubertal has already been mentioned and Creglingen is a good centre for this with cycle hire facilities in the town and a leaflet of useful suggestions from the tourist office. Many hosts can provide cycles for their guests at no extra charge. Obviously a car is an asset in this area but travellers by public transport can reach Creglingen by bus from the railheads at Weikersheim or Ochsenfurt. The river Tauber is popular with an-

Archshofen

glers — the trout and other fish seem almost to be jostling for space in the shallow water.

Modest excursions from the town include the Fire Brigades Museum (housed in a former Renaissance *Wasserschloss*) at **Wald-mannshofen** about 6 miles (10km) to the north and 2 miles (3km) beyond there is the little Bavarian town of **Aub** where the parish church has a crucifixion group by Riemenschneider. The 1482 Rat-haus there overlooks the pleasant little square which has a notable baroque pillar bearing a gilded figure of the Virgin Mary. Outside the nearby village of **Burgerroth** is a chapel dedicated to St Kunigunde dating from about 1200 and in the churchyard is a lime tree reputed to be 1,000 years old. Unfortunately the chapel, which is in an isolated position, has suffered from vandalism and if one desires to see the interior the key must be obtained in the village. About 3 miles (5km) north-east of Creglingen in the village of **Frauental** one can find the former *Klosterkirche* founded by the Cistercian order in 1232. The church, which now serves as the Protestant church for the area, is well worth seeing. Just outside Frauental at the farm called Fuchshof, Herr Fuchs has assembled an interesting collection of old farming implements, fittings and furnishings which may be seen by prior arrangement. The tourist information office in Creglingen will assist if necessary.

There are endless rambling possibilities and numerous car parks in the countryside with marked circular walks. The 1:25,000 map *Oberes Taubertal* enables one to readily select routes which suit the capabilities of the walkers, the time available and the weather but the following easy ramble of about 7 miles (11km) may be regarded as typical.

Go southwards from Creglingen along the west side of the little stream called Herrgottsbach (waymarked by a blue rectangle) and after half a mile (1km), turn sharp left past the Kohlesmühle (Thimble Museum) to reach the main road near the Herrgottskirche. Turning right, continue to follow this for 457yd (500m). Turn right to re-cross the stream and resume the southerly direction along the west bank for a mile until **Münster** is reached. The meals at the Gasthaus Zur Traube near the church can be recommended. Following the way-marks, cross the stream and carry on to the far end of the village. Continue along the road close to the stream for about 457yd (500m) if it is desired to visit the camp site and bathing facilities mentioned. Otherwise turn sharp left to an almost due north direction and climb fairly steeply out of the valley on a minor road for about half a mile (1km). Turn sharp right reversing direction and continue to climb. Gradually this very minor road curves left to assume a roughly easterly direction towards **Archshofen**. Soon one is on the ridge between the valley in which Münster lies and the Taubertal. The road is called Archshofer Weg but there is no need to identify it. Once on the ridge the water tower in the village of **Schön** on the far side of the Taubertal will be visible and can be used as a point for which to aim. There are no waymarks between Münster and Archshofen which is a distance of about $2^1/_2$ miles (4km), but by whatever road or track, one will eventually join a more important road to drop down steeply into Archshofen. About 229yd (250m) past the first houses note the signs where the *Liebliches Taubertal* cycle route crosses the road, turn left and follow this back to Creglingen about 2 miles (3km) away.

Again leaving Creglingen, travel either along the Romantische Strasse, a picturesque and fairly quiet road or, if cycling or walking, along the designated route on the south side of the river. After about $2^1/_2$ miles (4km), just past the village of Archshofen a turning off the main road leads steeply up the valley side to a splendid viewpoint, the *Panoramablick*. A round walk is marked from the nearby parking space. The road leads on through Schön to the village of Freudenbach for the swimming pool mentioned previously. The riverside road continues through the villages of **Tauberzell** and **Tauberschecken-bach**. In the latter a bridge over the now quite small river enables a visit to be made to the Flax Museum in **Burgstall** about half a mile

The 1,000-year-old church of St Peter and St Paul in Detwang

(1km) to the west. Prior arrangements are necessary — see under museum details at the end of the chapter.

Shortly before the road climbs out of the valley to the historic town of Rothenburg, a stop should be made in the village of **Detwang**. The little church of St Peter and St Paul was founded here in 968. It belonged to the Neumünster monastery in Würzburg until 1258 when it was taken over by the Teutonic Order and when the order was dissolved in 1544, it became the Lutheran parish church. Romanesque elements in the architecture date from 1200-50 and Gothic ones from the fourteenth century. Baroque elements were added later; the gallery with its balustrade decorated with garlands of flowers in about 1650, the painted font in 1720 and the inlaid and gilded pulpit in 1723. There are many treasures in the church but the outstanding work is Tilman Riemenschneider's altarpiece of the Holy Cross. It was originally made for St Michael's Chapel in Rothenburg in 1508 and was moved to Detwang in 1653. It is one of the great master's finest works and time is needed to absorb every detail of the carving. The lifelike faces and hands of the figures depicted are quite remarkable.

A description of **Rothenburg** would not be appropriate in the

present volume for it is one of the most popular places on the tourist
trail. This is by no means an undeserved honour for it is a really
lovely town and if the reader is not already familiar with it, then a
visit should certainly be paid, preferably in an evening when the
hundreds of coach-borne visitors will have departed, or at a quiet
time in spring or autumn when there is peace to enjoy the old place.

Further Information
— The Tauber Valley —

Buildings and Gardens

Weikersheim
Schloss Weikersheim
6992 Weikersheim
☎ (07934) 8364
Open: daily April to October, 8am-
6pm, November to March, 10am-
12noon, 2-4pm.
Mighty Renaissance palace from
around 1600; splendid baroque garden.
Conducted tours of the interior included in admission price. Entry to
grounds only also possible.

Wertheim
Ruins of twelfth-century castle complex. No admission charge.

Churches

Bronnbach
Former Cistercian Abbey Church.
Baroque interior from seventeenth to
eighteenth centuries. Fine choir-stalls.
Gothic-Romanesque cloisters.
Open: from Easter to mid-October with
daily (except Monday) guided tours
8am-12noon, 2-6pm.
At other times tours possible by prior
arrangement.

Creglingen
Herrgottskirche
Half a mile (1km) from town centre.
Noted for its fine works of art, espe-
cially St Mary's Altar by Riemen-
schneider.

Open: April to October, daily 8am-
6pm, November to March, Tuesday to
Sunday 10am-12noon, 1-4pm.
Admission charge.

Detwang
St Peter and St Paul
Many fine works of art, in particular
the altarpiece of the Holy Cross by
Riemenschneider.
Open: June to 15 September, daily
8.30am-12noon, 1.30-6pm. November
to March 9-11am, 2-4pm, at other times
9-11am, 1.30-5pm. Closed on Monday
in winter.
Admission charge.

Stuppach
Parish Church
Four miles (6km) south of Bad Mergen-
theim on B19.
Famed for its *Madonna* by Matthias
Grünewald painted 1517-19.
Open: April to October.
Admission charge includes explana-
tory talk in German.

Cycling and Cycle Hire

From April to October cycles may be
hired at the DB stations at Bad Mergentheim, Möckmühl, Rothenburg,
Tauberbischofsheim, Weikersheim and
Wertheim or from the following:

Creglingen
Schlosserei Haag
Hauptstrasse 34

6993 Creglingen
☎ (07933) 507

Wertheim
Gertrud Arnold
Kaiseräcker 6
6980 Wertheim-Bettingen
☎ (09342) 3284

Erika Rösch
Eichler Höhenweg 1
6980 Wertheim
☎ (09342) 6123

Museums

Bad Mergentheim
Auto-Mobil-Museum
Burgstrasse 2-4
6990 Bad Mergentheim
☎ (07931) 8244
Open: daily 1 February to 31 December, 10am-6pm.
Collection of motor vehicles including many racing cars, also motor-cycles.
Memorabilia of famous racing drivers.

Deutschordensmuseum
Schloss
6990 Bad Mergentheim
☎ (07931) 57359 or 57232
Open: whole year. Saturday, Sunday and holidays 10am-12noon, 2.30-5.30pm and March to October, Tuesday to Friday 2.30-5.30pm. Closed 24 December to 5 January.
Rooms furnished in baroque, rococo and classical styles with a wide variety of impedimenta of these periods housed in the palace of the Teutonic Order.

Creglingen
Flachsbrechhüttenmuseum
Burgstall
6993 Creglingen
☎ (09865) 497
Situated mid-way between Creglingen and Rothenburg.
Open: throughout the year.
Guided tours by prior arrangement with Herr Strauss at above number or contact Creglingen tourist office. The story of flax-growing and preparation.

Bäuerliches Museum
Fuchshof
6993 Creglingen-Frauental
☎ (07933) 572
Four miles (6km) north-east of Creglingen.
Open: throughout the year.
Guided tours by prior arrangement with Herr Fuchs. Old farming implements and furnishings, etc.

Feuerwehrmuseum
Waldmannshofen
6993 Creglingen
☎ (07931) 45959
Six miles (10km) north of Creglingen.
Open: daily 10am-12noon, 2-5pm and at other times by prior arrangement.
Comprehensive display of fire-fighting equipment, etc housed in former Renaissance moated palace.

Fingerhutmuseum
6993 Creglingen
☎ (07933) 370
Opposite the Herrgottskirche.
Open: April to October daily 8am-6pm and November to March, Tuesday to Sunday 10am-12noon, 1-4pm.
Thimbles from all over the world dating from Roman times to present day.

Lauda
Heimatmuseum
6970 Lauda-Königshofen
☎ (09343) 4517
Situated in Lauda between Tauberbischofsheim and Bad Mergentheim.
Open: April to October, Sunday and holidays 3-5pm and at other times by prior arrangement.
Guild and workrooms, agriculture and wine-growing in the Tauber valley. Housed in the birthplace of the reformer of Franconian agriculture, Dr P.A. Ulrich.

Niederstetten
Jagdmuseum and Albert-Sammt-Zeppelin-Museum
Schloss
6994 Niederstetten
☎ (07932) 205

Open: April to October, Saturday and Sunday 10am-12noon, 2-5.30pm. Parties of ten or more can be accepted on other days by prior arrangement. General hunting museum with trophies from home and abroad and the history of the Zeppelins with many objects of interest, photographs, etc.

Röttingen
Rathaus
8701 Röttingen
☎ (09338) 208 or 308
In the town hall facing the market place.
Open: during business hours.
Collection of old furniture, Franconian costumes, guild treasures and flags, weapons, etc.

Tauberbischofsheim
Landschaftsmuseum
Im Kurmainzischen Schloss
6972 Tauberbischofsheim
☎ (09341) 2036 or 3377
Open: Easter to 15 October, Tuesday to Saturday 2.30-4.30pm, Sunday and holidays 10am-12noon, 2.30-4.30pm.
Varied collection of sacred art, furniture of Renaissance, baroque, etc periods, rural costumes, household implements, tools, etc.

Weikersheim
Tauberländer Dorfmuseum
6992 Weikersheim
☎ (07934) 8320
Open: April to 15 November daily 10am-12noon, 2-5pm.
Special arrangements can be made for parties of ten or more. Biggest collection of Franconian village culture in the Tauber area.

Wertheim
Historisches Museum für Stadt und Grafschaft
Mühlenstrasse 26
6980 Wertheim
☎ (09342) 301312 or 3
Open: April to December, Tuesday to Friday 10am-12noon, 2-4pm, Saturday and Sunday 2-4pm.

History of the counts of Wertheim, the fishing guilds, folk customs (costumes and ceramics), sacred art, furniture, etc. Housed in the seventeenth-century Residenz.

Wertheimer Glasmuseum
Mühlenstrasse 24
6980 Wertheim
☎ (09342) 6866
Open: April to October, times as above.
Special Christmas exhibition between first Sunday in Advent and 7 January. Glass technology from the time of the Egyptians to the present day. Exhibits from all periods of glass development.

Steam Railway

Dörzbach-Möckmühl
Jagsttalbahn
Deutsche Gesellschaft für Eisenbahn-
    geschichte
Geschäftstelle
Postfach 1627
7100 Heilbronn
☎ (07131) 160391

Local Address
SWEG-Betriebsleitung
Bahnhofstrasse 8
7119 Dörzbach
☎ (07937) 277
Twenty-five mile (40km) long narrow guage (750mm) line. Operates steam and other passenger trains Easter to October, mainly weekends and holidays. Great Whitsun Festival. Also St Nikolaus specials from about 6 December. Service details in DB *Kursbuch*, table 778.

Tourist Information Offices

Bad Mergentheim
Städtisches Kultur- und Verkehrsamt
6990 Bad Mergentheim
☎ (07931) 57232

Creglingen
Städtisches Verkehrsamt
6993 Creglingen
☎ (07933) 631/2/588 (outside office hours)

Niederstetten
Stadtverwaltung
6994 Niederstetten
☎ (07932) 534

Röttingen
Verkehrsamt
8701 Röttingen
☎ (09338) 208 or 308

Rothenburg
Kultur- und Verkehrsamt
8803 Rothenburg ob der Tauber
☎ (09861) 2038

Tauberbischofsheim
Gebietsgemeinschaft 'Liebliches
Taubertal'
Postfach 1254
6972 Tauberbischofsheim
☎ (09341) 821

Weikersheim
Kultur- und Verkehrsverein
6992 Weikersheim
☎ (07934) 7272

Wertheim
Fremdenverkehrsgesellschaft 'Roman-
tisches Wertheim mbH'

Postfach 1242
6980 Wertheim
☎ (09342) 1066

Zoos and Wildlife Parks

Bad Mergentheim
Wildpark
6990 Bad Mergentheim
☎ (07931) 41344
Situated on B290 south of town.
Open: daily from around Easter until
about end of October depending on
weather.
Extensive zoo with many animals in
natural surroundings. Free-flying birds
of prey, baby bears, large wolf pack,
animal museum. Restaurant. Children's amusements. Free parking.

Weikersheim
Tierfreigehege on the Karlsberg.
Deer, wild boars, etc in pleasant park
surroundings above the town. Baroque
country seat (1725-42) of Count Carl
Ludwig.
Forestry museum open Saturday and
Sunday afternoons.

9 • The Bayerischer Wald

The Bayerischer Wald, an area of outstanding natural beauty, lies at the most south-easterly corner of the Federal Republic of Germany and still retains an aura of old world courtesy and dignity. Tourism, with all its bustle and commercialism, is only just beginning to appear and for that reason alone the area must appeal to those who still prefer a get-away-from-it-all type of holiday.

It has two natural boundaries; to the south is the river Danube as it flows eastwards from Regensburg to Passau, while on its eastern flank lies the border with Czechoslovakia. The land lying between these two boundaries is part of the old Bohemian Forest that covered so much of Bohemia up to the last century. Bohemia was famous for its manufacture of glass and this tradition is still found in the Bayerischer Wald with Zwiesel as the main distribution centre.

Industry as such is only found along the Danube valley and is not an intrusion on the countryside. The economy is otherwise supported by agriculture, forestry and the newly found tourism. Each village and town is fiercely independent with a pride in its local history, which is passed on to visitors by way of festivals, museums and folk evenings. Most resorts are small but within each, visitors will find accommodation with modern comforts like television and rooms with private facilities, while food is of an excellent quality and well prepared.

The House of the Guest is an institution unique to Germany and basically offers the assistance and information that visitors require. Some provide other refinements such as reading rooms containing the German national newspapers as well as local ones. In resorts such as Garmisch-Partenkirchen, Bad Reichenhall and Berchtesgaden, foreign newspapers may be available as well. A television room is also fairly common. Unfortunately not all resorts do offer this facility but each year more are added. Prices in the Bayerischer Wald are the lowest in the whole of Germany but one feels however that this is a situation that cannot and will not last.

The air here is reputedly some of the cleanest and finest in Europe,

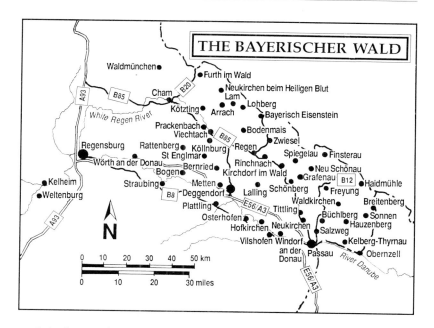

mainly due no doubt to the lack of pollution. Nearly all the brochures offer their town as one with a *Luftkur* (air cure) even if they have no medicinal waters to use as a bath or drinking therapy. Health in Germany is not taken for granted and each year many of its nationals take a cure of some sort for 2 or 3 weeks, some of which is paid for by their medical insurance while others choose to pay for their own treatment. This large demand therefore means that to attract visitors who like to combine therapy with a holiday, resorts are very willing to advertise the health benefits they can offer, ranging from the non-polluted air to all the various sophisticated treatments of sulphurous springs and vapours to mud baths, mineral waters and whirlpools. Relaxation is a key word in the German language.

Why then is the **Bayerischer Wald** not so well known as it might be? The answer is probably twofold. The first is transport, as it does not have an international airport within its boundaries but has to rely on Nuremberg and Munich with onward travel by either train or coach. The Deutsche Bundesbahn (German Railways) run a fairly comprehensive network over much of the area but it is true that sometimes journeys have to be finished by either bus or taxi, although quite a few hotels will organise this for the visitor. Having arrived, getting around presents no problem as every village has organised excursions as well as regular local bus services. For the private motorist there is the *Autobahn* which runs right through to Passau, and before long will join up with the Austrian *Autobahn* direct to Vienna.

The second factor may be because the people did not realise that there was scope for exploring further afield, a fairly valid reason until a couple of years ago when Czechoslovakia lifted its restrictions, and it is now possible to undertake day excursions to Prague. Anyone wishing to make this particular excursion should contact the local tourist office and ask for particulars well in advance as one requirement is that a form be filled in at least a week before the proposed date of travel together with a valid photograph. Other excursion destinations, to name but a few, range from Regensburg and Passau to Nuremberg, Munich and Salzburg.

Sporting facilities throughout the Bayerischer Wald are excellent with the emphasis definitely on water sports, tennis and riding. Walking however is the number one attraction whether it be from one village to the next, through woods or across open fields, to ascending the Grosser Arber the highest mountain hereabouts at 4,780ft (1,457m), or exploring the National Park covering 300sq miles (788sq km), with its wildlife reserve and forests.

The National Park issues a brochure called *Der Goldene Steig*, once the historic salt trade routes but now a network of marked walks, which shows the four main routes ranging from 7 to 19 miles (11 to 31km) in length. The two longest trails lead right to the frontier where they connect with routes on the other side but unless one is a practised long distance walker it is advisable not to try to continue.

The Prachatitzer Weg runs from Röhrnbach via Waldkirchen, Schiefweg, Böhmzwiesel, Fürholz, Grainet, Bischofsreuth and on to the border, a distance of 17 miles (27km).

The Bergreichensteiner Weg runs from Freyung via Kreuzberg, Mauth to Finsterau and the frontier, a distance of 19 miles (31km).

The Winterberger Steig runs from Hinterschmiding via Herzogsreut to Philippsreuth a distance of 14 miles (23km).

The Gulden Strass runs from Grafenau via St Oswald, Waldhäuser to Lusen, a mere 7 miles (11km).

For long distance walking either boots or stout walking shoes are advisable although all the above mentioned routes are by way of minor roads or good paths with wayside halts providing benches and tables while on the longer routes there are huts for shelter. The rolling countryside is adorned with small villages and ancient castles, some of which are only ruins but often the setting for historical plays or pageants which abound here. The most famous and colourful of all is probably the Drachenstich (Dragon Sticking Festival) at Furth im Wald.

The churches found in the rural parts of the Bavarian Forest are on the whole small and without the rich paintings and stucco work found elsewhere in Bavaria. In the seventeenth and eighteenth centuries when most of this work was carried out the area was sparsely populated and most definitely off the beaten track to the more famous artists. However this in no way detracts from the many delightful interiors that have been lovingly undertaken by local artists. For example it is impossible but to admire the wonderfully carved 'Fisher of Men' pulpit at Weissenregen on the outskirts of Kötzting.

Although the area is small it has two of the finest and loveliest cities in the whole of Germany in Regensburg and Passau. Both owe much of their delightful architecture to the Italian influence through trading with the Venetian merchants in the Middle Ages. The cathedral at Regensburg is undoubtedly a Gothic masterpiece and the organ in the cathedral at Passau the largest in the world.

The Danube Valley

Regensburg and Passau

The historic town of **Regensburg** is the gateway to the Bavarian Forest and is therefore a natural starting point, especially as it is also the capital of East Bavaria.

This gracious city, whose history goes back as far as the Stone Age, offers its visitors one of the warmest welcomes to be found anywhere in the whole of Germany. In Celtic times (500BC) it was called *Radasbona* , then came the Romans who built a fortified camp and renamed it *Castra Regina*. The settlement had four gates and above one was placed a 26ft (8m) stone slab in 179 to commemorate the fortification. This historical monument is now on view in the town museum and part of the massive walls erected during the Roman occupation can still be seen at the Porta Praetoria.

Regensburg attained its greatest fame during the Middle Ages which is why the Alt Stadt (Old Town) is so important for it is here that the real heart and soul still flourishes as it did centuries ago amidst the gracious buildings erected during this period.

The cathedral of St Peter is one of the few Gothic cathedrals to be found in Germany and by any standards is a masterpiece. Even from the motorway that bypasses the city it still dominates the surrounding countryside. It was built in 1275 on the site of a previous building of which the Eselsturm (Donkey's Tower) still remains, but its twin towers and west façade were added during the fifteenth century. It is a little difficult to appreciate the full beauty of the interior but the baroque high altar, the Gothic side altars and superb stained glass windows do give some indication of the wealth that remains hidden.

The Alter Kornmarkt stands on what was the inner fortification in 200 and is the setting for the Ducal Court, the Roman Tower and St Ulrich's Church. The Ducal Court was once the Ducal Palace, in Carolingian times known as the Herzogshof, and one of the most important palaces in southern Germany under Charlemagne. The Great Hall is Romanesque with a timbered ceiling adorned with coats of arms.

The Roman Tower still contains some of the original masonry in the 12ft (4m) thick walls which form the base. Its original function was that of a keep; later it became the treasury and could only be reached by an enclosed bridge linking it to the palace. St Ulrich's Church dates from the early thirteenth century and is also currently being restored and will then house the diocesan museum.

The Alte Kapelle is the oldest church in the city as its foundations date back to the Carolingian period but its fame dates from 1000 when it was restored to full glory. Additions and alterations were made in the thirteenth and fifteenth centuries. The detached bell tower was constructed with Roman blocks of stone. The interior is rococo with the high altar and golden triumphal arch flanked by statues of Henry II and his wife Kunigunde as patrons of the church. In the tiny Chapel of Grace there is an icon of the Virgin Mary reputedly given to Henry II by the pope in 1014 and is set in an exquisite frame made of silver gilt and embellished with precious stones. The painting unfortunately is now known to be of the thirteenth century and because it was painted in a Byzantine style, the legend maybe destroyed, but the beauty remains.

The Niedermünster Church was once a convent but in 1806 became the cathedral's parish church and while renovations to the cathedral were in progress the Domspatzen (Cathedral Sparrows) were heard. They are the Regensburg equivalent to the Vienna Boys Choir and have the same excellence of quality.

The Altes Rathaus in the Kohlenmarkt was built between the fourteenth and sixteenth centuries. The main entrance is reached by a flight of well worn stone steps. The door itself is a massive wooden one black with age and embedded in the masonry, by its side, are the old iron rods which were the official measures used in the settlement of disputes. The Reichsaal (Imperial Hall) has a beautifully timbered ceiling supported only by a massive central beam that is held in place

Schloss Weikersheim, in the Tauber Valley
above: seen from the baroque garden; below: the Knights' Hall

Creglingen in the Tauber Valley

St Peter's Cathedral and Steinerne Brücke (Stone Bridge)
across the river Danube, Regensburg

by the roof framework. The ceiling is studded with 22-carat gold studs, and in the centre of the main beam is the city coat of arms. The walls are hung with Flemish tapestries from the late fifteenth or early sixteenth centuries. The Reichsaal became the home of the Imperial Diet from 1663 until the dissolution of the Holy Roman Empire in 1806.

At the far end of this long chamber and raised on a dais is the Imperial Throne, flanked by two benches covered in a red cloth on which the electors sat while the side walls have benches covered in a green cloth for the princes temporal and spiritual. The benches across the floor of the chamber were for the representatives of the Free Imperial Cities and other visiting dignitaries. Other interesting rooms to be seen are the Electors' Chamber with its single handed clock dating from 1624 and massive furniture. The Antechamber is delightful with its Renaissance panelling but in some respects the adjoining room with its deep blue ceiling and silver stars denoting secrecy is more romantic.

The dungeons house the medieval torture chambers with many of the original gruesome instruments which are on show to the visitor. Two of the well preserved rooms are the Inquisition Room and the Folterkammer Chamber where the furniture includes such items as the 'Spanish Donkey' and 'The Maiden's Chair'. Spine chilling is almost an understatement but children seem to revel in it.

One item down here not connected with torture is the old salt scales. It is very crude to look at having only two pans either side of a moving pointer, but if one piece of paper was to be placed on one of the pans the pointer would register.

Another feature of the old town are the patrician houses built by wealthy merchants during the thirteenth and fourteenth centuries. Some were built as towers while others were erected around court-yards but both show the influence of Venetian trading partners. Many of these noble houses have fallen into disrepair but it is the policy of the city council to renovate them for use, for example, as student residences for the university.

The Runtingerhaus was originally built in the year 1200 by the Runtinger family who were as rich and famous as the Fuggers of Augsburg. The first dwelling was built in tower form but, with increasing wealth, the family pulled down the tower and rebuilt it on a lavish scale to include a large banqueting hall. After restoration in the 1970s it has now become the home of the City Archives whose collection contains the 'Runtinger Book' a ledger which shows the family's trading from 1383-1407.

The oldest stone bridge in Germany and certainly the first to span the Danube is the Steinerne Brücke, a medieval engineering feat of the first magnitude taking only 11 years to build (1135-46). The original bridge was constructed with sixteen arches and three towers but time has seen the removal of several of the arches and two of the towers. On the parapet halfway across is the famous statue of the Bruckmandl (Little Bridge Man). The stories surrounding its origins are many but one amusing theory is that the engineer in charge of the construction made a pact with the Devil in order to complete the bridge as quickly as possible. The payment was to be that the first eight legs to cross the bridge would be handed to the Devil. The engineer honoured this bargain but instead of sending four humans across he sent a dog and two chickens.

On the waterfront at the city end of the bridge is the Historische Wurstküche (Old Sausage Kitchen) whose history is as old as that of the bridge. It was built to provide food and drink for the workmen employed on the bridge construction. Eight hundred and fifty years later it is still fulfilling the same function but the clientele is some-what different; the working man has now disappeared and tourists as well as some of the local inhabitants have taken his place. The fare provided is excellent; home made potato soup, pork sausages and *Sauerkraut* (pickled cabbage) washed down by beer brewed by the local prince. Ruling over the hot kitchen stove is a great character, Elsa Schricker, born at the turn of the century and still working everyday, apart from Christmas Day when the premises are closed.

There are so many interesting places to visit, most of them being in the confines of the old town, guided walking tours are the finest method of getting to know this city and are arranged by the local tourist office which is situated on the ground floor of the Altes Rathaus. The following are just a few of the important places that should not be missed.

Keplerstrasse is named after the famous astronomer Johannes Kepler who lived with his family at No 2. Number 5 is now known as the Kepler House for it was here that the great man died in 1630 and is, today, a museum showing his work on the Copernican theory of the solar system together with instruments and drawings that helped him in his work.

The Bischofshof (Bishop's Palace) whose foundations are the old Roman walls, was built round a central courtyard which contains one of the most delightful and original fountains in a land that produces so many. Called the 'Goose Sermon Fountain' the central figure is a fox dressed up as a cleric preaching to some geese. The back of the cassock is slightly open to reveal the face of the fox leering at the innocent geese. The water from the fountain spills into a trough whose sides show four historical episodes connected with the palace and the courtyard in summer is an outdoor restaurant for a first class hotel.

Haidplatz is a large elegant square dominated by the Haus zum Goldenen Kreuz (House of the Golden Cross), five storeys high and surmounted by battlements and a tower. Its function from the sixteenth to the nineteenth centuries was that of an hotel where the famous and wealthy used to stay while in Regensburg. It was also the setting of a true romance when Emperor Charles V fell in love with a commoner, Barbara Blomberg, whose father was a city alderman. This alliance produced a son who later became famous in his own right as Don Juan of Austria, the victor of the naval Battle of Lepanto against the Turks in 1571 and later governor of the Netherlands.

The building is no longer an hotel although a café still remains together with a violin workshop, an art gallery and a set of small boutiques, known as the Golden Cross Arcade.

The Thon-Dittmar Palace is also on Haidplatz and it originally consisted of two fourteenth-century patrician houses which were amalgamated in the early nineteenth century. Built round a central courtyard with balconies on two floors it has now become a natural open-air theatre during the summer. Shakespearian plays find much favour and figure prominantly in the season's programme. The German-American Institute is also to be found within its portals.

Schloss Thurn and Taxis is the home of the family who bear this name and who in the past were known as the postmasters of Europe through founding the first post and mail coaches back in the sixteenth century. The castle was originally St Emmeram's Monastery but after secularisation in 1808 it was taken over by the Prince of Thurn and Taxis who proceeded to turn the south wing into a turreted palace. When the family are not in residence, and they do have other homes throughout Germany, the palace is open to the public and includes the state apartments, Throne Room, Ballroom, Chamber of Mirrors and the Green and Yellow Drawing Rooms.

The Marstallmuseum housed in the indoor riding school contains a fascinating display of horse transport, from ceremonial coaches and carriages, phaetons which were used around the extensive parkland, to sleighs and sledges. Upstairs in the gallery are equestrian paintings and ornate harnesses used over the years.

Last but by no means least is the City Museum in Dachauplatz in what was a former monastery of the thirteenth century. It has over a hundred rooms on three floors which gives some indication of the magnitude of wealth that is and was in Regensburg.

The ground floor contains relics from prehistoric and Roman times and includes the foundation stone of 179 as well as a model showing boats bringing the stone up river, being unloaded and carried away to where the fortifications are being built.

On the first floor are exhibits illustrating the historical development of the city while the second floor concerns what is loosely termed as art history from medieval to present day in the form of paintings, sculpture, tapestries and craft work which naturally includes glass and furniture. A series of rooms also shows the varying styles of different centuries. The third and top floor draws attention to the cultural pursuits that have been enjoyed in east Bavaria.

This is not a comprehensive analysis of Regensburg but merely an introduction as to the treasures and pleasures that are on offer to the discerning traveller.

Regensburg is blessed by having not only the mighty Danube flowing past its walls but also because the Regen joins its larger brother. The Rhine-Main-Danube canal will bring new prosperity by opening up the navigable waterways right through the heart of central Europe. This new project can be visited by motor boat and is proving a popular pastime. It is a journey of approximately 17 miles

A wayside shrine in the Bayerischer Wald

(27km) upstream to Kelheim and is spectacular. The excursion by river takes about 2 hours but includes passing the Befreiungshalle (Hall of Freedom), a rotunda-shaped building in Greco-Roman style designed by Leo von Klenze and built in 1842 to commemorate the War of Liberation against Napoleon. Adorning this eighteen-sided edifice are eighteen buttresses, each topped by a female statue holding a plaque with the name of a German tribe inscribed upon it. The number '18' has been deliberately incorporated to remind those who care that it was on the 18 October 1813 that the Battle of Leipzig was fought and Napoleon defeated. The interior is reminiscent of a Greek marble temple with Valkyrian figures illuminated only by the small amount of daylight which finds its way through the cupola high above.

Kelheim is a small town at the confluence of the Altmühl and the Danube and is extremely picturesque with its old town gate. It has a long and noble history for the dukes of Bavaria resided here from around 1200. The main attraction though is undoubtedly the Benedictine monastery of Weltenburg dating back to 612 and even then built on the site of a former Roman settlement. To reach **Weltenburg** the Danube flows through a rocky gorge known as the Donaudurchbruch. Here the rugged limestone cliffs rear up to a height of 400ft, (122m) and at the end where the river bends, stands the monastery with its splendid baroque church built by the Asam brothers in the early eighteenth century. Inside is St George's Altar with its larger than life sculpture of St George attacking the dragon.

For the energetic it is not only possible but extremely rewarding to take the well marked footpath from Befreiungshalle to Weltenburg as it follows the ridge close to the river taking approximately an hour. The return journey can be made by boat in order not to miss the gorge from the river.

Downstream from Regensburg is **Donaustauf** and yet another famous landmark — Walhalla, a classical white marble temple perched high on a wooded hillside with commanding views over the winding river to the flat and fertile plains beyond. It was built on the orders of King Ludwig I of Bavaria by Leo von Klenze in 12 years and he took the Parthenon in Greece as his inspiration for this German Hall of Fame.

The temple (one can call it nothing else) can be reached by road or more romantically by river steamer even though it entails climbing the 366 steps leading up to the main entrance flanked by a double row of Doric columns. Inside the floor is a colourful marble mosaic. Set back against the outer walls are plinths holding marble busts of famous men and women, most of whom are German as one would expect, but there are quite a few exceptions. Outside the view is superb along the river valley. It stretches from Regensburg in the west and southwards over the vast plain known as the 'Grain Store of Bavaria', a reference to the maize that flourishes here. Another good viewing point nearby is from the ruined Romanesque castle that was once the seat of the bishops of Regensburg.

From here onwards the river winds its way past the low fertile plains to the south while on the northern shore the foothills of the Bavarian Forest begin to rise. Apart from the motorway that also runs to the north of the river there are tiny farming communities, sometimes with castles or monasteries, not all of which are inhabited for some have fallen into ruins. Minor roads lead up into the foothills and so into the hinterland of the forest itself. One such road is at Wörth an der Donau, a small community which boasts a fortified castle adorned by eight turrets. Courses in painting and sketching are among the facilities to be found here.

From Wörth the minor road leads to the small village of **Falken-**

stein recommended for its views over the surrounding countryside. The village is unpretentious with its small main street, a couple of *Gasthöfe* and a few shops but the climb up through the woods to the summit for the panoramic views of vast tracts of forest interspersed with tiny communities is a reward for the long toil involved. The castle up here on the heights is, during the summer, the setting for a drama festival mainly during June and July. Falkenstein is also called the 'Pearl of the Bavarian Forest'.

Rejoining the Danube valley one can follow the river as it flows placidly on to the town of **Straubing** on its southern bank. Twentieth-century Straubing is a flourishing market town but it has a long and varied history. Once a Celtic and then Roman settlement the old town grew up around the church of St Peter in about 1180. For once the old town did not form the nucleus for expansion, and it remained outside the fortified new town which was developed in 1218. St Peter's was built in Romanesque style although the towers were added as late as 1886. The focal point of the interior is a particularly fine crucifix from 1200, but it is the burial vaults of 1486 with their Dance of Death frescoes (1763) that have become famous. In the churchyard there is the chapel and tomb of Agnes Bernauer whose fame or notoriety, depending on one's point of view, is due to the fact that she was the daughter of an Augsburg barber and because of her outstanding beauty caught the eye of the heir to the dukedom of Bavaria. Albrecht married her in 1432 against the wishes of his father who in turn sought to discredit his unwanted daughter-in-law. Three years later he managed to do this by successfully accusing her of witchcraft and sorcery. The penalty was death by drowning in the Danube. Friedrich Hebbel wrote a tragedy recalling the life and death of this woman and it is now performed every 4 years in the Ducal Palace.

The so-called new town with its fortifications became the capital of an independent duchy in 1353 but lost this status in 1425 when it was incorporated into the duchy of Bavaria.

The main square in the centre of the town is the Theresienplatz notable for its fourteenth-century, 200ft (61m) city tower surmounted by five pinnacles. Opposite is the Gothic town hall of 1382. Also occupying a central position in the square is the Tiburtius Fountain of 1685 and the tall graceful Trinity Column erected in 1709 to commemorate the town's liberation after Austrian troops besieged it.

There are some fine old medieval houses with high gables to be found in the Ludwigplatz and the Fraunhoferstrasse. The parish church of St Jakob is fifteenth century, and its most notable feature is the high altar with valuable figures, and painted panels of 1590 from an altar in Nuremberg. The side chapel of the Maria Hilf contains some early fifteenth-century paintings. The altar and paintings in the Maria Tod Chapel are by the Asam brothers. Other churches of note are the Carmelite church, begun in 1371 but not finished until the fifteenth century, and the extremely ornate even sumptuous Ursuline church of 1738 which is again the work of the Asam brothers.

The Schloss or Ducal Palace by the bridge across the Danube was built in 1356 by Duke Albrecht I. The chapel was added during the fourteenth and fifteenth centuries and the courtyard is the venue of the Agnes Bernauer Festival.

Straubing is also a noted agricultural centre for cattle and grain, both of which have long flourished on the well irrigated land surrounding the town. Each year, during the month of August, the Gauboden Folkfest (Fertile Land Festival) takes place with its processions, singing, dancing, barbecues and vast quantities of ale to refresh the revellers. The Gauboden Museum houses a prehistoric collection together with the Römischen Schatzfund (Roman Treasure Trove) with its wonderful array of gold masks, bronze figures and armour which were only excavated in 1950. A point of interest is that a model of the medieval town of Straubing was made in 1658 by Jakob Sandtner and is now considered so important that it is in the Bavarian National Museum in Munich.

Eight miles (13km) north-east of Straubing is **Bogen** a small town with a pilgrimage church up on the Bogenberg. It is an old established place with a museum and a reading room for visitors to use. The Marienkirche on the Bogenberg dates from the thirteenth century and is the setting for the annual Whitsun Festival. Close by is Oberalteich a former Benedictine monastery church of 1630 with a splendid rococo interior containing a hanging staircase that leads up to the galleries.

Before reaching Deggendorf it is worth visiting Metten and the Benedictine monastery of St Michael whose origins date back to the eighth century when it was founded by the Emperor Charlemagne. The present church with its fine carvings and lavish baroque interior dates from only 1720. The superb entrance porch has a frescoed ceiling which is rather unusual. Above the high altar is a particularly fine painting of St Michael destroying Lucifer by C.D. Asam but even more interesting is the wonderful monastery library; a veritable work of art and Aladdin's Cave all rolled into one. The ceiling

Deggendorf

frescoes all relate to the books that can be found in the very ornate bookcases that line the walls. The equally elaborate decor of the vaulting and cornices are of marble and held up by Atlas like figures mounted on plinths. The banqueting hall continues in this ornate style with rococo stucco work while the ceiling is as fresh and vibrant as when it was painted 250 years ago. In the inner courtyard there is a fountain which is dedicated to the founder Charlemagne.

Deggendorf, a pleasant town with a delightful promenade, is at the confluence of the three rivers, namely the Regen, Isar and Danube. Trees give shade in the heat of the day and it is from here that the river excursions call to load and unload passengers. This prime site has enabled Deggendorf to be an important town since 750, and the only one of any size to be located on the north bank of the Danube. Naturally it is a busy commercial centre these days and the main thoroughfare, especially on weekdays bears witness to this fact when it is lined by stalls selling everything from fresh produce to clothing. Like all modern towns, Deggendorf is subject to traffic problems and the stalls, although colourful, do not exactly aid the flow of traffic. The Luitpoldplatz at the centre of the town has a sixteenth-century Rathaus incorporating the St Martin Chapel of 1296, and two charming fountains of the same era. There is a local museum containing many fine paintings, weapons, clocks and local craftwork and a prehistoric section illustrating the life and times of the early settlers.

The church of the Maria Himmelfahrt (Assumption) was Romanesque but destroyed by fire in 1240. The succeeding years have seen reconstruction in varying styles but something to admire on the wall of the Wasserkapelle is a relief over the door which dates from the mid-thirteenth century. At present the church is closed for interior restoration. The other noteworthy church in the town is that of the Holy Sepulchre with a Gothic nave and basilica of 1360.

Deggendorf is also the scene of several festivals which include the annual Music Week in August covering a wide range and taste in this field. July sees what is called the Deggendorfer Kaffeehaustage which recreates the old coffee house traditions. The Volkfest (Folk Festival) is now held annually at the end of July to the beginning of August, when processions, games, music, drinking and jollifications become part of the town scene.

Across the river lies **Plattling**, a pleasant old town on the Isar and also on the fast railway line from Passau to Munich and Nuremberg. This provides a first class service for visitors without their own transport. The Isar provides an excellent venue for oars-men and during the summer rowing regattas are held there.

The Danube now flows in a more southerly direction away from the foothills and in this particular stretch the Benedictine monastery of St Mauritius can be seen. It was at its most powerful in the Middle Ages and the foundations which are fourteenth century are all that remained after a disastrous fire. The current building is early eighteenth century.

The river now forms a loop and on the southern bank is **Osterhofen** with the monastery church of St Margaretha in the Altenmarkt. The original medieval building fell into decay but in 1727 the best artists of that period, namely J.M. Fischer and the Asam brothers, were commissioned to undertake its restoration. Taking 13 years to complete but now regarded as the most elaborate baroque church in Bavaria, some may perhaps feel it is too elaborate but that is a matter of personal choice. Let us just say that the sheer beauty is almost overpowering!

Once again the river forms a long loop before straightening out where the village of **Hofkirchen** on the north bank is to be found. This peaceful rural community has an ancient but picturesque ruined castle, the Hilgartsberg, perched high above a narrower stretch of the valley. It has had a chequered history with ownership chang-

The river Danube with a view of the Veste Oberhaus, Passau

ing hands many times but has been used since the last century as a setting for festivals as well as a viewing platform. Hofkirchen may be small but there is a heated open-air swimming pool and other sporting attractions, river cruises and easy access to the *Autobahn* or alternatively train services from Vilshofen on the southern bank. **Vilshofen** has grown up between the river Vils and Wolfach just as they enter the Danube and its history goes back 1,200 years, as

witnessed by the Renaissance Tower, the baroque parish church and
the twin towers of the Benedictine Abbey of Schweiklberg. There is
a splendid new leisure centre complex with swimming pool and
medicinal salt baths. Many sporting activities are held here as well as
lessons at the flying and gliding school.

Windorf is a little old market town on the north bank of the
Danube slightly downstream from Vilshofen. Offshore it is the largest river island between Ulm and Vienna with its nature reserve
attracting many species of birds who find this a haven especially
during the nesting season. Along the banks there are over 40 miles
(64km) of marked country walks and because of its location and
proximity to Passau, Windorf has now become a summer resort with
two 'holiday villages'. **Ebersberg,** the larger of the two, is set on
rising ground and affords splendid views over the city of Passau.
Each chalet contains two or four furnished apartments and within
the complex is a restaurant, swimming pool, sauna, table tennis and
children's playground. **Buchelberg** is both smaller and quieter,
surrounded by gentle wooded hills and facilities for riding, tennis
and bowling are near at hand.

Aicha vorm Wald, lying just north of the river before it reaches
Passau, is a small village surrounded by green pastures. Its origins
date back to the tenth century and details together with its subsequent history can be found in the local museum housed in the
moated Schloss Aicha. The village lies on the banks of the Gross Ohe
river as it flows through a narrow but pretty valley, providing an
ideal location for anyone wishing to find peaceful surroundings
linked to an activity holiday. Accommodation is of the simple traditional variety, but it is advisable to have a car for staying here.

Passau is said by some connoisseurs, including Alexander von
Humboldt, to be one of the seven most beautifully situated cities in
the world. Its setting is certainly delightful with the old city being
built on a spit of land that narrows to a point as the rivers Danube and
Inn come together. The waters mingle to become mosaic of blue and
brown and the modest yet little Ilz is the third river to join the tide
here.

The old waterfront is lined at the narrowest point with old buildings of varying heights and colours. On the north bank of the Danube, wood covered slopes sweep up to the Veste Oberhaus, a
mighty fortress dominating the skyline. It began life in the early
thirteenth century in quite a small way, but succeeding generations
of prince bishops added to the complex turning it into the vast
domain that it is today. It has now become the home of the town

Hotel Wilder Mann, Passau

museum, art gallery, Bohemian Forest Museum and Fire Brigade Museum. There is also a restaurant and observation tower here.

The old city is dominated by St Stephen's Cathedral which took 113 years to build (1407-1520). The architecture is mixed; Roman-

The Glass Museum, Passau

esque, Gothic and baroque are all to be found here. It is however the organ that attracts the vast crowds that flock each day for the concert given at noon. The seats in high summer are all taken half an hour before the concert is due to commence and then there is only standing room left in order to listen to the wonderful instrument with 17,000 pipes and 208 stops which makes it the largest church organ in the world.

Flanking the cathedral is the shady Residenzplatz on which stands the New Residence Palace of the prince bishops with a beautiful staircase leading to the state rooms which are all in an ornate rococo design. The Residence may be the largest and grandest but the other houses here are stately patrician homes that once belonged to the wealthy merchants.

There are many interesting places to visit in Passau such as the

Rathaus Ratskeller (1298), the Old Residence of the prince bishops (now the Law Courts) and the Jesuit church of St Michael. Niedernburg is a former benedictine convent of the eighth century with the Maria Parz Chapel containing the tomb of the abbess Gisela, sister of the Emperor Henry II and widow of St Stephen, King of Hungary.

Passau does not live in the past. It is a modern city with first rate theatre and concert programmes and is the host city to the European Weeks Festival each year. All sports either for watching or participating, are given first rate facilities.

The town is one of the major departure points for the short cruises to Regensburg while longer ones can go as far as the Black Sea. This would seem to be a city of perpetual movement. Large and small craft load and unload passengers from all corners of the world while every language imaginable assails the ear. All this however just seems to lend enchantment to the cosmopolitan city.

Down by the waterfront stands the Hotel Wilder Mann. Apart from being a first class hotel it is unusual that it also incorporates a unique collection of glassware which has now been established as the Passauer Glass Museum. It is also home to the suite of rooms once occupied by the Empress Elisabeth of Austria and still furnished as it was during her stay. More than 10,000 pieces of glassware are on show here, Biedermayer to Art Nouveau are displayed in over 150 show cases. All the principal glass manufacturers are represented here with either full collections or several pieces covering the last 200 years and grouped together period by period in separate rooms. Every colour and shade of glass imaginable can be seen. Some of it is engraved, some is hand painted, some is small, and some large, but all have a story to tell. The museum is open daily and the visitor is permitted to wander at leisure and even take photographs. The hotel also has a rooftop café and a lift to whisk visitors up to the top floor. One of the cakes on offer here is called Sissi's Delight and it is extremely rich.

Six miles (10km) downstream from Passau is **Kellberg-Thyrnau** , noted for its clean pure air. Surrounded by meadows and gently rising hills it is an excellent centre for exploring this corner of Germany together with the adjoining countryside belonging to Austria and Czechoslovakia. The riding school here has acquired a first class reputation. Other activities include swimming, tennis and bowling and as an alternative there are well marked nature trails to delight walkers and naturalists. Concerts, folk evenings and a lending library all help to create a full programme and there is also a bus connection to Passau.

The last town in this section of the Danube valley is **Obernzell**, a market town and once the summer residence of the prince bishops of Passau who had a castle here. It is now part of the Bavarian National Museum, includes pottery for which Obernzell was once famous and is strategically placed on the banks of the Danube as the river begins to enter a gorge. There is a ferry to convey passengers to the opposite shore and a boarding point for travellers by river steamer to Austrian territory. The town itself is well laid out with an imposing market square and an eighteenth-century church with twin towers. An additional sporting facility here is the 11 mile (18km) stretch of water for skiing enthusiasts. Cycling is another popular attraction here thanks to the 30 mile (48km) long track which runs alongside the river. The local tourist office organises a weekly programme of events guaranteed to keep visitors well occupied with sporting and cultural activities. A local speciality here is the fruit wine, more associated with the Black Forest area but very welcome as an alternative to wine and beer on warm days.

Bavarian Forest

The South

From Passau the B12 road runs along the valley of the river Ilz till it reaches **Salzweg**; a small rural community that offers its visitors a warm welcome, but especially to those who are interested in flora and fauna. A river information trail with a total length of over 45 miles (72km) has been set up here in the Ilz valley enabling those interested in such things to see for themselves the unique species of flora and fauna found here. Swimming is in a dammed up section of the river while other sporting activities on offer are tennis and shooting. A bus service from Salzweg to Passau, only 4 miles (6km) away, allows the attractions found there to be enjoyed quite conveniently.

Following the B12 northwards one reaches the fair sized village of **Hutthurm**, lying in a sunny part of this wild but romantic valley. Holidays here are simple and relaxing, spent in small private pensions and private houses where the cost can be quite inexpensive depending on the length of stay. Sporting attractions consist of tennis and a bowling alley, while swimming has to be undertaken in the neighbouring village of Büchlberg less than a couple of miles away. However the village does offer its guests a reading room and arranges local folk evenings. There is a distinct advantage in having one's own transport here as it enables one to cover the delightful surrounding countryside without having to rely on the local bus service. The nearest railway station is 10 miles (16km) away at Passau.

East of Hutthurm is the slightly smaller **Büchlberg** on what used to be the old salt trade route known as the Golden Path, for in the Middle Ages salt was as precious as gold is today. Close to the winding river Erlau, Büchlberg is fast gaining a reputation as an ideal centre for leisure activities with its keep fit trails, riding, tennis, fishing and swimming in the heated outdoor pool. Relaxation is catered for with excursions by old stage coach and in the evenings there is music and dancing as well as special folk performances. The newly found prosperity is reflected by the medium sized hotels that have recently been built. Like Hutthurm the close proximity to Passau makes this an attractive destination.

Hauzenberg is ideal for a relaxing holiday amidst the unspoilt forested countryside which surrounds it, and is still only 13 miles (21km) from Passau to which it is connected by a regular bus service. It is very much a family resort with children warmly welcomed, both in the self-catering apartments as well as the many farms that offer accommodation and allow the children to 'help' in feeding the farm animals. Children's adventure play areas have been set up to help keep them fully occupied.

Other facilities here are a reading room, cinema, open-air chess and stage coach trips. For the past 10 years, normally in May, Hauzenberg has been running cultural weeks. The school hall becomes a theatre and the new church, with its excellent acoustics, is transformed into a concert hall with seating for 800 people.

On the sporting front, both indoor and outdoor tennis, swimming and smallbore shooting are available. There is also a well organised rambling association which awards special commemorative badges to those who cover enough mileage. There is an animal museum which attracts many who come here, but without doubt the biggest attraction is the Kropfmühl Graphite Mine which is the last working mine to be found in Germany. A visit enables one to descend to the fourth floor where the mining is now carried out. Also on show is the machinery used to extract this mineral both now and in the past. Woodcarving is a local interest and courses in this subject are held.

Heading north-east from Hauzenberg and passing the small Freudensee the road reaches **Sonnen** which, true to its name, is a dear little village on a sunny plateau. As the border with Czechoslovakia draws closer, one really begins to realise that nothing could be more off the beaten track and away from tourist routes. Here the local people really enjoy meeting visitors from other parts of Europe and further afield. Absent are the hotels and larger pensions and in their place stand the small traditional inns that have seen many a year, together with houses let out as apartments and a few private houses and farms. After a day spent in the open air discovering the pleasures of nature, the evening is a welcome time for relaxing over a glass of beer, watching television or making merry at a barbecue. There is a local bus service to Passau but a car is really essential.

Breitenberg is tucked into a corner where the three countries of Germany, Austria and Czechoslovakia meet. It is also one of the finest and loveliest of rambling areas with the Dreisessel mountain rising to a height of 4,333ft (1,321m). Although this is real border territory the paths and trails are well marked and, providing one does not attempt to stray from them, there is no real likelihood of crossing any borders unwittingly. Additionally there are red and woods, lakes and rivers all near at hand. One certain factor is that you will be hospitably welcomed here for in 1986 Neukirchen received a commendation in the competition on hospitable Bavaria; quite a feat for a village. There are plenty of outdoor activities here with woodland and river trails, keep fit courses, riding, tennis and fishing, all of which may be necessary to those taking advantage of the bread that has been baked in the old style ovens — the warm bread not only smells delicious but tastes it as well. Neukirchen is a quiet oasis to the more hectic life of Passau 11 miles (18km) away.

The North

Regen stands on the Black Regen river which flows on eventually to Regensburg. On warm sunny evenings the riverside walks under leafy trees give the relaxation that the area is known for. They are also just as pleasant in the evenings when illuminated by electric light.

The large town square is overlooked by shops and cafés, as well as the parish church of St Michael, while on the fourth side is the House of the Guest with its reading and television rooms and information office all under the same roof. A decorative touch to the square is the flower beds and the old fountain.

Courses on glass painting and pottery are to be found here, but details should be obtained from the local tourist office. There are also many sporting facilities with two swimming pools, an excellent riding school with its own jumping arena and well defined country rides up to 7 miles (11km) long. In addition there is tennis and football. Fishing is definitely a major sport here and rules are laid down and strictly adhered to regarding the quantity and size of fish that may be caught in any one day. Apart from fishing the river is used for rowing and canoeing and even shooting the rapids is a possibility for those with a strong nerve.

The last weekend in July sees the Pichelsteiner Festival celebrated. It is without doubt the longest extended weekend in the Bavarian Forest as it lasts for 5 days. The origins of this festival are certainly strange as it is derived from a stew called the 'Pichelsteiner' which is made from meat, vegetables and seasoning. The result is an excellent and very filling meal which even the Iron Chancellor Otto von Bismarck was delighted with. Apart from eating and drinking during the day, there are water sports and musical processions with those taking part wearing the historic *Tracht* (a local costume). At night gondola trips illuminated by Venetian lighting all contrive to make this a genuine Bavarian carnival.

To the south of the town is the ruined castle of Weissenstein where, or so it is alleged, a certain Count Hund buried his wife alive in retaliation for having drowned their baby in the river. Here also is the Frassenden Haus Museum where the Baltic poet Siegfried von Vagesack and his Swedish wife, also a poet, lived and worked, producing more than eighty literary works. The ground floor is in fact devoted to their work and the rooms are furnished with their belongings. The first floor houses a collection of snuff boxes, 1,300 examples in all, and is claimed to be the largest private collection in Europe. It is the work of a former Bürgermeister, Alois Reitbauer, over a period of more than 46 years.

The second floor has varying themes from the world of literature, art and folklore, but the exhibitions change from time to time so it is not possible to state categorically just what will be on view at a given time. The third floor is set aside for special exhibitions by well known artists of which there may be two or three during the summer months.

The attics up under the roof are given over to the linen industry that once flourished widely in these parts. Both implements and illustrations show the entire process, from the growing of the flax to the final woven linen.

The name Weissenstein means 'White Stone' and the entrance hall shows the geology of the quartz with its strange formation that creates this phenomenon known as Pfahl. The Pfahl is in fact a quartz ridge which stretches from Freihung in the north to Freyung in the south and is estimated to be around 150 to 300 million years old. It can only be seen above ground at certain locations, namely Thierlstein near Cham, Viechtach and Weissenstein where it appears as a white rock. Outside the museum a massive dragon has been sculptured from this rock and then beautifully coloured in blues, greens and red with its jaws wide open showing its wicked fangs as if ready to swallow unsuspecting visitors.

Following the river Regen upstream one comes to **Zwiesel** which is acknowledged as the centre of the glass industry as well as that of the loveliest part of the Bavarian Forest. The town itself consists of a steep main street which, until the new bypass was opened this year, was heavily congested. It is still very busy but at least the queues are not quite so long for anyone wishing to drive through the town.

There is a small well laid out garden at the lower end of the town with benches and a pool whose fountain seems to attract birds who use it as a shower in summer. This peaceful haven also has a small free car park adjacent to it, with no limit making this a very useful starting point for exploring the town and various glass works. Most

Attractive half-timbered buildings in Creglingen, the Tauber Valley

The market place at Bad Mergentheim, in the Tauber Valley

Master glass-blower at work, Theresienthal

of these works have their own showrooms which the public may browse round and purchases are beautifully packed to ensure no breakages on the journey home however far that may be. The main street also has some showrooms for works that are not as central. At the top end on the north side in a quiet courtyard is the Wald-museum. The ground floor mounts a comprehensive introduction to the forest in the way of trees and insects that they often harbour to their detriment as well as the uses that the felled trees are put to. One may also see a representation of a forester's house in bygone days. Animal life in the forest is also there together with the fungi that grow within its boundaries and information on how to distinguish between those that are edible and those that are poisonous, even fatal. The upper floor shows the glass that has been produced in this area over the years. The parish church is noted for its statue of *The Whipped Christ*.

Zwiesel can offer over 3,000 beds to visitors ranging from hotels to private houses and in addition there is a youth hostel and a camping site that is open all year round. Recreational facilities here are also good with two outdoor pools, one of which is heated, as well as the indoor swimming pool. There are also guided walking tours as well as an information trail to the Grosser Falkenstein. Seven miles (11km) to the north of Zwiesel at Scheuereck is a nature reserve where you can see wild animals being fed without prior booking.

Zwiesel and the glass industry are synonymous and glassware bought here is far cheaper than in the shops or departmental stores in other parts of the country. Each manufacturer has a distinctive design and most are known for cut glass wares (eg Royal Bavarian Crystal). A good example which illustrates this art more fully is 'Theresienthal'.

The factory and showrooms are outside the main town of Zwiesel on the road to Bayerisch Eisenstein and the firm is one of the oldest and most famous in Germany. It produces the finest quality glass, 80 per cent of which is for the home market, the other 20 per cent being divided between Europe, America and Japan. It was founded in 1421 by the Rabenstein family and remained in their hands until 1636. From then on it passed through several family ownerships but since 1982 has been a public company.

The current production of Theresienthal glass has been developed from the old traditions. Indeed the company policy is to retain the old hand crafted methods and to this end the old wooden moulds are still used to give the final shape required. The molten glass is taken by a learner (glass industry term for an apprentice) from the gas fired furnaces to the glass-blower who blows through a long pipe to form the basic shape of the glass. This is then transferred to the wooden mould where the final shaping is undertaken before being passed to the master glassmaker who applies the decorative additions before checking the precision of the finished product. Each piece of glass, whatever its size, bears the unmistakeable stamp of Theresienthal in its superb colouring, shape and decoration. The mass production market is not for this firm; quality before quantity is their motto. It is no wonder the royal houses of Europe placed their orders here.

By modern standards the factory is quite small. Each morning the glass-blowers work from 8.30am-1.30pm and in summer the heat from the furnaces becomes almost unbearable — hence the amount of liquid that is consumed while working. After the glass-blowers have finished the men who mix and smelt the glass take over in order that the next day's shift may have enough molten glass to work with. When the glass has been fired and cooled some of it is passed on for hand engraving or painting. Factories, which can be visited, are well stocked with a wide range of table glassware, vases and decorative pieces which may be bought as single items or in larger quantities. There are at least ten glass works in the area which welcome visitors on scheduled visits.

The road from here to the frontier village of **Bayerisch Eisenstein** climbs up through an ever narrowing valley whose slopes are covered with dark green conifers. To the east is the 4,258ft (1,298m) high Grosser Falkenstein mountain while to the west is the highest peak within the forest, the Grosser Arber at 4,778ft (1,456m). This small resort is for the active. In winter it is a skiing area while in the summer the paths ring to the sound of boots and alpen-stocks (stout walking sticks), for it is here that the true alpine hiking and climbing comes into its own. At the far end of the main street is the border and customs post with a large car park. Once past the barrier the road continues to run on through the wooded heights for roughly another couple of kilometres before reaching the Czechoslovakian border post.

There is a winding narrow road which turns off westwards at the actual border or a slightly better road 4 miles (6km) back towards Zwiesel that leads directly to the Grosser Arber. Even before reaching the chairlift that carries one up this mountain, cars and coaches are parked along the roadside and in the parking bays. To avoid long queues at the chairlift it is advisable to arrive early — the lift commences at 8am! Having reached the top of the lift additional warm clothing can be a good idea as one is exposed to any wind that may be blowing. It is possible to continue on foot past a chapel to reach two rocky outcrops. The one above the chapel is the point where the visitor has extensive views over the Schwarzer Reger and on across the Czechoslovakian frontier to the almost hidden village of Zelezná Ruda. From the other rocky spur with its cross, one has the whole panorama of the Bayerischer Wald and the Lamerwinkel, albeit on fine days only. At least half a day is recommended to make this particular trip worthwhile. At the foot of the Grosser Arber is the enchanting and magical Grosser Arbersee lake with its surrounding pine trees reflected in its still waters; a very popular spot for family picnics and leisurely boating.

The road from here to Neukirchen beim Heiligen Blut covers some of the loveliest unspoilt and wooded landscape to be found anywhere in Europe with a rare elusive beauty that once found is hard to forget. The highest village in the forest is **Lohberg**, surrounded by woodland with a game enclosure for the deer and other wild animals. Marked walks radiate out from the village as well as a keep fit trail with its series of exercise stops along the shores of the Kleiner Arbersee. The open-air swimming pool, tennis courts and the fishing are gaining popularity with those in search of active holidays. A newly built House of the Guest with a reading and television room is an added attraction.

As the road commences its descent panoramic views over the Lamerwinkel unfold. The grandeur of the Grosser Osser towers over the gentler hills and the open sunny valley where the attractive but small resorts of Lam, Haibühl and Arrach form a triangle. **Lam** has a splendid new recreation centre which includes an indoor swimming pool and a gymnasium. There is a local folk museum with emphasis on the minerals found in these parts and a reading room in the House of the Guest. As well as the folk music and dancing there is a very good folk theatre which puts on plays dealing with some of the legends which the Bayerischer Wald is steeped in. Quieter forms of entertainment are zither music and for the railway enthusiasts on certain summer weekends there is the Regen Valley Railway steam locomotive *Mizzi* which operates, with nineteenth-century rolling stock, for excursions either between Kötzting and Lam or from Viechtach to and from Blaibach and Gotteszell.

Arrach, the third village of this trio, is linked for administration purposes to the tiny community of **Haibühl**. Whether one approaches this cluster of villages from either the north or the south they do represent some of the most attractive villages to be found here in the forest. Only a short distance separates Arrach from the wood covered slopes with their well signposted routes for walking. There is a riding stable with its own indoor school and jumping arena. Evening entertainments include folk evenings and film shows about the past and present Bavarian Forest.

Neukirchen beim Heiligen Blut is part of the developing holiday area in this region. It is surrounded by densely wooded slopes and has the longest chairlift in the forest which ascends the 3,482ft (1,061m) high Schwarzriegel which is part of the Hohe Bogen ridge. At the top there is a restaurant and a newly constructed summer toboggan run. Neukirchen is a 500-year-old village due, in no small way, to the fact that pilgrims were drawn here to pay homage to a miracle that is alleged to have occurred back in the Middle Ages. The village itself is neat with some rather nice old houses and a well tended park. Sporting facilities on offer here are tennis, riding and hang-gliding.

Furth im Wald is an old border town and famous for its Drachenstich (Dragon Sticking Festival) which takes place from the second Sunday in August for a week and is the oldest folk festival in Germany. Nowadays this is no ordinary country pageant but a first class production that costs over a million Deutsch Marks. The festival and play are performed in the main street which is closed during this period; seating for 2,225 people is erected along the route. The seats

The Dragon Festival, Furth im Wald

at the front are the most expensive but as it is tiered all have a good view of the proceedings. Its fame has spread worldwide, mainly due to television coverage as well as having been filmed by Walt Disney.

The real origin of this particular festival is obscure although it probably had something to do with the Magyars who used to sweep down from the Hungarian plains and terrorise this region. In fact until a 100 years ago this pageant was always performed at the religious festival of Corpus Christi. With a 500-year-long history the play has changed slightly as successive authors have rewritten the script. The current production is the work of Josef Martin Bauer in 1952 and shows the fate of a frontier people during the worst moments in the Hussite Wars of the fifteenth century. The heart of the story is simple; a young and lovely maiden falls into the clutches of a wicked dragon and is rescued by a gallant knight. The play itself is performed on a raised stage, with a procession through the streets consisting of 1,100 participants in medieval costume. Some are dressed as mounted knights in full armour, for which 200 horses are needed, not forgetting the flag bearers, musicians and dignitaries.

The Dimpl family have long been associated with the pageant and many a son has played the noble knight who wins the lady. In 1967 Volkmar Dimpl and Rosemarie Percher were the *Ritterpaar* (leading lady and gentleman) and a few years later actually married.

Once the procession is underway the dragon must be attacked by

The town hall, Furth im Wald

the mounted knights with spears until the final death blow. Only then is the maiden free to be claimed. In a way the real hero is that of the dragon who, in these modern times, is a fabulous creation. The current monster was designed by the Pyrkos family and built by the engineering firm of Fischer in Mühlausen, close to the city of Nuremberg. The sensation caused when the finished article was mounted on a long trailer and towed by lorry for around a hundred miles over well used roads probably had to be seen to be believed.

Fountain, Furth im Wald

The monster, for that is what it really is in more ways than one, measures 58ft (18m) long, 13ft (4m) wide, 10ft (3m) high and has a comprehensive hydraulic system enabling its wings to flap. It is also fully mechanised and has two drivers ensconced inside. Painted red and green with flashing eyes, the huge jaws open and shut to show the wicked teeth while the nostrils emit billowing smoke. It is strange but for all this the spectacle is not a frightening experience. Children adore the dragon and when he is killed there are tears of real sorrow to be mopped up. During the rest of the year the dragon may be visited in his lair in the Schlossplatz for a minimal fee.

Furth im Wald, even without the festival, is a delightful place with a charming Rathaus whose main entrance portrays St George slaying the dragon. A carillon of bells plays at 11am at the entrance to the Schlossplatz where the Landestormuseum can be found. It is housed in the former hospital and town tower and has a special collection of figures of saints as well as paintings of them. The museum has recreated a furnished room that would have graced a town house at the turn of the century and has a glass division which shows something of the glass and other local industries. It also outlines the history and geology of the town and surrounding countryside including that of Bischofteinitz in the Sudetenland over the border in Czechoslovakia. Overall it is a most interesting and comprehensive account of how people lived and worked throughout the ages.

The Voithenberghammer is an extension of the main museum although a little way out of town there is an old blacksmith's dwelling house and workshop in the Kalten Pastritz valley. Built in 1823 it has now been renovated to its former glory and displays the tools and implements used by the smithy.

At **Steinbruch** on the other side of the town, is the Waldmuseum with its animals, plants, flowers, insects and fungi that are, or were, found in the woods and streams in this part of the world. Amongst the larger stuffed animals on view are the brown bear, lynx, European bison and the capercaillie, a local and long extinct bird. Outside there is an enclosure for red deer and various species of wild goat that children find enthralling. Walks, fishponds, a children's play area and a restaurant make this a favourite haunt for a day out.

In addition Furth also offers its guests a wide choice in the way of accommodation. Sporting facilities are not forgotten with an indoor and outdoor swimming pool, tennis, riding, and golf, making this a really worthwhile place to stay for either a long or short period.

Just north of Furth is the 1,000-year-old town of **Waldmünchen** noted for its splendid network of marked walks. It is therefore a great favourite of those who prefer walking holidays alone or with a guide. It also has an annual pageant, known as Trenck the Pandour Pageant, and is performed during July and August. This has nothing to do with the world of dragons as it originated during the eighteenth century. A certain Baron Trenck and his mounted troops pillaged the town of Cham. The inhabitants of Waldmünchen were afraid of what would happen to them and so they gathered together a large sum of money and offered it to the baron in order that he would leave them in peace; this he agreed to do. The pageant is now celebrated by the enactment in full costume of the baron and his troops arriving and being paid off. The standard of riding, coupled with the colourful costumes as well as the merrymaking that ensues, makes this a joyful occasion.

The small town square has a Rathaus with a gilded statue outside. This forms the focal point around which the compact town has arisen. A modern riding school with its own grounds takes groups of riders out to discover the surrounding countryside. Sailing and

Totenbrett boards on the side of the road

The following resorts are all situated on the western side of the Ostmarkstrasse beginning with **Rattenberg** which is perched on a small ridge overlooking the rolling countryside that appears almost as a patchwork quilt with its fields, farms and small woods rising and falling as far as the eye can see. This scattered farming community comes together on a Sunday morning for church services and then goes on to the local inns where, over *steins* of beer, the latest news is discussed with vim and point.

The district of Neurandsberg, a little way from the main village, has a ruined castle and is also one of the remaining places where the old Totenbrett boards can be seen at the side of the road. These boards are an old east Bavarian custom which derived from the deceased being placed on a funeral board and taken to the church-yard for burial. Afterwards the board was decorated and inscribed with the loved one's details before being placed near wayside shrines or on walls of houses and so acting as a memorial.

Haibach is another small hamlet and together with Elisabethzell offers peace and tranquility in open countryside which both walkers and naturalists enjoy. There is swimming in the open-air pool and hang-gliding.

St Englmar is known for its winter sports but is nevertheless an ideal choice in summer as well, with wooded slopes that lead up to the Proller (3,406ft, 1,038m), the Predigstühl (3,328ft, 1,014m) and the

Hirschenstein (3,559ft, 1,085m) by well marked and timed routes. There is an annual festival held on Whit Monday incorporating the old religious and folk play of Englmari Suchens (Englmar Search) which recalls how the holy hermit Englmar was murdered around 1100 and the body later found in the forest without having decomposed. The festival commences at 9am in the Kirchplatz with an opening fanfare by the town band followed by a mass and the blessing of the animals.

St Englmar has first class riding facilities with an indoor swimming pool as well as medicinal baths, massage and sauna. There are indoor and outdoor riding arenas as well as tennis courts. For entertainment there are plays and folk evenings in the local folk theatre and concerts or zither music at one of the hotels.

Köllnburg is set on a broad ridge away from the sound of traffic but in a particularly delightful part of the Bavarian Forest with its panoramic views over the surrounding countryside. The village is clean and neat with a baroque church and a twelfth-century castle that once belonged to the Nussberg family before its partial destruction in 1468. Like Viechtach this is also a fog free climate. Sporting facilities within the village are tennis and bowling but with a quick and easy access to Viechtach the extensive facilities there can be used with little inconvenience.

Bernried is a small resort in a sheltered sunny position at the commencement of the foothills of the Bavarian Forest, just above the Danube valley and only 7 miles (11km) from Deggendorf. The Bernriederbach is a clear mountain stream that rises close to the summit of the Hirschenstein and flows past the wooded slopes and the village of Bernried before joining the Schwarzach which then flows into the Danube. The trees that surround Bernried are mostly silver birch and make a pleasant contrast to the darker conifers. In spring and early summer the meadows are carpeted with flowers adding to the already colourful scene. Although very much a walking area, Bernried has an open-air swimming pool as well as riding and tennis.

Halfway between Bernried and Deggendorf in the Perlbach valley is Schloss Egg, a real fairytale castle, built in the twelfth century high above the surrounding forest and now open to the public from April to November to view the chapel and the main hall. The castle is guarded by ramparts while in the courtyard is the Hungerthurm (Hunger Tower). This is a tall square windowless building except for the narrow lancet windows that throw a minimal amount of light on the stairs leading to the top of the tower with its pyramid shaped roof and the four small turrets that decorate each corner. An ideal setting for Rapunzel to let down her long golden tresses.

The castle now forms part of an hotel. In fact the former stables and coach house have been turned into first class restaurants in historic surroundings; meals enjoyed here are not cheap but a splendid way to wind up an excellent holiday.

Further Information
— Bayerischer Wald —

Museums and Places of Interest

Bodenmais
Museum Bodenmais
Bahnhof Strasse
Open: daily 10am-4pm except during November and December.
Hours of guided tours vary. A car park is at hand.

Breitenberg
Weberei Museum
Open: daily during main summer months but only on three afternoons a week in early and late season.

Finsterau
Freilichtmuseum Bayerischer Wald
Open: daily from May to September; afternoons only in January to April and October.

Zwiesel
Theresiental Glass Factory
Open: 9.30am-1pm for factory visits.
Showrooms open: 9am-4pm Monday to Friday.

Tourist Offices

Regional Office for east Bavaria
Fremdenverkehrsverband Ostbayern
Landshuter Strasse 13
8400 Regensburg
☎ (0941) 57186

Aicha vorm Wald
Gemeinde Aicha vorm Wald
Am Kirchplatz 1

8359 Aicha vorm Wald
☎ (08544) 281

Arnbruck
Verkehrsamt
8498 Arnbruck
☎ (09945) 414

Bayerisch Eisenstein
Verkehrsamt
Schulbergstrasse
8371 Bayerisch Eisenstein
☎ (09925) 327

Bernried
Verkehrsamt
8351 Bernried
☎ (0995) 217

Bischofsmais
Verkehrsamt
Rathaus
8379 Bischofsmais
☎ (09920) 337

Bodenmais
Verkehrsamt
Bergknappenstrasse 10
8373 Bodenmais
☎ (09924) 7001

Bogen
Stadtverwaltung
8443 Bogen
☎ (09422) 1661

Breitenberg
Gemeindeverwaltung
8391 Breitenberg
☎ (08584) 412

Büchlberg
Verkehrsamt
Hauptstrasse 5
8391 Büchlberg
☎ (08505) 1222

Cham
Verkehrsamt
Rosenstrasse 1
8490 Cham
☎ (09971) 4933

Deggendorf
Verkehrsamt
Oberer Stadtplatz 34
8360 Deggendorf
☎ (0991) 380169

Eging am See
Verkehrsamt
Rathaus
8359 Eging am See
☎ (08544) 617

Falkenstein
Verkehrsamt
8411 Falkenstein
☎ (09462) 244

Frauenau
Verkehrsamt
Rathausplatz 34
8377 Frauenau
☎ (09926) 719

Freyung
Direktion für Tourismus
Rathaus
Langgasse 5
8393 Freyung
☎ (08851) 4455

Furth im Wald
Fremdenverkehrsamt
Lorenz Zierlstrasse 3
8492 Furth im Wald
☎ (09973) 3813

Grafenau
Verkehrsamt
Rathaus
Rathausgasse 1
8352 Grafenau
☎ (0855) 2085

Haibach
Fremdenverkehrsamt
8441 Haibach
☎ (09963) 1030

Haidmühle
Gemeindeverwaltung
8391 Haidmühle
☎ (08556) 2691

Hauzenberg
Verkehrsamt
Rathaus
Schulstrasse 2
8395 Hauzenberg
☎ (02691) 1586

Hofkirchen
Marktverwaltung
8359 Hofkirchen
☎ (08545) 213

Hutthurm
Marktgemeinde
8391 Hutthurm
☎ (08505) 833 and 834

Kellberg-Thyrnau
Verkehrsamt
St Blasius Strasse 10
8391 Kellberg-Thyrnau
☎ (08501) 320 and 282

Kirchdorf im Wald
Gemeinde
8371 Kirchdorf im Wald
☎ (09928) 355

Köllnburg
Verkehrsamt
8371 Köllnburg
☎ (09942) 8691

Kötzting
Verkehrsamt
Rathaus
Herrenstrasse 5
8493 Kötzting
☎ (09941) 8921

Lalling
Verkehrsamt
Lallinger Winkl
8351 Lalling
☎ (09904) 374

Lam
Verkehrsamt
Marktplatz 1
8496 Lam
☎ (09943) 1081

Lohberg
Verkehrsamt
Rathaus
Rathausweg 1
8491 Lohberg
☎ (09943) 760

Neu and Alt Schönau
Verkehrsamt
8351 Neu Schönau
☎ (08558) 610

Neukirchen vorm Wald
Verkehrsamt
Pfrundestrasse 1
8391 Neukirchen vorm Wald
☎ (08504) 1763

Obernzell
Verkehrsamt
Rathaus
8391 Obernzell
☎ (08591) 1877

Osterhofen
Verkehrsamt
8353 Osterhofen
☎ (09932) 1061-1064

Passau
Fremdenverkehrsverein
Neuburgerstrasse 7
8390 Passau
☎ (0851) 51408

Plattling
Stadtverwaltung
8350 Plattling
☎ (09931) 2042

Rattenberg
Verkehrsamt
8441 Rattenberg
☎ (09963) 703

Regen
Verkehrsamt

Haus des Gastes
Stadtplatz 2
8370 Regen
☎ (09921) 2929

Regensburg
Tourist Information
Altes Rathaus
8400 Regensburg
☎ (0941) 5072141

St Englmar
Verkehrsamt
Rathaus
8449 St Englmar
☎ (09965) 221

St Oswald-Riedlhütte
Verkehrsamt
8351 St Oswald
☎ St Oswald (08552) 750
or Riedlhütte (08553) 383

Salzweg
Fremdenverkehrsverein
Goldener Steig Salzweg
Passauer Strasse 18
8391 Salzweg
☎ (0851) 41372

Schönberg
Verkehrsamt
Rathaus
8351 Schönberg
☎ (08554) 821

Sonnen
Gemeindeamt
8391 Sonnen
☎ (08584) 808

Tittling
Verkehrsamt
Im Grafenschlossle
Marktplatz 10
8391 Tittling
☎ (08504) 2666

Viechtach
Verkehrsamt
Stadtplatz 1
8374 Viechtach
☎ (09942) 1661

Vilshofen
Fremdenverkehrsbüro
Stadtplatz 29
8358 Vilshofen
☎ (08541) 8022

Waldmünchen
Fremdenverkehrsamt
Marktplatz
8494 Waldmünchen
☎ (09972) 262

Windorf
Verkehrsamt
Marktplatz 24

8359 Windorf
☎ (08541) 8500

Wörth an der Donau
Verkehrsverein
8404 Wörth an der Donau
☎ (09482) 472

Zwiesel
Verkehrsamt
Stadtplatz 27
Rathaus
8372 Zwiesel
☎ (09922) 1308 or 2041

10 • Munich

The German Federal Republic is today a country without a true capital: Bonn is merely a provincial city where the diplomats meet. But there is, in the BRD, a capital city that truly deserves its name — Munich, the capital of Bavaria.

Bavaria enjoyed a long history as an independent state before it was reluctantly absorbed into the German Empire in 1871. Even today the blue and white flag of Bavaria is seen more often than the black, red and gold of the Federal Republic and there is much, somewhat sentimental, talk of Freistaat Bayern. The many fine buildings and gracious town plan of Munich bear witness to the enlightened and sometimes romantic rulers of the Wittelsbach family who guided the destiny of Bavaria for over 700 years up to 1918.

As a city, Munich can hardly be described as off the beaten track, though comparatively few English speaking tourists spend more than a couple of days there. Even those who do pass through seldom succeed in getting the feel of the city as a whole. In order to do so a walk through Munich will establish its basic shape.

After Venice and perhaps Dubrovnik, Munich must be just about the pleasantest city in the world to walk in. You can stroll for half an hour in the very centre of the city without seeing a motor car. Start at the Karlstor, one of the old gates in the city walls, and make your way down the pedestrian zone, lined with shops and passing the Michaelskirche, the Frauenkirche and the Jagd-und-Fischerei-Museum (Hunting Museum) to the Marienplatz, the centre of Munich. Here there is the old fifteenth-century Rathaus and the splendid Gothic-revival new Rathaus (1867) on which automata of knights and folk dancers give a daily performance at 11am. From here turn to the right past two churches, both worth visiting (the tower of the Peterskirche provides a good view of the city), to the Victualienmarkt, still a market for vegetables and every kind of food, whose stalls loaded with produce bring an air of the Bavarian countryside into the heart of the city. Statues of Karl Valentin and other figures of popular entertainment (whose museum can be visited

211

The pedestrian zone, Munich

later) are daily provided with posies of flowers by the stall holders.

Returning to the Marienplatz and, going on in the opposite direction, pass through the Alter Hof, the earliest (1255) ducal residence of the Wittelsbach rulers, to the Nationaltheater (Opera House) and the Residenz (the later Wittelsbach Palace), and then where the street widens out to the Feldherrnhalle, a loggia built by Ludwig I in 1844 in imitation of the Loggia dei Lanzi at Florence. Why not pause here, for so much of Bavaria's history has been played out before these stones.

For Ludwig, though the statues of generals in the loggia cannot compare with those at Florence, this Feldherrnhalle symbolised his dream of creating Munich as a Florence beyond the Alps, a capital of art and culture. Here, in the nineteenth century, Baedeker's Guide states that a military band played on 4 days a week at mid-day. Here, in 1914, a vast crowd assembled to hear the declaration of war against

Pavement cafés near the new town hall

Russia and France, and in a photograph of the crowd taken on that August day one can pick out the face of a lean and hungry young man with blazing eyes who has been recognised as a certain Adolf Hitler. Not far from here, in 1919, Kurt Eisner a professorial type of man though actually a journalist, and prime minister of the newly declared independent Socialist Republic of Bavaria, was gunned down in the street by a right wing student provoking, in reaction, the establishment of a soviet regime that was only ended by the arrival of troops from Berlin. It was near here that the Beer Hall Putsch of 1923 met its inglorious end when the Nazi column of would-be revolutionaries scattered in flight before a volley of rifle fire, leaving Hitler flat in the gutter and eighteen of his followers dead. After the Nazis achieved power in 1933, a shrine of remembrance to these fallen comrades was set up here, which every passer by was required to honour with a Hitler salute. The little passage behind the Feld-

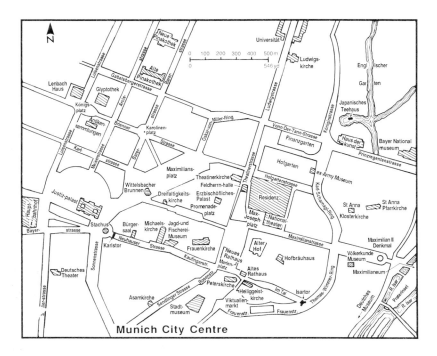

Munich City Centre

herrnhalle became curiously popular with those citizens who did not wish to pass in front of it and became known as 'Drückebergergasse' (Dodger's Passage). It was on the side of this monument that the little desperate band of students, known as the Weisse Rose, daubed their pathetically ineffective protests against the Nazi regime before they were identified and executed in 1943. In a final moment of history, it was here that Charles de Gaulle, whose meeting with Chancellor Adenauer in 1958 paved the way to the end of a long chapter of Franco-German bitterness, spoke to the people of Munich, not only of the end of French and German conflict but of the revival of French and Bavarian friendship.

There are no monuments to the Nazi period today in the city that saw its birth, and Germans in general are still reluctant to talk about it. But the foreign visitor who feels no such inhibitions can, if he or she wishes, visit a few places associated with that terrible chapter of history. When Hitler first arrived in Munich from Vienna he lodged for a time at 34 Schleissheimerstrasse in the north of the city. After the war he lived in two bare rooms at 41 Thierschstrasse, still a rather run-down area near the river. The beer hall which he used for many meetings and from which the 1923 Putsch set out was the Bürger-

Marienplatz and the old town hall

bräukeller in Rosenheimerstrasse on the other side of the river; it has now been demolished, but Hitler used several beer halls for his meetings; the 1920 meeting to launch the German Workers' Party, the fore-runner of the Nazi Party, was held in the Hofbräuhaus, which Hitler often painted as souvenirs for tourists and which is very much still there. After the Nazi Party became powerful he had a smart apartment at 16 Prinzregentplatz, and it was here that his niece, Geli Raubel, with whom he had apparently had an unsatisfactory relationship, committed suicide in 1931. The headquarters of the National Socialist Party were at the top of Maximiliansplatz, now named Platz der Opfer des Nationalsozialismus (Square of the Victims of National Socialism). If it can be faced, the concentration camp site at Dachau, reached by *S-Bahn*, has been preserved as a memorial to those who suffered and died there.

Resuming the walk through Munich, turn left at the Feldherrnhalle which leads to the Egyptian obelisk (not a genuine one from the Pharoahs) and on to the Königsplatz, an imposing square with a reproduction of the Propylaon on the Acropolis at Athens and with classical museums on either side. This was a culmination of Ludwig I's ideal of creating here an Athens of the north.

Alternatively, the branch right from the Feldherrnhalle leads into the Hofgarten. This is a pleasant place to sit on a fine day, with the Residenz on one side and low arcades with cafés on two others. On the fourth side is the bombed ruin of the former Army Museum, an impressive if heavy domed building, which has not been restored but has been safeguarded from further decay. After much debate about the future of the building a scheme was put forward in 1987 to extend it with wings in similar style on either side so as to serve as the administrative and government offices of the *Land* of Bavaria. This has set Munich in an uproar. Its proposers can logically claim that such a site deserves a building of equal importance, and that the necessary additions should be in matching architectural style. Its opponents claim that a huge stone classical structure would ruin the atmosphere of this pleasant garden, dwarf the old royal palace and the arcades, and merely serve as a monument to the vainglory of the late Franz Josef Strauss, Bavaria's highly conservative prime minister. The socialist city council has refused planning permission, but the battle is not over yet.

A few steps beyond the Hofgarten leads to the Englischer Garten. This was laid out by a British-American scientist, Sir Benjamin Thompson later Count von Rumford, at the end of the eighteenth century in the new 'natural' park-like style of landscaping. It is fairly narrow but immensely long and you can walk in it for miles. There is a lake, a Greek temple, a Chinese pagoda, and lots of restaurants and cafés, but mostly just grass and trees. The police sometimes raid the slope under the Monopteros (the temple) for pot smokers. If you bear off to the left you soon come out into Schwabing, the traditional students' quarter, but few students can afford the price of drinks and meals here now. There are, however, a clutch of fringe theatres and

The Englischer Garten, Munich, with the Frauenkirche (left) and the Theatinerkirche in the background

political cabarets and many pleasant restaurants and cafés.

Taking a different direction from the Viktualienmarkt (but this is no longer walking distance) you can come to the Theresienwiese, the great open space where the Oktoberfest is held. This is an enormous fair, with everything from performing fleas to a giant wheel. But as the way here is an extremely well-beaten track there is no need to linger here for long. Not many people, however, take the trouble to go up inside the huge bronze statue of Bavaria, the guardian of the land, depicted as a woman clad in a bearskin with a lion by her side, through whose hollow eyes you can look down on the city below.

Working round to the far side of the Isar, the river that runs through Munich, you may be lucky enough to catch the Auer Dult, an open-air market with stalls ranging from flea market goods to antiques and curiosities of all kinds with traditional fairground entertainments like a merry-go-round and a Kasperl theatre. It is held on the Mariahilfplatz three times a year, in April, July and October. Not far from here you can join the bank of the Isar and walk pleasantly on to the Maximilianeum, the present seat of the Bavarian parliament but designed by Maximilian II in the mid-nineteenth century for the higher education of civil servants.

Maximilian II (1848-64) was the worthy but rather boring king who came between Ludwig I and Ludwig II. Ludwig I (1825-48) loved beautiful buildings and beautiful women, but had to abdicate because of his too notorious love affair with an Irish dancer who had taken the glamorous name of Lola Montez. Ludwig II (1864-86) supported Wagner and built romantic castles in the Bavarian Alps, but was forced to abdicate because the politicians thought he was mad. He was greatly loved by the peasants, and his portrait hangs to this day in many humble inns, but Munich was slow to honour his memory. Finally, a modest statue was erected in the park on the bank of the Isar, a little beyond the Maximilianeum, with which the tour may conveniently end.

Now, having looked at the outside, you can visit the palaces, churches, museums and art galleries, of which Munich can boast so many. It is impossible to ignore the most famous of these but as they are described in every other guide book they can be mentioned here briefly. However here are some descriptions of places not quite so well known, which many visitors miss, but which are well worth seeing.

Munich is home to three palaces. The Residenz in the centre of the city is a rather confusing sequence of rooms and courts, so numerous that only half are open at any one time; two visits are needed to see them all. Nymphenburg, the summer palace on the outskirts of the city, is a baroque masterpiece; every guide will show you Ludwig I's Gallery of Beautiful Women painted by his court portrait painter, and the pavilions in the grounds, especially the Amalienburg, are dreams of elegant rococo fantasy.

Schloss Schleissheim is further out, a short walk from the Ober-schleissheim *S-Bahn* station, and few tourists find their way there. It was originally planned in the seventeenth century to house the court collection of paintings and serves today as an overflow picture gallery for paintings that are not quite important enough to find wall space at the Alte Pinakothek. It gains from the fact that many baroque paintings of the seventeenth and eighteenth centuries are here, displayed in the architectural setting for which they were designed. The palace, with its magnificent staircase, bears the strong imprint of its builder, Duke Maximilian Emanuel, the 'Blue Duke', before whose onslaught the Turks had fled from the gates of Vienna in 1683.

Among the churches the Frauenkirche (Church of Our Lady, 1468) is the cathedral of Munich and a Gothic brick building. Note the small domes on its two towers; these are the father and mother of all the onion-shaped domes that were to sprout on innumerable church

The Nymphenburg Palace, on the outskirts of Munich

towers all over Bavaria and — by a curious geographical transmutation — all over Russia too. Like so many buildings in Munich, this shows photographs of the terrible ruin to which it was reduced by bombing in the war, and English speaking visitors have to ask themselves whether this obliteration of historic city centres was really necessary in order to defeat Hitler. However, as everywhere, the restoration has been superbly carried out, and in this case at least the artistic loss seems not to have been too serious as the result today has an almost Protestant simplicity.

Michaelskirche (1583) is a key building in the development of Bavarian architecture, being the first important baroque church built north of the Alps. Its wide nave and high vault, inspired by the Gèsu in Rome, create an impression of space and lightness, typical of the Counter-Reformation. Bavaria remained Catholic during the Reformation and the subsequent religious upheavals.

Theatinerkirche (1663) illustrates baroque architecture in a more florid stage. While it provides a splendid architectural feature to Munich's sky line, and is undoubtedly impressive in its interior, it lacks the charm and delicacy and sense of fun to be found in the later smaller churches in the rococo style. These are to be found everywhere, but only two will be described.

St Michael, Berg am Laim (1738) is a 10 minute walk from *S-Bahn* Laim, and is a magnificent example of the full flower of rococo art. To the Anglo-Saxon mind, churches ought to be dark, preferably Gothic in style, and with a 'religious' atmosphere. If you want to appreciate the wonderful rococo churches of Bavaria you will have to come to terms with a quite different conception, in which churches represent the vision of paradise of a simple, devout people. To the Bavarian peasants of the eighteenth century, the courts of heaven were pictured as something like the courts of their earthly rulers, but even more magnificent. It is a mistake, however, to regard these churches as no more than ecclesiastical ball rooms. One should first spend some time in absorbing the atmosphere, and then study the details with the aid of a guidebook. They are full of theological and biblical symbols but every building is conditioned by its period in history, and these buildings cannot escape the temporal overlordship under which they were created. The prince's arms may be emblazoned in the arch of the vault, and notice here the flag of Bavaria waved by an angel flying over the pulpit!

A rococo church is almost always flooded with light streaming in from concealed windows upon walls of white and gold, with altars framed in marble stucco pillars. Saints sway in ecstasy, cherubs gambol in childish fun, while up above in the vault of the dome the Mother of God and the Divine Trinity hold out their hands in welcome. The artists who combined to create these masterpieces were architects, sculptors, fresco painters and, most important of all, stuccatori, or artists in stucco, for there is no real marble or stone, all is paint and illusion. It will greatly assist your appreciation of these buildings if you learn the names of some of these artists, for their work can be seen and recognised everywhere. Johann Michael Fischer was the architect at Berg am Laim; J.B. Zimmermann was the

Looking down Ludwigstrasse, Munich, towards the Feldherrnhalle and the Theatinerkirche (right)

stuccator (his stucco work in the Amalienburg at Nymphenburg has already been encountered), and J.B. Straub was the sculptor.

Two other very gifted artists were the Asam brothers. Egid Quirin was a sculptor and stuccator, and Cosmas Damian a fresco painter. They decided to build a private chapel adjoining one of their homes in Sendlingerstrasse, and as this is near the centre of Munich it is easily visited. Unlike most rococo churches, Asamkirche (1733) is rather dark, but it represents a brilliant attempt to create an atmosphere of architectural exuberance in an almost domestic setting. The church is very narrow, rising in three tiers to a superb symbolic group of statuary representing the Holy Trinity in the traditional form of the Gnadenstuhl (Mercy Seat), in which God the Father supports Jesus upon his Cross while the Holy Spirit, in the form of a dove, spreads its wings overhead.

The great rococo churches of Bavaria are mostly attached to monasteries and are outside Munich, but among the many small churches in the city that should be sought out by anyone with a feeling for this style of art is St Anna in Lehel in St Anna Strasse between the Prinzregentstrasse and Maximilianstrasse. This was designed by J.M. Fischer, with work by the Asam brothers and J.B. Straub. There is a very elegant small hotel almost opposite. Another at the end of Maria-Theresia-Strasse, is St Georg in Bogenhausen, an elegant residential district on the other side of the Isar, with sculptures by Straub and his pupil, Ignaz Günther. Günther was one of the finest sculptors of all, and his house is now a small museum opposite the Stadtmuseum.

Munich is richly provided with museums of every kind. The Schatzkammer in the Residenz has a superb collection of antique jewellery; the Deutsches Museum is a large and important museum of science and technology, and the only museum in Munich open on Mondays; the Völkerkunde Museum is a museum of ethnology and there are many more. Here are three others, not quite so well known.

The Bavaria Nationalmuseum in Prinzregentstrasse is mainly devoted to objects of Bavarian origin. There are superb sculptures, a fascinating collection of folk art, and a wonderful collection of Christmas cribs in the basement, the finest of which are Neapolitan. There is nothing like this anywhere else in the world.

The Munich Stadtmuseum in St Jakobs Platz is the city's own museum and comprises five distinct collections. One floor illustrates life in Munich by a series of domestic interiors of different periods; one tells the story of beer making, which is very much a Bavarian speciality; one is a museum of photography, with a cinema in the basement, one is a collection of musical instruments, and another is a museum of puppet theatre. This, too, is an art in which Munich has a strong tradition and is the finest collection of puppets anywhere in the world.

The Stuck Villa, in the Prinzregentstrasse but over the other side of the bridge, is a museum of Art Nouveau. Franz von Stuck, an artist of that movement, created the décor of the rooms in which the objects are displayed.

Beside these, if there is time or enough wet afternoons, a small but interesting collection of toys can be seen in a tower of the Altes Rathaus. Or, if your interests are quite different, the BMW Museum at Petuelring, opposite the Olympia Tower, tells the story of the motor car that is conquering all Europe and represents Bavaria's most successful industrial export. This is far more than a museum of one motor car: it demonstrates in effective visual displays the whole development of travel and machinery in the past and looks forward into the future. Similar is the Siemens Museum at Prannerstrasse, just off the Maximiliansplatz, which demonstrates technical achievements in electronics and computer science. The most unusual museum in Munich is the Karl Valentin Museum, housed in the old gateway at Isartor. Karl Valentin was a Bavarian comic actor who

The Olympia Tower

gained a great following in the early twentieth century and who is still remembered with affection. The museum is crammed with souvenirs of the popular entertainments in which he took part, and on the top floor there is a very amusing café in the style of the 1920s, where you can have tea or coffee. Finally, Munich can offer the first 'Nachttopf-Museum' in the world, that is to say a museum of chamber pots, in Böcklinstrasse near Schloss Nymphenburg. It contains

600 examples of this important domestic utensil from 2,000 years of civilisation.

While mentioning the Olympia Tower, one should not ignore the whole sport complex here which includes not only the tower, which you can ascend in a lift, but a great hall that is used for all sorts of purposes from the opera ball to the 7-day bicycle race, an ice stadium, and a fine football stadium that is the home of the famous FC Bayern München. Horse races take place at Daglfing and consist of *Trabrennen*, that is trotting races, which provide a more attractive visual spectacle than the momentary thundering down the track of conventional horse racing. This *Galopprennen* however, can be seen at the racecourse at Riem, near the airport.

Amongst art galleries the Alte Pinakothek is one of the great picture galleries of the world, with vast canvases by Rubens and works by many other Old Masters. The Neue Pinakothek, adjoining, contains paintings from the end of the eighteenth to the early twentieth century and provides a fascinating panorama of the development of artistic taste from Classicism through Romanticism to Impressionism. The Haus der Kunst, a building of the Nazi period intended to house pure Aryan Germanic art, now displays the kind of contemporary paintings that would make Goebbels turn in his grave. There are three other galleries that are not well visited but no less interesting to all students of art.

The Lenbach Haus, just beyond the Königsplatz, was the home of the fashionable nineteenth-century portrait painter, Franz von Lenbach. It now houses a selection of his canvases in a fascinating reconstruction of his studio, which illustrates the style of life a successful painter could achieve in those days. There is also a good collection of paintings by the Munich school of nineteenth-century landscape painters, which eloquently convey the atmosphere of the Bavarian Alps through the eyes of romantic artists and, most important, a very fine collection of paintings by the Munich Blue Rider School, led by Wassily Kandinsky in the early twentieth century, representing the earliest purely abstract school of painting. There is no collection to match this anywhere in the world. Like most of the Munich museums and galleries, the Lenbach Haus has a pleasant café and restaurant (the Deutsches Museum has the best restaurant of all).

The Schackgalerie, in Prinzregentstrasse, will interest you if you enjoy nineteenth-century landscapes and genre subjects. The love affair between German artists and Italy is well depicted here in many charming romantic canvases.

Aub town hall and baroque Virgin Mary pillar, in the Tauber Valley

Stuppach parish church, in the Tauber Valley

The Glyptothek, in Königsplatz, is probably the most interesting museum building in Munich and perhaps in Europe. It was built in 1816 by Ludwig I to house the collection of Greek statuary he was assembling. It is quite small, with overhead natural lighting that displays the fine sculptures admirably. Opposite, on the other side of the Königsplatz, the Antikensammlungen contain a complementary collection of Greek and Roman antiquities.

In addition to these permanent collections there are numerous private art galleries offering works for sale. In Maximilianstrasse alone there are over a dozen modern art galleries offering works by contemporary artists, some of whom are amongst the most important in the Federal Republic. There is also the 'Galerie in der Lothringerstrasse' near the Gasteig Concert Hall, which is run by the city of Munich and which offers exclusively works by living artists, mostly young and, needless to say, mostly avant-garde.

Munich is rich in entertainments of all kinds. The monthly listing, *Der Monat in München*, gives details of dozens of theatres, concerts and fringe offerings. The Nationaltheater is an opera house of international standard, built in 1811 in French Empire style (the French influence upon Bavarian high society was very important). Burnt down in 1823 it was rebuilt in the same style. Bombed to ruins in the war, it was again, after much debate, rebuilt exactly the same. It looks wonderful, but from some seats you can see only half the stage and from a few cheaper seats you cannot see the stage at all. Advance booking opens only 7 days before the performance and the available seats usually go on the first day, but don't despair. If you are staying in a smart hotel it will often have a small stock for its guests, (and provide a young lady to accompany you if you wish) and, if you are in more modest accommodation, you can often pick up returns at the Abendkasse 2 hours before the performance.

The Gärtnerplatz Theater stages light opera (up to Mozart and Rossini) and operetta, sung always in German. Prices are a little cheaper than at the Nationaltheater.

The Cuvilliés Theater (1751) is the court theatre of the Residenz and perhaps the most elegant little theatre in the world. It is named after its architect, a Walloon dwarf called François Cuvilliés, who also designed the Amalienburg at Nymphenburg. The theatre was destroyed in the war, but fortunately the plaster decorations had been removed to safety, and after the war they were re-erected, though on a different site. Performances and concerts are given here regularly, and it provides a perfect setting for a chamber concert or a Mozart opera.

If you can understand German there are two important theatres for dramatic works — the Kammerspiele (municipal) and the Residenztheater (state). The Kammerspiele has a high reputation for its more avant-garde productions and to become a member of the Kammerspiele company is regarded amongst many actors as the crowning of their careers.

The fringe theatre scene in Munich is extremely lively. There are actually about forty such theatres of varying standards, a good number of them subsidised by the city. Next to Berlin, perhaps, Munich is just about the liveliest theatrical place in Germany today. Among the fringe theatres a particularly interesting one is the Alabama-Halle, a rather bleak place in the northern part of the city off the Schleissheimerstrasse (but it can be reached by tram). This houses, as a rule, rather way-out theatre, dance and musical productions. Peter Brook has showed his productions there several times. This is funded by the city, with the help of a special foundation set up by BMW. The aim was to attract to the living theatre the type of young audience that would not naturally go to the opera houses or the conventional dramatic theatres.

Puppet theatres, as seen in the Stadtmuseum, have long been part of the Munich tradition. There are two professional theatres, staging regular performances. The older of these, in Blumenstrasse, was built in 1900 for Papa Schmid, a greatly esteemed puppet player whose first theatre had been opened in 1858 through the encouragement of Count Pocci, an official at the court of Ludwig II. Pocci wrote many plays for Schmid to perform, and they are charming examples of dramatic fantasy. The Blumenstrasse Theatre has been carried on since Schmid's death by a succession of master puppeteers. Performances for children are given in the afternoons, and operas for adult audiences on one evening a week. The visitor may have a chance to hear an opera by Carl Orff, the Bavarian composer, whose works are greatly appreciated here.

More recently a traditional puppeteer, who found that his family repertory of folk plays and fairytales was not permitted to be played in East Germany, has opened a theatre at the corner of Zeppelinerstrasse and Bereiteranger, near the Mariahilfplatz. It is named the Ludwig Krafft Theater in memory of the first curator of the Puppet Museum in the Stadtmuseum. The *Doktor Faust* performed here, a folk play that inspired Goethe, has a full-blooded quality that is highly recommended. In addition to these, there are two amateur puppet theatres in Munich, details of whose performances can be found in the *Monat*.

Bavarian folk theatre, or Bauerntheater as it is called, with song, dance and dramatic sketches, can be seen at Platzl opposite the Hofbräuhaus. This is a popular tourist attraction for Germans, not necessarily to be scorned for that reason, and there are similar programmes at the Bairisches Raritätentheater in the Rheinhof Bierkeller at Bayerstrasse near the Hauptbahnhof. Knowledge of the Bavarian dialect is required to understand what is being said here. The visitor may be lucky enough to hear some genuine un-touristified folk songs at the Volksängerbühne in the Max Emanuel Bräuerei in Adalbertstrasse, up towards Schwabing.

Munich has a permanent circus building at the Zirkus Krone Bau behind the Hauptbahnhof. Carl Krone was a menagerie owner who, in 1903, was inspired by the European tour of the Barnum and Bailey Circus to develop his own circus which is now the largest in Germany. But like all European circuses it is presented in only one ring. European circus connoisseurs do not care for three ring circuses. Krone's first circus building in Munich was destroyed in the war, but a splendid new one has been built, presenting excellent programmes between December and March every year. This is one of the few permanent circus buildings in western Europe. During the summer tenting circuses sometimes pitch in the Theresienwiese or on a car park opposite the Pinakothek.

Concerts are held somewhere every day of every week. Munich seems to be obsessed with music. The main concert hall is the Gasteig, a vast arts complex opened in 1985 just over the Isar and beyond the Deutsches Museum island, where the excellent Munich Philharmonic Orchestra plays. The Herkules Saal in the Residenz provides an imposing setting for some occasions. Numerous churches and castles provide settings for Christmas oratorios and summer cantatas, in which the swooping curves of rococo plasterwork seem to find their complementary expression in the music of Handel and Bach.

Before the theatre you will need to eat and the meat eaten most in Bavaria is pork, and Bavarians eat a great deal of it. Every part of the animal is consumed, or used, in one form or another. Roast pork is *Schweinebraten*; pork cooked with *Sauerkraut* is *Schweinefleisch* and roast shin of pork is *Schweinehaxe*. All these are eaten with dumplings, *Knödel*, rather than potatoes; *Semmelknödel* are dumplings made with milk, egg, onions and parsley. Then sausages, *Würste*, come in many forms, too numerous to list, but a Munich speciality is *Weisswurst*, which is white as its name implies and is made from a mixture of veal and bacon with parsley and pepper; it should be accompanied by a special sweet mustard and is supposed to be eaten before noon. *Leberkäs* contains neither liver nor cheese, as its name might suggest, but is an inexpensive kind of loaf made up from the pig's lights. Lamb is not eaten much, and beef is sometimes described as *Tellerfleisch* and served with horseradish. A *Schnitzel* without *Wiener* before it may be assumed to be egg and breadcrumbed pork rather than veal. Gasthaüse, or inns, often offer *Jägerschnitzel* and *Zigeunerschnitzel*, which imply heaps of mushrooms and other embellishments, but it should be realised that these dishes are often supplied ready cooked by a wholesale caterer and are merely heated up in the microwave oven.

Munich is a long way from the sea and fish is not, in general, a local speciality. Two exceptions, however, are river trout, *Forelle*, sometimes kept in a pool outside the restaurant, which is served either *Blau* cooked in water and vinegar, or *Mullerin Art* fried in butter and carp, *Karpfen*, which is traditionally eaten on Christmas Eve. As everywhere in Germany, bread is available in many different varieties and are all excellent; mouth-watering cakes are on offer in every *Konditorei*.

To drink with all this the traditional Bavarian beverage is beer, either light, *helles*, or dark, *dunkels*. A special type that is refreshing on a summer day is *Weissbier*, which is made from maize rather than hops. Special brews of increased strength are produced at different periods of the year: *Salvator* is made in March, *Maibock* in May, and another special brew is produced for the Oktoberfest. If these are too alcoholic you can drink *Radler*, which is a shandy of beer mixed with lemonade.

The great place to drink beer is in a *Bierkeller* (they are not really cellars any more) or a *Bierhaus*. The typical *Bierhaus* consists of a number of large halls, sometimes with a stage, which have been, and still are, hired for political meetings. The Bavarians like to take beer with their politics. In the summer the customers move out into the adjoining garden. At a proper *Biergarten* beer is only served in a tankard called a *Mass*, holding two pints, but in a Gasthaus you can ask for a small beer, *ein kleines*, without shame. To nibble with the drink pretzels and radishes artistically cut into spirals are often served. If there is a sign, *Stammtisch*, over a table it means that table is reserved for regular patrons and you should not sit there.

These *Biergartens* are wonderful institutions, with long tables at which the line of drinkers link arms and sway, singing to the music of the band, as the night grows old. All class and social barriers cease to exist. If you are a foreigner with an elementary knowledge of German you need not feel embarrassed at taking your place at a table

A typical Bavarian beer garden

as you will be warmly welcomed.

The most famous *Bierkeller* in Munich is the Hofbräuhaus, not far from the Marienplatz, but this is the first port of call for every visitor to Munich and most definitely not off the beaten track. Still one should go there once. Others that might be recommended are the Augustinerkeller in Arnulfstrasse, near the Zirkus Krone; the Chinesischer Turm, by the pagoda in the Englischer Garten; the Kaisergarten in Kaiserstrasse at Schwabing; and the Hofbräukeller (not to be confused with the Hofbräuhaus) in Inner Wiener Strasse, across the river. Two *Biergartens* which are a bit more out of the way but which have their loyal clientele are Hirschgarten, between the Laim and Donnersberger Brücke *S-Bahn* stations north of the railway line, and Der Flaucher, on the river south of the centre of Munich where the Isar rafts land. Special beer tents are set up during the Oktoberfest.

The Munich region does not produce any wine, but there are any number of wine houses in the city. A haunt which can be recom-

The Hofbräuhaus is the most famous Bierkeller *in Munich*

mended is the Weinstadl in Burgstrasse, just off the Marienplatz, a sixteenth-century *Weinstube* which offers a wide selection of wines from the Pfalz (the Palatinate), which used to be part of Bavaria. Another *Weinstube* specialising in wines from the Pfalz is the Pfälzer-Wein Probierstube adjoining the Residenz; also near the Marienplatz is the Weinhaus Neuner in Herzogspitalstrasse, and the Weinhaus Schwarzwälder in Hartmannstrasse, with specialities from the Black Forest and wines from Baden. At all these places wine comes in quarter-litre glasses, *Viertels*, but smart restaurants and cafés tend to serve glasses at the same price, holding only a fifth of a litre.

The year in Munich is punctuated by a succession of festivals, and although these are now somewhat commercialised they are still celebrated with enthusiasm by almost everybody. *Fasching* (carnival) lasts from January to the beginning of Lent, and is marked by masked balls and parties and by the crowning in the Marienplatz of a *Fasching* prince and princess. After Easter the beer gardens set out their tables under the chestnut trees and the strong beers are produced. Corpus Christi, known as das Fronleichnamsfest, on the Thursday after Trinity Sunday, is celebrated with religious outdoor processions. At the end of September (perversely) the great Oktoberfest is opened on the Theresienwiese, and even if one does not go on the fairground rides it is good to watch the decorated horse-drawn beer drays as they process through the streets. With the beginning of December the Christkindl Markt is set up in the Marienplatz, to be opened by St Nikolaus accompanied by a black-visaged devil making dashes into the crowd in search of his victims. On the evening of 6 December any number of St Nikolauses, in hired or borrowed robes, may be observed visiting the homes of Munich citizens, carrying little presents for the good children and a birch at their belts for the naughty ones (but no one has ever heard of this being used), to be greeted by a carefully prepared little song and concert in every home. Christmas itself, in the land where Christmas trees came from, concludes the year with feast and joy.

Munich has an excellent public transport system in which buses, trams, underground (*U-Bahn*) and suburban services (*S-Bahn*) are totally integrated. But, as the fares are collected without any human element being involved, it is a little bewildering for the foreign visitors. If a short stay is being made the simplest thing to do is to buy a 24-hour ticket from automatic machines at the main stations; but if the stay is for a longer period of time the correct procedure needs to be mastered and is as follows:

There are two kinds of tickets: red for short trips and blue for longer journeys. They are both available in strips, called *Streife*, and are obtained by putting the correct amount of money (no change given) into automatic machines at stations and the main bus and tram stops. When you start a journey look at the chart at the station or stop which indicates how many tickets, and of which kind, are needed for the desired destination. A short journey in the inner city usually needs two red tickets; a journey from the centre to an outer suburb may need three or four blue tickets. Fold the *Streife* so that the required number of tickets are turned over, and insert them into a stamping machine at the entrance to or on the platform, or on the bus or tram. This cancels the tickets, and for the next journey use some fresh ones. A change from train to tram or bus is allowed, and a journey can be broken for a short visit, provided you keep going in the right direction.

Inspectors occasionally check that passengers have got tickets and have cancelled them correctly. If you have not done so a fine can be issued on the spot. But inspectors appear fairly rarely and the system works because the people are honest.

S-Bahn lines radiate out from Munich in every direction and, especially in the south, to wonderful countryside of woods and lakes, to villages bright with wall-paintings and blooming window boxes, and to the onion-shaped spires of rococo churches. Here are suggestions for just a few excursions to places that can all be reached in under an hour from Marienplatz.

Take the *S-Bahn* 1 to **Freising**. This is the home of the original cathedral see of Munich. The Romanesque cathedral, standing on a hill above the town (which has some pleasant features), was baroquized by the Asam brothers with stucco and fresco work.

The *S-Bahn* 4 leads to **Fürstenfeldbruck** and one of the largest and grandest of Bavarian baroque churches, constructed between 1701-66 and illustrating the development of church architecture from something similar to the Italianate Michaelskirche to the rococo decorations of the Asam brothers. The impressive interior is decorated in gold, orange and brownish scagliola (an artificial marble with a plaster of paris base). Note the high altar with twisted Bernini columns, inspired by St Peter's in Rome, and the clock above the chancel arch; this was not just for the congregation to be able to tell the time, but as a symbol of mortality! There are good level walks along the Amper valley and through woods; the distance can be reduced by returning from Schongeising station.

The *S-Bahn* 5 leads to **Herrsching** on the Ammersee. A short walk through the woods leads to the Andechs Monastery, a Gothic church with rococo reclothing by Straub and Zimmermann. Carl Orff is buried here. This is still very much a place of pilgrimage, with its own brewery. Alternatively the boat can be taken across the lake to Diessen (1732), a wonderful church designed by J.M. Fischer. The original onion dome was damaged by lightning in the nineteenth century and replaced with an inferior substitute; in 1986 this was removed and a replacement of the original shape and size restored. This is just one example of the care and taste devoted by the authorities to these Bavarian churches. The interior illustrates the close relationship between church and theatre architecture at the time, with boxes on either side of the organ, the side altars like wings leading the eye up to the high altar, which is fitted with panels that can be changed, like scenery, according to the liturgical season. It is no surprise to learn that the artist responsible for this superb altar was François Cuvilliés, the designer of the Residenztheatre. There are good walks on hills and through woods, or by the lakeside through a nature reserve. Return may be made by railway to the Hauptbahnhof.

The *S-Bahn* 6 to **Gauting**, leads to forest walks in every direction. The Wittelsbach family live at Leutstetten, and from Mühlthal you

A roofscape view of Munich with the Alps in the distance

can walk through the fields where they breed horses. The Mariakapelle on the hill in Gauting has six lovely examples of rococo carving; five of these saints have children in their arms. That surely illustrates something about Bavarian piety! A mill in the valley is supposed to be where Charlemagne was born.

Take the S-Bahn 7 to **Schäftlarn**, with another fine monastic church (1764) in a beautiful situation. The delicate stucco and frescoes are by Zimmermann, the altars and pulpit by Straub. Observe especially the sounding board above the pulpit with Mother Church pronouncing excommunication against a heretic in a highly dramatic manner. **Schäftlarn** lies on the upper waters of the Isar, and there are fine walks in either direction up and down the valley.

You can take it for granted that at all these places there are Gasthaüse with excellent food and drink. The only snag is that all inns in Germany are obliged to have one *Ruhetag* in the week, when they are closed. If you make an expedition in mid-week there is just the chance that you may arrive with tongue hanging out to find the Gasthaus closed. The visitor will be unlucky however if there is not another one open, as Gasthaüse in the same area stagger their closing days. A 'proper' Bavarian greets everyone with *Grüss' Gott*, and on leaving *auf Wiedersehen* for 'goodbye'.

Further Information
— Munich —

Museums and Places of Interest

Alte Pinakothek
Barer Strasse
Open: 9am-4.30pm, also 7-9pm Tuesdays and Thursdays. Closed Mondays and certain holidays.

Bayerisches Nationalmuseum
Prinzregentstrasse
Open: 9.30am-4.30pm.
Closed Mondays.

Cuvilliés Theater
Residenz
Open: weekdays 2-5pm, Saturdays 10am-5pm. Closed Mondays.

Deutsches Museum
Museuminsel
Open: daily 9am-5pm.

Glypothek and Antikensammlungen
Königsplatz
Open: 10am-4.30pm, 12noon-8.30pm Thursdays. Closed Mondays.

Haus der Kunst
Prinzregentstrasse
Open: daily 9am-4.30pm.

Karl-Valentin Museum
Isartor
Open: daily 11am-5.30pm.

Lenbachgalerie
Luisenstrasse
Open: 10am-6pm. Closed Mondays.

Münchner Stadtmuseum
St Jakobs Platz
Open: 9am-4.30pm. Closed Mondays.

Neue Pinakothek
Barer Strasse
Open: 9am-4.30pm, also 7-9pm Tuesdays. Closed Mondays and certain holidays.

Neues Rathaus
Marienplatz
Automata display at 11am daily.
Carillon chimes 11am and 9pm, also 5pm in summer. Elevator 8am-3.45pm except Saturdays, Sundays and holidays.

Residenz
Max-Joseph-Platz
Open: 9am-5pm.
Closed Mondays.

Schackgalerie
Prinzregentstrasse
Open: daily 9am-4.30pm.

Schlosschleissheim
(*S-Bahn* Oberschleissheim)
Open: April to October 10am-12.30pm and 1.30-5pm. Closed November to March.

Schloss Nymphenburg
(Trams 3, 21, 30)
Open: 9am-12.30pm and 1.30-5pm.
Closed Mondays.

Stuck Jugendstil Museum
Prinzregentstrasse
Open: 10am-5pm.
Closed Mondays.

Völkerkunde Museum
Maximilianstrasse
Open: 10am-4pm.
Closed Mondays.

Tourist Offices

Verkehrsamt
Bahnofplatz 2
8 München 2
☎ 089 2391 256 259

Fremdenverkehrsverband
Sonnenstrasse 10
8000 München 2
☎ (089) 597347

11 • The Bavarian Alps (Oberbayern)

T he state of Bavaria is the largest in West Germany and therefore
divided into various regions. The Bavarian Alps are found in the
extreme south of Upper Bavaria (Oberbayern) and form a natural
boundary with Austria. It is an area of striking contrasts, where the
lakes and flat plains in the north give way to the mountainous region
in the south and where the Deutsche Alpenstrasse runs from Lindau
in the west to Berchtesgaden in the east. Although the peaks here are
more dramatic than those found in the Bayerischer Wald, they are
still somewhat lower than the French and Swiss Alps.

This is the land of alpine villages whose balconied chalets are
garlanded in summer with a colourful floral profusion. Music is
never far away for every town, village or hamlet boasts a brass band.
Zither music in the inns helps foaming tankards to be downed to
slake thirsty throats and outside the air rings to the melody of cow
bells as cream coloured cattle graze in the lush village meadows or
high alpine *Almen*. Churches, usually rococo or baroque in style,
have interiors beautified by ornate carving and delicately hued
frescoes. From the late seventeenth to the mid-eighteenth century
Bavaria was fortunate to have the Asam family living in their territory. It is in no small way that the ecclesiastical art treasures found
here is due to them. Hans Georg Asam was born in 1649 and started
the family tradition but it was his two sons, Cosmas Damian born in
1686 at Benediktbeuern and Egid Quirin born in 1692 at Tegernsee,
that became so famous. The two sons did much of their work together and so became known as the Asam brothers.

In winter, when the snow comes, many of the mountain villages
turn into winter wonderlands and the inhabitants put away their
agricultural implements and become ski instructors, while the
sports shops change their summer wares to those more suited to
skiing. For those interested in trying a winter sports holiday off the
beaten track, an application to any of the local tourist offices will
bring information regarding facilities in their area.

The region is well served with means of transport. The main

airport is at Munich Riem which is capable of taking the biggest transatlantic jet aircraft. Hire of cars from firms like Avis and Hertz is a mere formality at the airport or the main railway station (*Hauptbahnhof*). Fast inter-city trains from all parts of Germany will convey the traveller by day or night services in comfort. Travellers coming from those channel ports which do not have a through service change at Cologne, but there are seat reservations for the entire journey; thanks to the computerised system the required carriage in the next train is opposite the one just vacated. The budget conscious traveller can make the journey by coach and be whisked at high but comfortable speeds along what must be one of the finest motorway systems outside of America.

The private motorist is well taken care of with good and frequent filling stations, restaurants (waiter and self-service) as well as parking bays with toilet facilities on all the motorways. A free motorway service booklet can be obtained from the German Tourist Office in London or at filling stations on the *Autobahn*; it provides valuable help in calculating distance and services available on route. Most towns and villages have their own local tourist office that helps visitors to find accommodation as well as giving out local information on transport and places of interest; some are incorporated with the House of the Guest.

The climate during the summer months ranges from warm to very hot but in the more mountainous regions thunderstorms can break out quite quickly especially during July and August. Walkers are therefore well advised to have a small rucksack into which protective clothing as well as insect repellent can be carried. Snakes are rarely a hazard.

Accommodation varies from farmhouses to first class hotels but all offer well kept rooms. A simple room will contain a bed, chairs, wardrobe, bedside table with reading light and a washbasin with hot and cold running water. At the other end of the scale the rooms have balconies, bathrooms or shower and a WC, some may have televisions and refrigerators for drinks but naturally these are mostly found in the bigger establishments.

Self-catering standards, whether in apartments or whole houses, are first class with fully fitted kitchens containing ovens and refrigerators; some even have washing machines and dryers. Bed linen is usually supplied but sometimes towels have to be taken (always check at the time of booking just what will be on offer). The cost of heating may or may not be included in the price and the final cleaning charge is usually extra.

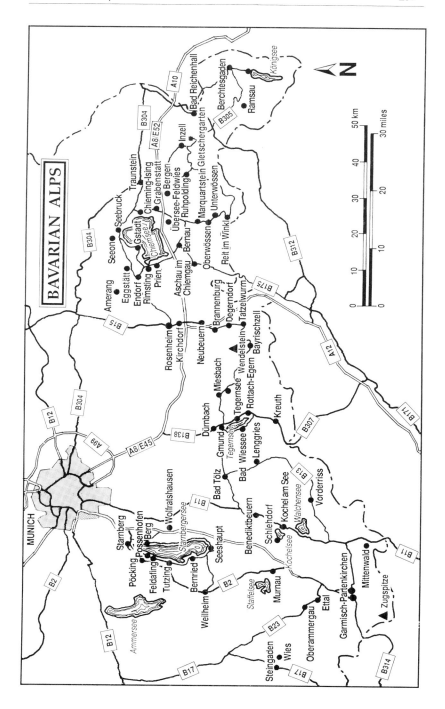

BAVARIAN ALPS

Meals, whether in hotels or restaurants, are of excellent quality and quantity, not highly seasoned and therefore usually very acceptable to the majority of palates. *Konditorei* (confectioners) have mouth watering displays of luscious cakes attracting either personal shoppers or those wishing to sit down and avail themselves of coffee as well. Regrettably though this does prove rather an expensive pleasure.

The cost of accommodation varies enormously depending on the number of people, length of stay and the type of accommodation chosen.

Bavaria is where comfort, leisure, kindness and geniality are combined and known as *Gemütlichkeit*. Although it is a holiday area popular with the Germans this region is well worth exploring. Even the better-known places, especially those associated with King Ludwig, will reward the visitor, despite being busy during the peak periods. Try to avoid the German school holiday times to avoid the crowds, advice which applies to much of Continental Europe, not just Bavaria.

The Deutsche Alpenstrasse

Back in the 1930s an alpine road was constructed to enable visitors to enjoy the splendours and hospitality to be found in this rural corner of Germany. The route to be covered commences at Steingaden, south-west of Munich where Oberbayern and the Allgäu meet, and ends where the Alpenstrasse finishes at Berchtesgaden.

Steingaden is an unpretentious village with a lovely old Romanesque church of St John; built in the twelfth century it has twin towers with saddle roofs which are unusual in this part of the world. During the Peasants Rising of 1525, some 15,000 peasants attacked the church and set fire to some of the outer buildings; the damaged areas were subsequently rebuilt but again suffered in 1646 at the hands of the Swedish army during the Thirty Years War. This is very much a rural community and the inhabitants are mainly farmers or employees of the factories which turn the milk from the famous Allgäu cattle into cheese.

Coupled with Steingaden is **Wies** whose fame lies in its church which was built between 1746-56 on the orders of the abbot of Steingaden. This glorious rococo church is set in alpine meadows, shielded by dark pine forests and was the work of two famous brothers, Dominikus and Johann Baptist Zimmermann. Viewed from the outside this yellow and white church gives no indication of

The famous rococo church at Wies

the wealth or beauty that lies within. The interior walls are painted white as is the stucco work, but this merely serves to enhance the rich glowing colours of the painted ceiling which represents the Day of Judgement. The side altars form a marked contrast with a rich red marble (in truth it is merely layers of red stucco, polished to a high degree) and the main altar has been treated in the same way. In the central alcove pay particular attention to the rough wooden statue of Christ, for it is this statue that attracts pilgrims from all corners of the world; a legend decrees that real tears were seen running down its cheeks. At the moment the interior is undergoing examination for roof damage and scaffolding has had to be erected to enable workmen to examine the roof in great detail. During the past 2 years plaster has been falling down and it is feared that aircraft vibration may be the cause. It is hoped that the church will be restored to its full

The Echelsbacher Bridge

beauty as soon as possible.

On the way to Oberammergau the road crosses a 250ft (76m) gorge, spanned now by the Echelsbacher Bridge built in 1929. Prior to that, motorists had to cross the river Ammer by raft pulled by oxen. There is a commemorative monument on the left bank.

The road runs south through the Ammergebirge to reach **Oberammergau,** home of the famous passion play which is performed every 10 years; the next performance is in 1990 but in the intervening years this village is well worth a visit. Situated at the foot of the Kofel it is a good centre from which to explore the surrounding areas which include the Zugspitze and the Karwendel mountains.

The village itself, although not strictly off the beaten track, when not overcrowded with tourists coming for the play, is delightful. The houses are gaily painted and two great favourites are those painted with scenes from *Red Riding Hood* and *Hansel and Gretel*. The parish church was built in the early part of the eighteenth century and the interior has some first class frescoes.

Oberammergau is famous for its woodcarving and houses an international school to instruct pupils in this most delicate of crafts. There is an arts and crafts museum in the Dorfstrasse exhibiting all manner of local craft work. One of the finest pieces is that of a crib made almost 200 years ago.

With the mountains rising all around this is definitely walking

The painted façade of the Hansel and Gretel Haus, Oberammergau

territory — either on the well defined paths or real mountaineering if preferred — for which guides are available. Each year, on 24 August, there is an organised walk (*Gebirgswandertag*) in King Ludwig's footsteps. As dusk falls bonfires are lit and the mountain peaks catch the reflected glow turning a rich rosy red.

A few kilometres further on is **Ettal** in the Ammergauer range; a mere hamlet but dominated by a magnificent Benedictine monastery. It was founded in 1330 by the Emperor Ludwig after a traumatic journey from Rome where he had been crowned by the Pope. His homeward route had taken him to the northern Italian cities where he had tried unsuccessfully to obtain taxes from the wealthy merchants. A battle ensued and Ludwig was soundly defeated and had to flee for his life. Weary and dejected he knelt and prayed for help, whereupon a monk appeared and offered him money and a statue of the Virgin Mary. In recompense the monk required him to found a monastery in his homeland of Bavaria. To this Ludwig agreed and when his horse eventually collapsed in a lonely valley he took it as a sign that this was where the monastery should be built.

The façade is decorated with figures representing the twelve apostles and its magnificent green dome is about 200ft (70m) high. The eighteenth-century interior is a combination of baroque and rococo and is comparatively modern. The paintings adorning the dome are the work of Jakob Zeiller. The cloisters that surround the church are now a school and the pupils are taught by the monks when they are not distilling a potent liqueur made from twenty-six different alpine herbs and known as Ettal Klosterlikor. With the steady stream of visitors that the church attracts there is a ready market for this beverage. Across the road from the monastery is a general shop, a couple of inns and one or two houses.

After leaving Ettal the road claws its way upwards by a series of hairpin bends before descending to the Loisach valley and **Garmisch-Partenkirchen**, the famous expensive winter sports resort, a leisure centre for the American forces in Europe and also a base for some of the highest walking and hiking expeditions in Germany. It is possible to take advantage of the delights that Garmisch-Partenkirchen has to offer outside the main centre for a fraction of the cost and enjoy some of the superb natural facilities as well.

Grainau is a small village only 4 miles (6km) away and close to the Eibsee, a small delightful lake at the foot of the Zugspitze. For those who like gorges the walk to Partnachklamm, 2 miles (3km) from Garmisch, should not be missed. The river Partnach forces its way through a wild gorge while a path runs alongside the turbulent water which can at times dampen one with a fine spray; sometimes the path is cut out through the rock face and in other places becomes a platform built out over the river. The Riessersee, even closer to town, is another small lake with views across to the Waxenstein and behind that the towering Zugspitze itself.

A more strenuous walk is to the Höllentalklamm just below the Waxenstein where a path lies along a rocky gorge. The Zugspitze is the highest mountain in Germany and the summit can be reached by more than one route. There is a rack and pinion railway via the Riessersee, Grainau, Eibsee and Riffelriss and then by a tunnel to the Schneefernhaus from where a cable car makes the final ascent to the summit and viewing platform. On clear days the views are fantastic as one gazes across range after range of mountains into Austria, Italy and Switzerland.

The second route is by cable car from the Eibsee and is a must for those who enjoy an unfolding panorama. The third route is by cable car from the Austrian side of the mountain followed by a walk through the mountain with windows cut out of the rock face to enable visitors to look out onto the Schneeferner — a natural bowl that is used for skiing most of the year. Having passed through to the German side one can take the cable car to the summit.

A small detour from the Alpenstrasse which is well worthwhile is to **Mittenwald**, the last town in Germany before crossing the

The Riessersee with the Zugspitze in the distance

border into Austria. This medieval town might well have stepped straight out of *Grimms Fairy Tales*, set in the vividly green valley of the river Isar and protected by the towering massif of the Karwendel Gebirge to the east and the Wetterstein massif to the south. Added to this are five charming lakes around the town; the Schmalensee, Luttensee, Wildensee, Lautersee and Ferchensee which attract visitors who are happy to picnic on the shores and partake in the aquatic delights offered by these sheltered lakes.

The town has some beautiful old houses decorated with colourful frescoes which are mainly to be found in the Unter and Obermarkt. Here also is the church of St Peter and St Paul built in the mid-eighteenth century. In front of the church is a statue of a man seated on a stool carving a violin; this is Mittenwald's most famous son — Matthias Klotz (1653-1743).

Matthias Klotz was sent as a young boy to Cremona in Italy to

learn the art of violin making under a master craftsman Nicolo
Amati, where they also worked with Stradivarius (a native of Cremona). After 20 years of absence, gaining experience in various
locations, Klotz returned to his native Mittenwald. At the rear of the
altar in St Nikolaus Church in Mittenwald he carved the following
inscription 'MK 1684 violin maker for twenty years'.

Klotz found all the wood suitable for violin making in and around
Mittenwald and soon became successful in selling his instruments,
especially to monasteries and princely residences. He recruited tal-
ented members of his own family and then, to expand his trade,
extended this to other families. To start with they sold the violins
themselves which meant travelling a good deal, but eventually they
sold their instruments to merchants enabling the craftsmen to spend
more time on the manufacturing.

In 1858 a state violin-making school was founded at Mittenwald;
today the school is in the Partenkirchenerstrasse and has an annual
competition for the twelve places available. Applications are received from throughout the world and out of the hundreds only forty
are short listed and then the final twelve lucky ones are chosen.

The pattern of training has changed very little since the Middle
Ages. The successful applicant becomes an apprentice for $3^1/_2$ years.
The second stage as a journeyman lasts a further 3 years under a
master craftsman before the final examination is taken to become a
master. The time to make a violin is about 160 hours so it is not
surprising that these instruments are expensive to buy.

There are abundant facilities in the district but above all this is an
area for the walking enthusiast with routes ranging from a 10 minute
stroll to an all day 8 hour hike. The local tourist office will willingly
give further information on the choices available and on the special
guided tours.

This next section leaves the Alpenstrasse to take in some of the
lakes that lie in the Voralpenland. From Garmisch-Partenkirchen
one follows the road that runs along the Loisach valley until one
reaches the busy market town of **Murnau** which was on the old
medieval trade route between Germany and Italy. There is the fine
old parish church of St Nikolaus as well as the charming Mariahilfe-
kirche here and was the home of Wassily Kandinsky, a painter of the
early abstract Blue Rider School. Murnau is also noted for its water
sports facilities on the Staffelsee and Riegsee. The Staffelsee is the
larger lake and has sharply indented shores forming reed-fringed
bays. The lake itself is dotted with small wooded islets and sailors
make full use of these obstacles in races. There are two excellent

Alpine meadows near Mittenwald

bathing beaches close to Murnau and accommodation in the district to suit all tastes and prices, including a large camping site.

Weilheim is a small but busy market town between Murnau and the Starnbergersee, dating from Roman times. During the Middle Ages the town was encircled by a city wall built, so it is said, by prisoners from the local jail. Much of the old fortification has disappeared but it is possible to see some remaining parts which give an indication of the size of the town during that period.

Weilheim, in the Middle Ages, was used to store that most precious of commodities, salt. Another interesting historical fact is that the small village of **Polling**, now a suburb of Weilheim, was the major community back in the eighth century, as it housed a Benedictine abbey while the abbot ruled over the surrounding countryside. It is well worth stopping to see the abbey church and the ancient houses that still remain in its shadows. From Weilheim the road goes on to Starnberg, the main resort on the Starnbergersee, but before reaching it there is one place of particular interest and that is **Pöcking**.

It is a small unpretentious town and the home of the now famous chain of Post Hotels found throughout German speaking countries. In the days when everything had to travel by road, including the mail, coaches pulled by teams of horses and carrying a few passengers as well, needed a few stopping places where horses could be

Weilheim

changed and passengers provided with a meal and overnight accommodation. Local inns were used and eventually the regular ones became known as Post Hotels; the first of them is at Pöcking.

The Starnbergersee covers an area of approximately 22sq miles (8sq km) and is a mere 18 miles (29km) from Munich, the capital of Bavaria. It is naturally a great attraction to the city dwellers who, during the summer months, come by car or train for a day on or near the lake. The wealthy have villas in the small resorts that lie around its shores. From Starnberg there is an *Autobahn* link into the city centre as well as a fast electric train service as far as Tutzing on the western shore. The lake itself is plied by large ships very similar to those used on the Rhine for daytime cruises. Why not take a complete tour of the lake or use it as a ferry to one of the lakeside resorts?

During the sixteenth and seventeenth centuries the Starnbergersee was the venue for many great water carnivals while the guests watched from luxurious gondolas. Even now there are wooden gondolas that take passengers on short excursions.

The resort of **Starnberg** lies at the northern end of the lake and is overlooked by a sixteenth-century castle, once the home of the prince bishops but now alas a mere tax office. In the centre of the town the tall blue and white maypole, like those found in most communities in Bavaria, is decorated with figures representing the various trades carried out in and around the town. Perched on the top is a starling which is the town symbol; Starnberg means Starling Hill.

The parish church of St Josef dates from 1765 and is built in the rococo style. The main altar is flanked by white marble figures and gives a pleasant lightness to the interior. In the Possenhoferstrasse is a local history museum showing the various activities in this area down through the ages. As befits the largest resort there is a fine yacht harbour and during the summer months regattas take place most weekends and holidays.

The eastern shores of the lake are less populated than the western side but **Berg**, a short distance from Starnberg, is where Ludwig II, famed for his fantastic castles of Neuschwanstein, Linderhof and Herrenchiemsee, met his untimely end. After being declared insane and deposed from the throne, Ludwig was sent to Schloss Berg under the supervision of a doctor. Two days later he and the doctor took a small rowing boat out onto the lake. When they failed to return a search party was sent out and found the boat overturned in shallow water and the bodies of the two men who had drowned. The actual spot is marked by an iron cross rising from the lake and on the shore is the tiny Votivkapelle. Each year, on the 13 June, a service is held here in memory of this tragic king who nevertheless left behind a rich heritage that succeeding generations flock to see.

Berg is essentially for those wishing to spend their days out on the lake and evening entertainment is sought either in Starnberg or Munich. Except for the small hamlets of Leoni (named after the Italian baritone Giuseppe Leoni), Aufkirchen and Ammerland, most of the shore is inhabited by wildlife.

This quieter shore has attracted some famous names who value the peace it affords and have made their homes here — Christian Morgenstern the poet and currently the well known German baritone Dietrich Fischer Dieskau.

On the western shore after leaving Starnberg is **Possenhofen** and the *Schloss* that looks out over the lake. This was the childhood home of the Empress Elisabeth (Sissi), wife of Franz Josef of Austria. Sissi and her sisters loved this castle and would ride through the woods and countryside; after this carefree existence it is little wonder that Sissi found the life at the Austrian court in Vienna stifling and rebelled against the restriction it imposed. The castle is not open to the public but a pleasant walk across the public park enables the inquisitive to see the exterior.

The neighbouring village of **Feldafing** is a busy little resort which offers splendid water sports facilities as well as one of the most delightfully laid out golf courses in Germany. Its view is of the lake

and, in the distance, the rising alps. Feldafing boasts only one large
hotel, the Golf Hotel Kaiserin Elisabeth, which is renowned for its old
world charm and hospitality as dispensed in the halcyon days when
the Empress Elisabeth returned to the scene of her childhood and
stayed in this hotel for several weeks during the summer. In the
course of her stay she would cross to the small offshore Rosen Insel
(Rose Island) to meet her cousin Ludwig II for whom she had a great
affection. Doubtless these two unhappy people exchanged confi-
dences and sought comfort in each other's company.

The hotel is the starting point for excursions in the old yellow and
black post coaches drawn by four horses, and is where courses are
held for driving four in hand.

The hill rising at the back of the town is the Kalvarienberg (Hill of
Calvary) with its Stations of the Cross, and is also a good vantage
point for surveying the surrounding countryside.

The town also boasts a well laid out park thanks to Maximilian II
(father of Ludwig II) who had intended to build a castle as well; in the
event he only managed the Roman villa, in the style found at *Pompeii*
on the Rosen Insel, before his early demise.

The Rosen Insel can only be reached by boat; at weekends one can
cross by a pole propelled gondola, but during the week visitors either
have to hire a boat or swim. On the island one can visit the villa or just
stroll along the paths that have been laid out amongst the thousands
of rose bushes; the perfume-scented air on a still warm afternoon is
wonderful. Richard Strauss, the composer, used to come here frequently, perhaps to gather inspiration for his next work.

Lothar Günther Buchheim, noted painter, author, photographer,
publisher and collector, lives in Feldafing. His work known as *The
Boat* was the story of a U-boat crew during World War II, and has
subsequently been televised and received with warm acclaim in this
country.

The next lakeside resort is **Tutzing** where the emphasis is again
on the water sports facilities with sailing and windsurfing predominating. Just outside the town at Deixlfurt is another golf course and
at weekends and holidays is extremely popular. While on the subject
of golf it is in theory possible for visitors to use local courses. However in practice it may prove more difficult because golf courses are
not as numerous here as in Britain or America and therefore those
that there are in Germany become well patronised. Prior contact with
a club or course is advisable to save disappointment. Golf is still
regarded in Germany as a sport for the few rather than the majority.
Tutzing also offers shooting as an alternative sport and in fact the

local club organises tournaments and welcomes entries from visitors.

Another local sport (perhaps craft might be a better explanation) is that of fish sticking. Instead of rod and line a long pole, sharpened to a fine point at one end, is used. This method does not yield a large catch but it does provide an insight into the lengths the fisherman in bygone days used to go to. Anglers employing the more conventional method are rewarded with pike, renke, rainbow trout, carp, eels and tench.

Every 5 years Tutzing holds an historical play which depicts a fisherman's wedding. As one might imagine it is a highly amusing affair with one of the funniest parts centring round the bridegroom and the party he holds the night before the wedding.

The castle, Schloss Tutzing, was originally built during the early part of the seventeenth century but was completely rebuilt at the beginning of the nineteenth century and now houses an evangelical college.

Bernried, with its lovely old timbered houses, is the last resort on the western shore and in 1983 was awarded a gold medal and title of *Schönstes Dorf* (Most Beautiful Village). Peace and tranquility prevail here and is an ideal place for anyone in need of relaxation. A former Augustinian monastery founded in the twelfth century is close to the lakeshore and after restoration is now used for educational purposes by the Benedictine Order.

Over 70 years ago an American, Wilhelmina Bush-Woods, came to Bernried and was so enchanted with the place that she built a castle, Schloss Hohenried, on the northern slopes overlooking the village. She also founded a trust which supports the nature reserve here. In 1950, with a view to ensuring the future environment and welfare of the local people, she made arrangements that on her death her Bernried estate (195 acres) was to be given to the community in perpetuity for all classes of people but with special reference to mothers and children, nature and animal lovers for their relaxation and enjoyment as well as to stimulate and inspire artists and students. In 1952 Wilhelmina Bush-Woods died in a Munich hospital at the age of 62 and is buried in the now private grounds of the Schloss Hohenried Clinic.

The final lakeside resort is situated at the southern end of the lake and is **Seeshaupt**, a mere hamlet where accommodation and pastimes are simple. Apart from the sailing and windsurfing school the only other sport is tennis. Visitors who come here are mainly ornithologists and are attracted by the numerous birds which find a haven for nesting within the tall reeds which grow in profusion.

Wolfratshausen is an old eleventh-century market town to the north of Seeshaupt in the valley of the Isar. The Munich to Garmisch-Partenkirchen *Autobahn* almost clips the western side of the town but does provide for quick and easy motoring. In the Marktstrasse there are some very fine old houses to be seen, dating back several hundred years. The ancestral home of the counts of Diessen-Andechs was built in the eleventh century to withstand marauders but not unfortunately, a thunderstorm that occurred in 1734. The parish church of St Andreas with its dominating 210ft (64m) high tower was built in 1484 but partially destroyed in 1619 by fire. The real gem here though is the early baroque church of 1286 in Nantwein which is dedicated to St Nantovinus, a pilgrim who after being falsely accused of treachery was burnt at the stake.

At the confluence of the Loisach and Isar rivers is the Pupplinger Au, now the largest nature reserve area in Europe. An added attraction for visitors are the raft trips that ply between Wolfratshausen and Munich. These large rafts, made of logs and propelled by a long oar, have wooden benches for the passengers to sit on. The 2 hour journey is a merry one as beer is dispensed straight from the barrel and there is often music to which the passengers are invited to join in and sing.

Leaving the Starnbergersee area, head south-east through the tiny village of Penzberg to **Benediktbeuern**. This village is at the foot of the Benediktenwand that rises to a height of 5,853ft (1,784m). The village offers simple accommodation, a few shops and is the home of a magnificent Benedictine abbey which was founded in 730. It is the oldest monastery in Upper Bavaria and the present building dates from the latter half of the seventeenth century. It is baroque in style with frescoes painted by Hans Georg Asam whose son Cosmas Damian was born here. Scenes from the life of Christ are depicted in rich glowing colours in the painted frescoes that adorn the ceiling and walls of the basilica and are the work of Hans Georg Asam. The pillars and arches are literally smothered in white plaster stucco and very reminiscent of Grinling Gibbons work in wood. Above the high altar is a clock, probably the only one in such a prominent position inside a church. According to the guide one of the abbots considered that sermons should not exceed 45 minutes and so had the clock installed to ensure that the preacher did not overrun the allotted time.

The separate chapel of St Anastasia is situated at the northern end of the abbey and was built in 1751. It is the work of Johann Michael

The monastery at Benediktbeuern

Fischer, who later went on to build Ottobeuren in the Allgäu in the same style, and now recognised as a masterpiece of baroque architecture. Concerts are held in the precincts of the abbey during the summer and guided tours are available daily, one in the morning and afternoon, to other parts of the abbey including the old refectory now used as a library; note the frescoed ceilings by J.B. Zimmer-

The rich baroque interior of Benediktbeuern

mann. The Alte Festsaal on the second floor is now used for concerts and is an extremely elegant room with six full length windows that light up the ornate ceiling with its glorious paintings of 1674 by Kaspar Feichtmayr. The Kurfurstensaal, again the work of J.B.

Zimmermann and his son Josef in 1731, is now used as a house chapel and has modern seats and kneeling rests. Hanging from the ceiling are four sparkling glass chandeliers.

Originally the occupants of this abbey were of the Benedictine Order but since 1930 it has been inhabited by the Salesian Order who have established a theological college here in the cloisters of the church. One point of interest is that the text used by Carl Orff in 1937 for his choral work, *Carmina Burana*, was written by a monk here in the twelfth century.

The Frauenhofer Museum in the Frauenhoferstrasse is the old workshop of the scientist Josef von Frauenhofer (1787-1826). It is hard to believe in this modern age that the almost crude apparatus here helped to improve the specialised field of optics.

The Alpenstrasse now runs on to the pretty lakeside resort of **Kochel am See** that nestles at the foot of the rising alps with painted houses adding to its charm; the Hotel Zur Post built in 1356 and the Alpenhotel Schmied von Kochel are two such buildings that prove this point.

One cannot fail to notice that the name of Schmied von Kochel is uppermost in this village; translated it means Smith of Kochel. The main square bears the name as well as the bronze statue of this mighty man, a giant in more ways than one, who in 1705 died fighting in Munich and became the hero of the Peasants Uprising. The parish church of St Michael is typical of the area with white walls and a steep black roof with an onion dome on the tower. Franz Marc, the famous painter, was killed in France in 1916 and now lies buried in the churchyard here.

Its situation on the shores of the lake makes Kochel a popular place for holidaymakers and town dwellers at weekends who are happy to take part in all sorts of aquatic sports which includes a splendid outdoor swimming pool. Wildlife abounds in the marshy territory at the northern end of the lake and especially at nesting times. This is also a good starting point for walking and hiking with a choice of taking the low or high routes. There is plenty of accommodation for visitors whether in hotels, private houses, farms or camping sites.

Schledorf is a farming community that is adjacent to Kochel but dominated by yet another Benedictine abbey. The first church to be built was in the fifth century by the Kochelsee, but in 742 the holy Tertulin persuaded Otto von Freising to found and endow a Benedictine abbey here in Schledorf; alas in 907 it was destroyed by the Hungarians. Rebuilt again in 1140 as an Augustinian monastery it was replaced in 1718 with another new building but this time with an inner courtyard and then greatly extended in 1812 to become the imposing edifice that stands today. From 1892-1904 it was a Dominican convent but changed hands to become a missionary monastery. The abbey church of St Tertulin, with its double staircase leading up to the main entrance, is incorporated in the main buildings; the views afforded from here over the Kochelsee to the Herzogstand are magnificent. The interior of the church is in marked contrast to that of Benediktbeuren with its plain classical features and simple geometrical patterned decoration; the work is that of J. Mayr and Johann Fischer in the late eighteenth century. The high altar with its massive painting of the *Shepherds Paying Homage* was the work of J. Zick in 1735.

At the southern end of the Kochelsee is the hydro electric power station which draws its supplies from the neighbouring and much larger Walchensee. From Kochel the road runs alongside the lake before climbing and twisting up through the woods to reach the vividly deep blue Walchensee ringed by dark green woods against the rising majesty of mountain ranges to the south, the Karwendelgebirge in the foreground and the Stubai Alps on the horizon. The Walchensee is not overpopulated, but one or two small hotels and camping sites can be found at Urfeld and Walchensee.

From the village of **Walchensee** there is a chair-lift taking visitors to the Herzogstand, the ascent affording visitors glorious panoramic views over the surrounding countryside. From the top of the chairlift a 30-40 minute walk along a well defined path leads to the summit itself. On clear days the mountain ranges that can be identified include the Karwendel, Stubai, Wetterstein, Zugspitze, Grossglockner and the Gross Venediger.

From Walchensee it is possible to follow the road to Wallgau and the Isarfall. Use the small side road to visit this cascade of water, which has been formed by diverting part of the river Isar before taking the toll road which follows the main stream of the Isar as it passes through the mountains to **Vorderriss**. Here, the visitor will find a cluster of chalets a *Gasthof* and the long Sylvenstein lake with its dam at one end constructed in 1959 to regulate the river and control any flood of water. The excess water is now used by an underground power station. At Vorderriss the small toll road continues alongside the river Rissbach before crossing the border into Austria and the tiny mountain retreat of Eng.

From Vorderriss the national road runs along the southern shore of the Sylvenstein before crossing back in mid-lake via the magnificent high stone bridge where once again the road divides. One branch continues to the end of the lake and the Walchental to the frontier, from where the Achen Pass leads to the Achensee and eventually to the Inn valley. The other branch is the B13 which continues to follow the Isar as it flows northwards to reach the small town of **Lenggries** in the area known as the Isar Winkel, lying between the Tegernsee and Walchensee.

The town itself is mainly situated on the eastern bank of the river and in the centre, with the 182ft (55m) high tower topped by a copper dome, stands the parish church of St Jakob built in 1772. First and foremost Lenggries caters for those interested in activity holidays for which it offers excellent facilities for sailing, windsurfing, canoeing, hang-gliding and tennis.

For the walker this is an area of natural unspoilt beauty and in early summer the surrounding countryside is a picture with a profusion of wild flowers which includes some protected species such as the ladys slipper orchid, the turks-cap lily, alpen roses and gentian.

Opposite the town on the west bank the cable car will whisk visitors up to the Brauneck from where even more splendid vistas burst forth. In winter this open sunny plateau becomes a skiers paradise with its connecting network of lifts producing runs of various gradings. In summer the ski runs become trails for hikers who find much enjoyment in the sharp mountain air. The highest point is the Benediktenwand and can be reached from Brauneck with about 4 hours good walking. There are mountain *Gasthöfe* up here, some providing full meals and overnight accommodation as well as mountain huts selling drinks only. For the wildlife enthusiast, watch out for the ibex that can, on occasions, be seen perched on their rocky vantage points.

Overlooking the town is the Schloss Hohenberg, originally an eleventh-century fortress belonging to the lords of Thann but destroyed in 1707 during the War of the Spanish Succession. It was rebuilt in 1712-18 as a stately home with a chapel added in 1722 with a fine rococo altar. In 1953 the castle became the property of the Ursulines and is now a boarding school.

From Lenggries the road and river continues down the valley to **Bad Tölz**, whose history goes back as far as the fifth century when the Romans formed a settlement on the river bank. Today the river Isar divides the old town from the new spa that has developed on the west bank. It is here in the modern town with its wide tree lined streets and well kept parks and gardens that clinics and hotels offering cures for various ailments are to be found, together with the

The town hall,
Bad Tölz

municipally run Cure Centre. Here, as in most parts of Bavaria, guests pay a *Kur Tax*. In return they receive a visitor's card enabling them to use certain local facilities such as swimming pools at reduced charges. It may be noted that the waters on offer here for drinking are iodine based and slightly more palatable than the sulphur ones!

The old town with its steeply sloping Marktstrasse is the main shopping area where the small shops and cafés have gaily painted façades lending a piquant charm of its own, while at the top end of the street is the beautiful Rathaus with its delicately painted façade. In the centre of the street, opposite the main entrance to the Rathaus, is a statue of a warrior holding aloft a lance which is in memory of Kasper Winzerer, a knight and leader of a local mercenary band 450 years ago.

Bad Tölz offers visitors many attractions one of which is a delightful Marionette Theatre with a seating capacity for 161 persons. There is a most comprehensive Heimat Museum which opened in 1981 in the Marktstrasse exhibiting local arts and crafts, a geological collec-

*The pulpit, Wies Church,
in the Bavarian Alps*

*The old chapel at Museumdorf, in the
Bayerischer Wald*

Maria Gern, Ramsau, in the Bavarian Alps

tion and items of special local interest. A wander through the old side streets lined with venerable aged houses topped by steeply gabled roofs, painted façades and gay window boxes is a step back into history; worthy of note are the Marienstift, Höflingerhaus, Sporerhaus and the former Rathaus. Now that the new bypass is open it is possible for pedestrians to wander and view these delights less dangerously than before.

The parish church of the Maria Himmelfahrt dates from 1262 and is well worth a visit. The ecclesiastical gem however has to be the church and tiny chapel on the Kalvarienberg. The Kalvarienbergkirche dates from 1718 while the chapel is slightly later at 1743 and dedicated to St Leonard, a pious hermit who spent his life in the welfare of prisoners and horses. The chain that can be seen girding the chapel is a reminder of his prison work. Each year on the 6 November there is the Leonhardt Ride when farm carts and wagons, drawn by horses and attired in elaborate harnesses, form a stately procession up the hill bordered by the Stations of the Cross to the church and chapel where a special service is held.

A remarkable feature for this town is the number of specialists and other medical practitioners. Apart from this aspect of what is after all a spa town, Bad Tölz is a delightful place to stay; the riverside walks, tennis, fishing and even golf all add to the enjoyment of visitors of whom many are young and active.

At the top of the hill that leads out of Bad Tölz is a large American barracks occupied by American soldiers and their families; the amount of spoken English that one encounters in the town is therefore hardly surprising.

One of Bavaria's most beautiful lakes is the Tegernsee, east of Bad Tölz, surrounded on three sides by mountains whose tree-lined shores afford shade during the summer but in the autumn turn to a burning gold and with the mountain tops already white with snow make this a veritable paradise. The main resorts on the lake are Bad Wiessee, Rottach-Egern, Tegernsee and Gmund. **Bad Wiessee** on the western shores is now known for its spa facilities discovered only this century. Here the iodiferous and sulphurous sodium chloride springs are to be found which the clinics, sanatoriums and hotels offer to their clients who come to find relief for heart and circulation problems as well as rheumatics. There is a splendid partly open-air concert pavilion close to the lakeshore where orchestras as well as brass bands entertain. Lakeside gardens enable the afternoon stroller to combine light activity with perhaps a game of outdoor chess. For this particular pastime the chess board is at ground level and meas-

A quiet game of outdoor chess, Bad Wiessee

ures 12ft by 12ft (4m by 4m). The chessmen although 2ft high are quite light to pick up and move around the board.

The lakeside café's in the afternoon are well patronised as visitors partake of coffee and cake while enjoying the activities that are taking place on the lake from sailing regattas to the disembarkation of passengers on the lake steamers, or just listening to the background music from the afternoon concert. There is a theatre for more formal concerts as well as plays. Bad Wiessee is not just for the elderly who come to relieve their aches and pains for the young are catered for as well, in the shape of sailing and windsurfing; for inclement weather there is a first class swimming pool. Other sports include tennis and a nine hole golf course of which the whole of the Tegernsee is justly proud.

A whole range of walks either along the lakeshore or up into the surrounding hillside makes this a most attractive resort. For those wishing to walk further afield one of the local buses will take you to the departure points or there are ample car parks at all the strategic places which usually have large maps showing the area and suggested routes and times that each one takes. Most of the walks that commence at Bad Wiessee take between 2-3 hours but for most people it is quite simple to undertake only a part of a route. For those interested in idyllic views the walk to Bauer in der Au (Farmer in the Meadow), is a must. The building is in fact an inn where one can sit outside to quench the thirst that the walk has invoked while gazing at the green clad slopes surrounding the meadow on three sides. Cattle are up here grazing on their summer pastures and as they move the bells that hang round their necks jangle, filling the air with a melodious tune. After leaving the inn the ground drops away steeply and the whole panorama of the lake and hills rising on all sides unfolds.

To the south, where the road commences its climb towards the Achen Pass, are the villages of Kreuth, Wildbad Kreuth (a tiny spa) and Glashütte. These three tiny villages are strung out along the final stretch of road before the border. The further one goes the wilder and more remote the territory becomes as the mountains close in. **Kreuth** is the largest of these resorts and, in fact to begin with, is almost an extension of Rottach-Egern. It does however have its own delightful small Rathaus and a Bürgermeister and looks after its own affairs while offering a quieter alternative to the bustling lakeside resorts with some first class accommodation as well as the simple variety. Kreuth is an ideal base for those who are predominantly interested in walking in the day and by evening are content to sit and discuss the following days route over a glass of beer or wine. There is however an indoor tennis hall and squash courts for those still with energy to spend and indeed it takes only a few minutes to reach the other lake resorts for further evening entertainment.

Perched high above the south-west corner of the lake is the Schloss Ringberg. It is open to the public as it is part of the Max Planck Institute, a renowned scientific research establishment whose head-quarters are in Munich.

Rottach-Egern standing at the southern end of the lake is perhaps the most elegant and sophisticated town to be found in this valley. The lakeside is bordered with first class hotels including the five star Hotel Bachmair with its own night club that attracts international cabaret artists. Leading off the lakeside are small quiet roads and it is here that the small privately run pensions are to be found. All offer excellent accommodation but instead of having a lake view there is an equally attractive panorama across meadows to the mountains. The offer here is usually on a bed and breakfast basis but in the town itself or just outside there are plenty of restaurants so that it presents no real problem. Indeed one of the most popular restaurants with both visitors and locals alike is out at Berg. A pleasant stroll along-side the tiny Rottach stream takes about 20 minutes or even along the

Lake promenade, Rottach-Egern

road past meadows and cattle. Until early evening there is even a local bus service. This rural inn, the Angermaier, offers accommodation as well as lunches and dinners while during the afternoon a splendid array of home made cakes are on offer together with coffee and other drinks. Apart from one other restaurant in this neighbourhood the gastronomic delights are to be found in or around the centre of Rottach-Egern. Self-catering is widely featured here and is reflected in the fact that the town can boast three large supermarkets as well as smaller shops. Apart from food the shops are geared to the fashion market and *hautcouture* is displayed in the windows of the boutiques; footwear, from climbing boots to the latest fashion shoes from Italy, are also tantalisingly exhibited.

The House of the Guest is situated in the Rathaus on the main street next door to the Post Office. Accommodation, information, reading and television rooms are all housed here under one roof. Across the street is the office for the local tour operator whose windows display various excursions on offer ranging from a half day to extended day-long trips to Venice or Vienna.

There is a fine outdoor pool adjacent to the lake with wide sun bathing lawns and a restaurant; for cooler days there is a solarium. The concert hall is also part of this complex and can be used for plays and exhibitions.

The bandstand set in an open garden offers concerts at least two evenings a week and again on Sunday mornings. This is also a popular spot for feeding the swans and ducks that inhabit the lake, and seems to encourage anglers during the evening. In fact, by standing on the landing stage for the lakeside steamers, one can look down into the clear water and see fish of various sizes swimming just beneath the surface.

The author Ludwig Thoma lived in Rottach-Egern and is buried in Der Alte Friedhof (Old Cemetery) and is also the opera singer Leo Slezak. The parish church of St Laurentius dates from the fifteenth century with a pleasing interior. The nave was originally late Gothic but in 1671 was altered into baroque style. Although there are no paintings by internationally famous artists the work that decorates this church is pleasing to the eye. The Miesbacher School evidently believed in being slightly more restrained than Hans Georg Asam who was working in the area during this period.

It is hard to believe that Rottach-Egern was originally two villages (Rottach and Egern) and were primarily a farming and fishing community. In 1320 a road was constructed over the Achen Pass which opened up a trade route from Bavaria into the Tyrol and ultimately Italy, thus bringing prosperity to the area which over the years has continued.

Apart from the boating, swimming, surfing and fishing there are some splendid tennis courts on which is held an annual tournament with first class prizes. In this walkers' paradise escorted day hikes are arranged by the local tourist office twice a week, usually on Tuesdays and Fridays, providing the weather is good. The routes vary in length but range from around 4-8 hours; details of each excursion will be found in the tourist office.

For those who prefer to combine walking with a modicum of transport a pleasant stroll either along the road or up through the woods to Sutten and the Moni Alm is ideal. At Sutten there is a long chair-lift up to the Stumpfling Alm and its *Gasthof*. From here one can either take a second lift down into the next valley and the Spitzingsee or take one of the many mountain paths that eventually lead home. Moni Alm is a peaceful sunny valley with rough meadowland gay with flowers and where the dark green forests give way to more rocky pinnacles; the slience is broken from time to time by the call of one of the birds at the Greifvogelpark Adlerhorst. The birds on view here range from the great condor, vultures and eagles down to small owls under the care of a naturalist. Here, at close range, one can view these birds of prey that inhabit this region. Each bird is contained by a long chain attached to a foot enabling them to move around their

A picturesque corner of Tegernsee

tree-lined enclosure at will. They are also taken out hunting in order that they may retain their natural way of life. Close by is a small lake whose placid waters are broken only by small families of ducks that swim out of the reeds when strangers appear in the hope of food.

At the rear of the town is the 5,599ft (1,707m) Wallberg mountain which can be ascended by a twisting mountain road where James Bond survived a desperate chase, or by the cable car. At the foot of the cable car is the Alpenwildpark which is a reserve for the wild animals (mostly deer) while close to the top of the lift is the Wallberg Hotel with its large terrace used in winter by skiers for an extended lunch break and a chance to relax in the sun. In summer its function is the same but the boots and skis are replaced by somewhat lighter attire. A short but steep track leads to the Wallberg summit with its tiny mountain chapel. There are network of walks up here but it is advisable to have a map of the area because some parts are for climbers who have had some training or practice under difficult conditions.

The resort of **Tegernsee** on the eastern shores of the lake is, apart from Gmund, the resort with the smallest population. However that is of no consequence in the major role it has played throughout the

Tegernsee

ages. Dominating the town is the Schloss Tegernsee as it is known today but in fact its origins go back to the eighth century when a Benedictine monastery was founded and became, in the succeeding years, an important cultural focal point as can be seen in the Heimatmuseum housed in the *Schloss* itself. The present building dates from the seventeenth century with the frescoes and stucco work by H.G. Asam. In 1803 it was secularised and became a royal residence for Maximilian Joseph I, so receiving the title *Schloss*.

The twin towers that grace the castle are reputed to be the oldest in Bavaria. The church contains three aisles although many of the side altars have disappeared. The side chapels are embossed with ornate rococo decorations while the Rekreationsaal's stucco work is by J.B. Zimmermann. Apart from the church and rooms used for the museum this magnificent building is now the home of the local brewery which also provides good food at reasonable prices to go with the beer in its own *Stüberl* (a room where one can both eat or drink).

The large wooden boat houses on the edge of town house the lake steamers that provide not only round cruises but also a ferry service to the other lakeside resorts from dawn till dusk.

There is a privately owned train service known as the Tegern-seebahn which links up with the more modern Deutsche Bundesb-ahn at Schaftlach to take passengers on to Munich. Most Sundays during the summer special steam trips are arranged by the railways and the carriages are pulled by one of the lovely old steam engines that are now becoming such a thrill to young and old alike.

Tegernsee has a thriving yacht club and weekend sailing regattas are a regular feature. Windsurfing and rowing are also prominent. The town authorities have been busily renewing the *Kurpark* and the bandstand as well as the indoor swimming pool. The House of the Guest, situated on the main street in sight of the lake, houses not only the local tourist office but a library, reading room, television room and a music room.

The small streets that lead off the main road are an artist's dream and further on they give way to marked paths that wander the hillside, sometimes finding farms or *Gasthöfe* whose terraces look out over the lake before wending their way down into the next valley.

During the month of September there is an annual festival known as the Tegernsee Week when the streets take on a carnival air. The brass bands gather to play for the folk dancing and all the local customs and traditions are brought to the fore. The local theatre puts on plays and poetry readings and in the Baroque Saal of the *Schloss* concerts are given.

Gmund, at the northern end of the lake though the smallest resort, does have its own railway station as well as a seventeenth-century parish church, St Ägidius, with work by H.G. Asam. Today Gmund is probably better known for the traffic congestion that builds up here at weekends and fine sunny days. The T-junction is controlled by traffic lights but it still causes long delays at peak times. Unfortunately there is no real alternative route for those heading towards Holzkirchen and the motorway.

Once away from the traffic problems of Gmund the road reaches **Dürnbach**. It is only a couple of shops and inns but important to British and American visitors, for the Commonwealth War Graves Commission sign at either side of the traffic lights indicates the Dürnbach War Cemetery on the road to Miesbach. It is mainly for RAF personnel that died in World War II but there are others buried here that have, for one reason or another, been brought to make their final resting place in this quiet and peaceful corner of Bavaria. The cemetery is surrounded on three sides by trees; the fourth side is open and commands views across the fields to the distant mountains. The grounds are beautifully kept by gardeners who are all recruited locally, take tremendous pride in their work and are more than willing to talk to visitors. It is regrettable that the visitors' book shows a lack of British tourists; as well as the Austrians and Germans,

A wayside chapel at Schliersee

it does appear to be known to some North Americans and therefore it would be regarded that even the specialised tour operators have overlooked or forgotten that this cemetery exists.

The Alpenstrasse now continues eastwards and bypasses the old market town of **Miesbach**, but for those interested in making a short detour into town some history may be in order. The original town was destroyed in 1312 and was rebuilt only to be destroyed by fire in 1783. The old town now offers a peaceful setting with its houses and ancient Café Beer (1623) in the Marktplatz. Apart from being a busy commercial centre it has a museum covering the town's history together with farming and art exhibits from the seventeenth century. The parish church of the Maria Himmelfahrt was originally a pilgrimage church but rebuilt after the town fire of 1783.

Rejoining the Alpenstrasse the way leads to **Schliersee** that lies at the north end of the delightful lake of the same name. Set amidst vivid green meadows and dark green forests it also incorporates the districts of Neuhaus-Fischhausen and the charming mountain village of Spitzingsee.

This area has a long history going back to 779 when the monastery of Slyrse was founded but burnt down 200 years later by the Huns. In 1170 Bishop Otto I of Freising built another monastery where the present parish church now stands. This monastery survived even the troubles of the Reformation and the Thirty Years War. In the eighteenth and nineteenth centuries the peaceful charm of the area attracted painters and poets as well as the actor Konrad Dreher and his gifted pupil Franz Xaver Terofal who together created the world famous Schliersee Folk Theatre. Customs and costumes (*Tracht*) have remained unchanged in this area up to the present day. As in Bad Tölz there is a Leonhardt ride on the 6 November each year to the saints chapel in Fischhausen.

The Rathaus, which is well worth a visit, dates from the fifteenth century when its function was that of the law courts and offices. The parish church, originally built around 1350, was rebuilt in 1712 in a baroque style. The interior is light and airy, the woodwork being of walnut which, with the ornate gilding, gives an impression of eternal sunlight. The ceiling frescoes are again the work of J.B. Zimmermann and were done when the church was rebuilt. Three early pieces are the painting by Jan Pollack in 1494 of the Virgin, the statue of St Sixtus (1520) who was the patron of the church and the Throne of Grace dating from 1480. Schliersee is noted for its folk evenings and plays showing the history of the area as far back as the fourteenth century. Accommodation can either be in hotels, pensions, private houses, farms or the large camping site on the shores of the lake itself.

A tour of the lake by the small steamer takes about 45 minutes but is extremely pleasant. The further shore of the lake is for the most part uninhabited, although the railway line to Bayerischzell passes by. The lakeside gardens are attractively laid out and also provide a congenial setting for open-air concerts. Aquatic sports naturally flourish here and some of the hotel gardens slope down to the lakeside where they have their own moorings and bathing platforms which are sometimes used for fishing as well. Swimming, apart from in the lake, may be undertaken in either the indoor or outdoor pools.

After leaving Schliersee the road leaves the lake and runs on through increasing mountain grandeur. Another short detour is to the Spitzingsee, a tiny lake surrounded by mountains which can be reached by a good but steep and winding road, up over the 5,473ft (1,668m) Brecherspitze. Around the lake a small resort is emerging with good facilities so that in a relatively short time this quiet mountain retreat will attract many more visitors.

The return journey to the valley below is quite spectacular. Descending from a height of this magnitude the views alone are well worth the effort but not really recommended for those who do not have a head for heights.

Bayrischzell, a quaint and picturesque mountain resort well patronised in both winter and summer, has grown up over the years at the foot of the Wendelstein, a mighty giant of just over 6,000ft (1,829m). Ascents can be made by either cable car or the oldest rack and pinion railway in Germany. Near the terminus is the Wendelsteinkirchl which was designed at the end of the last century by Max Kleiber. He carried the cross that adorns the roof from the foot of the mountain on his own back. This small chapel is the scene of weddings for those who prefer something different and can afford the price. The summit itself is marked by the tiny stone chapel of St Wendelin built in 1718. From this vantage point some of the finest panoramic views are to be found. To the north lie the low, flat open plains around the Chiemsee giving way to the Berchtesgaden Alps, Loferer, Leoganger Steinberge, the grey limestone massif of the Kaisergebirge and finally the Tauern Heights with their glittering glaciers.

From Bayrischzell the way lies amidst the mountains; the Tatzelwurm waterfall is a sight to behold in early summer when the melting snow high above increases the velocity and volume of the flow of water. It can only be reached on foot but it is not really hard or difficult walking. From Tatzelwurm to **Degerndorf** a toll road descends fairly steeply and runs through the mountains by means of a tunnel. When emerging at the other end one finds that the scenery has undertaken a dramatic change; the high encircling mountains disappear and instead the green fertile plains irrigated by the river Inn are in view, stretching away in the distance as far as the Chiemsee. Degerndorf's most noticeable features are the sturdy chalets whose wooden balconies from late spring to early autumn are a riot of colour with their flower filled boxes spilling over. Further on the villages of Brannenburg and Kirchdorf follow the same pattern being quiet and attractive as well as offering reasonably priced accommodation to those who wish to explore this part of Germany.

Chiemsee and Berchtesgadenerland

The Chiemsee is part of the Chiemgau region which is the flat and mainly agricultural land lying south-east of Munich. The centre is dominated by the Chiemsee, the largest of all the Bavarian lakes. This area being close to Munich attracts not only visitors from all parts of

Germany and Europe but the city dwellers who pack into their cars in the early morning to enjoy a day in rural surroundings combining fresh air and aquatic facilities from yachting to surfboarding.

Small pretty villages are the norm here and accommodation for those wishing to stay overnight or longer is to be found in small family run pensions and hotels. It is a great camping area and camp sites are both numerous and well equipped. Because of its proximity to both Salzburg and Munich, should the weather be inclement the attractions offered by these two major cities can be easily reached.

Although much of the region is flat it is the beginning of the alpine territory which becomes Berchtesgadenerland, and in fact places like Aschau, Marquartstein, Inzell, Reit im Winkl and Ruhpolding are true mountain resorts offering both winter and summer sports.

Berchtesgadenerland is the mountainous region from Bad Reichenhall to the Austrian border with Berchtesgaden as its focal point. It is first and foremost a centre for alpine activities, from walking to mountaineering, riding to kayaking or the more gentle although not always less strenuous sports of golf and tennis.

Here, on fine summer days, the sky is a really deep blue against which the giant peaks of the encircling mountains rise majestically, also etched against the sky the dark shadow of a circling eagle looking for its prey. Lower down the mountainside is the dark green forest, quiet and tranquil except for the occasional call of a bird or the sound of rushing water forcing its way over rock strewn channels.

It is also an area strong in keeping the old traditions alive, from the ceremonial return of the cattle from the high alpine pastures to their winter quarters in early to mid-autumn depending on the weather. The Buttnmandle is celebrated at Christmas time when Santa Claus and his wife escort the Buttnmandl as devils covered in straw and wearing grotesque animal masks make a hideous noise shaking chains and cow bells while Whitsun is the time to see the Miners Annual Day with its 400 year old ceremony consisting of a parade with bands and festive uniforms and an open-air concert.

Rosenheim is not technically part of the Bavarian Alps but as it lies just off the main Munich-Salzburg *Autobahn*, as well as close to the Chiemsee and Chiemgau region that do form part of the Bavarian Alps, it has been included. The town itself dates back to Roman times when two major roads (routes is perhaps more accurate), namely the one from the Brenner Pass to Regensburg and Salzburg to Augsburg, formed a cross roads. Later a medieval town grew up around Burg Rosenheim which currently is a thriving industrial centre and railway junction. The old and new towns are separated by the Mittertor

Painted houses in Neubeuern

Gate, now home to the town museum. The Heimatmuseum shows the cultural history of the town as well as shipping on the river Inn and prehistoric and Roman collections. The Inn Museum on the Innstrasse houses a collection of boat building and shipping on the river Inn. There are displays of models of the old boats as well as the flora and fauna found around the river banks.

The old town is of the most interest with the old shopping arcades which can be found as well as graceful aged buildings like the Altes Rathaus, Ellmaierhaus (1568) and the Nepomukbrunnen fountain. The parish church of St Nikolaus was originally built in the fifteenth century but only the tower and some cross beams remain from the original building for the church was rebuilt in neo-Gothic style in the late nineteenth century. The church of the Holy Ghost was built by a wealthy merchant, Hans Stier, in 1449 and connected to a domestic dwelling; its *Volto Santo* mural dating from 1499. The hospital church of St Josef (1618), the Capucine monastery of St Sebastian founded in 1635 but rebuilt in 1889, and the Loreto Chapel of 1635 are some of the ecclesiastical buildings of the town.

Two villages well worth a visit lie on the west side of the *Autobahn*.

Neubeuern must rank as one of the loveliest gems to be found even in this land of enchanting villages. It is hardly surprising therefore that in 1981 it was awarded the title of 'Loveliest Village in Upper Bavaria' and is now in great demand with film and television companies who are in the market for picturesque locations. This small community owes its existence to the river Inn on whose shores it has grown up — the reason being that in olden times one method of transportation was by river. The boats that used the Inn needed places to moor and their crews had to take provisions on board, so communities like Neubeuern were established. The main square with its old houses is a photographer's dream, decorated with sepia tinted murals and crimson geraniums spilling over the window boxes. It would seem that time has stood still. Perched on its rocky outcrop stands the castle which is now a hotel and a chapel dating from 1751. The parish church is even earlier, being built in 1672.

The neighbouring village, a mere kilometre away, is that of **Altbeuern** whose church dates from 1494 although the high altar is of a much later date, namely the seventeenth century.

The other picturesque village is **Aschau im Chiemgau**, through which the river Prien flows and, along with the following resorts, is in the area known as the Chiemgau. Overlooking Aschau is the Burg Hohenaschau, a fortified castle set on a rocky cliff and the perfect setting for any fairytale. The outer walls date from the twelfth century, while some additions were made during the sixteenth and seventeenth centuries. The chapel was built in 1637 with a rococo style interior, although the high altar is of early Italian baroque, purported to have come from Verona and is a recent addition. The two side altars are again the work of J.B. Zimmermann.

Inside the main building the ballroom with its gallery of ancestors, containing twelve gigantic statues on pedestals and the ornate stucco work of the ceiling and walls, have to be seen to be believed. The parish church of St Maria dates from the fifteenth and eighteenth centuries and has a baroque chancel and rococo side altars. Jacob Laub's *Madonna*, with a protection cloak should also be seen. The Hotel Zur Post next to the church is a relic of the seventeenth century and many of the houses in this village are extremely old. Accommodation here ranges from hotels and pensions to farms and camping. Sporting facilities are also extremely good with hang-gliding, minigolf, riding and swimming in both an outdoor and indoor pool. Entertainment is not forgotten with a library and reading room, folk theatre with folk evenings and concerts.

Close to the castle is a cable car which ascends the 5,330ft (1,625m)

Prien

Kampenwand from whose summit the glories of the Chiemgau unfold. There is a café and terrace to welcome those returning from one of the many walks that radiate from here and for those wishing to venture no further.

Bernau, separated from the Chiemsee only by the *Autobahn*, is small but in quiet rural surroundings and prides itself on being *Gemütlich* — a word that has different meanings to different people.

It is true however, that Bernau extends a warm welcome to its visitors and trusts that they will enjoy themselves. With the Chiemsee in the foreground, mountains in the background and green pastures all around, it certainly makes an idyllic holiday setting. Naturally all the facilities of the Chiemsee are open to anyone staying in Bernau and it does have its own windsurfing school. Swimming is either in the lake or in the new indoor pool. The new tennis and squash complex has its own sauna and a small restaurant, while those more attracted by the mountains can take the cable car from Aschau to the Kampenwand. Accommodation here is extremely good but it is a popular resort at weekends and the vacancies are quickly filled.

Chiemsee is the largest lake in Bavaria covering 32sq miles (83sq km) and it naturally attracts a large number of visitors. Not all of them are holidaymakers who camp or stay around its shores for some are city dwellers who enjoy a day out on the unusually placid waters. Another reason for its popularity is easy access, with the Salzburg-Munich *Autobahn* running along its southern shores. By far the most popular sports here are aquatic but it also attracts the anglers as this lake is as rich in fish as any in the country with renke, bream, pike, eel and trout. Naturalists also abound in the areas where the reeds grow in profusion for it is possible to see up to 250 types of bird as well as a multitude of different plants around Bernau. This incredibly beautiful lake, sometimes called the Bavarian Sea, could hardly have a better setting — an immense sheet of blue water with partly wooded surroundings, reed-fringed banks and a backcloth of mountains to the south and east.

Prien in the south-west corner is the major resort but the others, although small, are equally attractive in their differing ways. The town of **Prien** is situated about half a mile from the actual shores of the lake but its baroque and rococo buildings provide an attractive ambience. The Heimatmuseum is housed in a delightful old farmhouse dating back to 1837. Inside the rooms are given over to different periods and traditions. There is a farmhouse living room together with a kitchen and bedroom. Other rooms are furnished in the Biedermeier or baroque style while another displays local costumes. There is also a dug out canoe which was used for fishing on the Chiemsee and handwork that includes painting on glass. Outside is a charming garden which makes a visit here almost a necessity. The art gallery in the Altes Rathaus has some delightful pictures, the work of many a local artist, especially over the last 200 years. The parish church of 1735, which is larger than one would imagine, is adorned with frescoes and stucco work by the celebrated J.B. Zim-

The Chiemsee ferry at Prien Stock

mermann. The intricately worked wrought iron handrail that leads
up to the pulpit is a fine example of local craft.

There is a nineteenth-century steam locomotive known as the
Fiery Elias that runs from the main railway station to the lake shores,

Fraueninsel

and judging from the numbers who avail themselves of it this mode
of transport is extremely popular with both young and old alike.
Situated on the lakeside is the heated outdoor pool surrounded by
green lawns but by mid-day they are covered with sun bathers. The
town's harbour (Prien Stock) is close by and it is from here that the
ferries ply, not only to the other resorts but also to two islands. The
Fraueninsel or Ladies Island derives its name from the Benedictine
convent founded on it in the eighth century by Duke Tassilo III who
was later disposed of by the Emperor Charlemagne.

It is ironic that Charlemagne's granddaughter Irmengard later
became abbess here. The present building is Romanesque and dates
from the eleventh century while its interior is baroque with a beautifully painted ceiling and high altar with a carved Madonna all
dating from the seventeenth century. Its bell tower is distinctive with
its octagonal shape and was built beside the church to be a place of
refuge. The dome was added in 1626, almost 600 years later. The
Torkapelle (Gate Chapel) of St Michael and St Nikolaus probably
dates from Carolingian times and parts of the wall paintings from the
eleventh century. The picture of Christ on the east wall is thirteenth
century. The convent is now a boarding school.

The village, that has grown up over the years around the convent,
offers sanctuary to the many artists who come here to paint the
surrounding landscape as well as the ever hopeful fishermen who

Herrenchiemsee

try their luck and skill. Courses in both painting and pottery work are on offer here.

The larger and more famous island is that of **Herrenchiemsee** and it is here that Ludwig II was to build his largest and also last palace. The entire island was bought by the king in 1873 as a fit setting for his replica of Versailles. For those not familiar with the royal castles it should be noted that it was this final extravagance that brought the king's downfall. Although not so spectacular to look at as Neuschwanstein it is larger and the fittings are so lavish that both he and the state were bankrupted.

The craftsmanship is superb; the Meissen porcelain chandelier is quite exquisite in its delicacy and detail. The palace is surrounded by formal gardens (again copied from Versailles) and offer the visitor a chance to wander and reflect on this strange young man and his dreams of everlasting beauty. During the summer the ballroom, or to give it its correct name the 'Hall of Mirrors', is the venue for candle-lit concerts.

The island's history goes back to the eighth century when a Benedictine abbey was founded in conjunction with the Fraueninsel convent but regrettably destroyed by the Magyars. It was re-established again in 1730 and prospered until secularisation in the early nineteenth century. Part of what was the Bishop's Palace is now used as a hotel and restaurant.

On the north-west shores of the Chiemsee are the lakeside villages of Rimsting, Breitbrunn, Gstadt and Gollenshausen. Nearby Eggstätt on the small Hartsee offers visitors the choice of swimming, sailing, windsurfing, boating and fishing. **Rimsting** and **Eggstätt** also have indoor pools even though the Chiemsee is the warmest of all Bavarian lakes on account of its size. All these resorts share in offering other activities especially to those seeking an active type of holiday, well catered for with tennis and riding including short courses of instruction in these pursuits.

Endorf is not on the lake and is known more for its iodine thermal springs and the benefits these can offer. In addition there are concerts and plays as well as a good range of sporting facilities.

North of Endorf is **Amerang** a quiet village surrounded by gentle wood-covered slopes. The parish church of St Rupert was originally Gothic in design but was altered into baroque in 1720. Perched on a hill above the village of Amerang is a delightful old *Schloss* with a picturesque wedge-shaped Renaissance courtyard three storeys high with Tuscan columns. The balconies are bedecked with flowers and trailing creepers which relieve the stark white walls. The acoustics are so good that during the summer regular concerts and plays are performed here with seating for 255 people.

Entry to the *Schloss* is by guided tour only at rough hourly intervals but should the visitor have to wait he or she is invited to visit the fish pool teeming with carp, golden trout as well as several other varieties of fish. On reaching the pool there is a machine dispensing food with which the visitor may entice the fish to fight over tasty morsels. At the same time chickens scurry underfoot to catch pieces that are dropped; a notice helpfully informs one that the chickens like the granules intended for the fish.

After crossing the stone bridge over the moat one enters the outer stone flagged hall where entrance tickets are purchased as well as postcards, home baked bread, smoked fish and new-laid eggs. One cannot fail to be amused that during the summer visitors not only pay to feed fish and fowl but are then encouraged to buy the produce as well.

The guides are young students, some of whom are members of the von Grailsheim family who own the *Schloss*, are well informed and do welcome questions. From the courtyard the tour enters the main building where one can see the Rittersaal with its restored frescoes and hunting trophies and the music room with a delicately painted ceiling from which hangs a chandelier in shot glass with hues of blue, pink and green. The games room with its Biedermeier furniture and billiard table is housed here, along with the sitting room with intricate inlaid furniture. On the first floor is the Gothic St George's Chapel which was established in 1245 and extended in 1512. Under the recently cleaned walls Gothic paintings have been found. The painting at the rear of the altar dates from 1762 while on a side altar stands the small wooden sixteenth-century figure of Anna, the Virgin Mary's mother.

On the top floor is a small museum housing a collection of fishing and household utensils used in days gone by. There is also a cabinet with military uniforms and caps.

East of Amerang and north of Seebruck is **Seeon** known for the former monastery founded in the tenth century by the Count Palatinate Aribo whose monument in the form of a tomb is in the St Barbara Chapel of the monastery church of St Lambert. Aribo's feet are shown resting on his faithful hound. The church has had a Romanesque basilica added and converted to a Gothic style in the fifteenth century. The flat roof was changed to net vaulting whose unusual green and gold designs contrast with the white columns supporting them, thereby focusing attention on the representation of the Ascension and other themes.

The original famous *Madonna of Seeon* sculpture, also of the fifteenth century, is now in the Bayerisches Nationalmuseum in Munich, but a copy is on the high altar. Other interesting parts are the chapterhouse, refectory and chapel of St Nikolaus built in the eighteenth century.

Seeing the whole complex as one approaches, it is quite understandable why this small island was chosen for the site of what was to become such a massive building. The setting really is superb as the red roofs and white walls contrast with the green grass and the leafy trees surrounded by the deep blue of the lake water. Then, rising above everything else, the twin octagonal towers from the eleventh century which received their onion domes in 1561 are in view.

This prosperous monastery was able to encourage art and science so that among its visitors were Haydn and Mozart. Nevertheless with secularisation at the beginning of the nineteenth century, this work was destroyed and the buildings are now in private hands. In the monastery courtyard a 6 week season of plays is held in July and August. Shakespeare's *Twelfth Night* was one of the choices in 1987.

Of special interest to motor enthusiasts is the Oldtimer Museum with some twenty-two veteran cars and motorcycles. It is open on Wednesday and Sunday afternoons at the Hotel Schanzenberg.

Seebruck was originally a flourishing Roman military camp called *Bedaium* on the Salzburg to Augsburg road. This is substantiated by the treasures that have been unearthed over the years and which are now in the museum.

Today Seebruck is a holiday resort at the northern end of the Chiemsee where the river Alz leaves the lake. The church of St Thomas belongs to the Fraueninsel convent and was built in 1474. In the entrance are two antique fragments.

During the summer this resort is a busy water sports centre with its sailing and windsurfing school together with a fine yacht marina and bathing beaches. For entertainment there are concerts and folk evenings. The local museum Römerhaus Bedaium exhibits Celtic and Roman items discovered locally.

The road out of Seebruck towards Chieming soon reaches **Ising** which is well known for its pilgrimage church of the Maria Himmelfahrt. It was probably built in the late fourteenth century but there is conjecture that a villa was erected here in Roman times. Although the church was altered in the eighteenth century there are some interesting carvings and paintings, some of which recall disasters on the Chiemsee.

The last resort on this eastern shore is **Chieming** with 4 miles (6km) of beach, and a charming lakeside promenade. A well equipped House of the Guest provides an indoor swimming pool. Other sporting facilities here include riding, shooting and an eighteen hole golf course.

Traunstein is an old market town approximately 5 miles (8km) from the eastern shore of the Chiemsee and only a short distance from the Munich-Salzburg *Autobahn*. With a history dating back to the thirteenth century this town has seen many changes. During its early days it suffered from the plague and was plundered by foreign troops and often partially destroyed by fires, the last of which was in 1851. Today it is known as a flourishing health resort thanks to its salt and mud bath therapy. Even with its chequered history there are some fine old houses together with the fourteenth-century Brothausturm (Breadhouse Tower) and the sixteenth-century Lindlbrunnen (a small lime-tree fountain) which have managed to survive.

The town museum houses a collection of household effects as well as various implements and costumes that have been in use through the ages along with religious and secular art. There is a separate section devoted to the salt trade with which the town was and still is associated.

The parish church of St Oswald, originally built in the fourteenth century, was rebuilt in the late seventeenth century. The Salinenkapelle dedicated to St Rupert in der Au was built in 1630 in early baroque style. The frescoes with which it is decorated also date from this time.

As befits a town of this standing, there are many facilities to be found here with concerts, folk plays and good sporting attractions. On Easter Monday the Georgiritt (George Ride) takes place with a mounted procession of over 400 and includes a sword dance.

Bergen is a small village on the south side of the *Autobahn*. It is not, at first sight, any more remarkable than some of the other places that surround it, but if one was to visit the church one would not only see its slender delicate spire but also a lump of rock! According to legend it is the rock that Tannhäuser had to carry on his back as a penance. For those not acquainted with Tannhäuser the story tells how he had sinned by having an affair with Venus the Goddess of Love on the Venusberg. Tiring of her he wished to return to his mortal love but in order to do so had to receive absolution from the pope himself who in turn imposed this burden. Tannhäuser carried this heavy rock back across the Alps but on reaching Bergen dropped it and to this day it still remains there. The opera written by Richard Wagner was taken from this legend.

Just outside the village is the cable car that will take visitors up to the Hochfelln at 5,440ft (1,646m) in a two stage journey which can be terminated at the middle station if desired. The summit itself can be reached by a rough path and the weary can regain their breath by taking a look inside the wooden chapel, or watch the hang-gliders launching themselves into space. This is one of the many places in the Chiemgau where one can enjoy the superb views of both mountains and extensive plains.

Übersee-Feldwies is an attractive quiet village in rural surroundings with flower decked chalets lining the roads. The village is justly proud of its local theatre where plays, quite a few of them comical, are produced. The local brass band gives concerts as well as accompanying the folk songs and dances at the folk evenings. Sporting facilities include tennis and riding as well as a full aquatic programme on the Chiemsee. Accommodation ranging from hotels to self-catering and camping can be found here.

Once again the visitor rejoins the Deutsche Alpenstrasse as it parts company with the *Autobahn* at Grabenstätt, known for its Roman museum, as the former now heads directly towards the Alps as it follows the merry little Tiroler Ache stream. At first the way is flat until **Marquartstein** is reached; a lively village whose way of life is steeped in the old traditions which include its own folk theatre. On

Sundays and feast days (of which there are plenty) the local costume is proudly worn. The women are attired in full black skirts with velvet bands. The matrons wear black tops with long sleeves edged with white lace, white kerchiefs tucked into their necklines, pinafores of blue or mauve silk and small black boater style hats trimmed with gold tassels perched on their heads. The unmarried girls are clothed in a black velvet bodice over crisp white blouses. Their pinafores are white with gaily coloured embroidery and they wear white knitted stockings and black shoes with silver buckles. Their bodices positively jangle with silver medallions that are looped from side to side by silver chains. All the women wear fresh red flowers (usually carnations) and sprigs of rosemary tucked into their necklines.

The men are just as gaily attired in their *Lederhosen* with massive chased leather belts around their middles as well as gaily embroidered braces and knee length socks. But as often happens in rural areas, the part from ankle to mid-calf is missing; in other words there is only the foot and top piece. The reason for this is not really clear. Two favoured explanations are that it economised on wool when these areas were poor and the other one is that when' walking through long wet grass the wool got wet and uncomfortable — there may be other reasons as well. White shirts are worn under either brown and green or grey and green jackets. Their hats are of green velour adorned with long white feathers. Activities here are of the simple outdoor variety with the emphasis on walking although there are plenty of organised excursions with the local tour operator or by one's own transport.

Leaving Marquartstein behind, the scenery once again becomes more and more alpine as the road climbs steadily to the next villages of Unterwössen and Oberwössen of which Unterwössen is the larger. Both villages have grown up along the road that runs through them. **Unterwössen** has an indoor swimming pool and is the home of the German Gliding School. Halfway between the two villages lies the Wössnersee — a pretty little lake at the foot of the Rechenberg. Sheltered from the wind it offers an ideal place for swimming, a large children's play area and rowing boats for hire. This is only open during the summer months as the lake is fed from streams coming straight off the mountain side and therefore the water is fairly cold. At Oberwössen there is an enclosure for feeding the wild deer that make their homes in the surrounding woods. In winter these shy wild creatures need this regular source of food if they are to survive but even in summer, when food is more plentiful, they will probably come once a day.

The road swings in a wide arc past the Walmberg before reaching the open and sunny plateau and the attractive, peaceful village of **Reit im Winkl**, perhaps best known as a winter sports paradise. Here the mountains rise on every side in majestic splendour and the dark green forests sweep down into the valley. From the first moment one is never in any doubt that this is a true alpine resort. At an altitude of 2,500ft (762m) the air has taken on the crisp fresh tang that comes straight off the mountains. Pass the daylight hours in exploring the surrounding countryside on foot, over meadows gay with wild flowers, through the woods or take a chair-lift to the high pastures where some of the cattle are grazing. On the rocky outcrops you may find the deep blue gentian and the deep pink alpine roses — edelweiss is found only on the highest peaks and in any case is a protected flower and must not be picked; the penalties for doing so are quite severe.

Facilities here include first class swimming pools, indoor as well as open-air. There are several small lakes set amidst meadowland and are popular venues for families who bring inflatable dinghies and picnics. Other pursuits include riding, tennis, rock-climbing and minigolf. Due to open in the spring of 1988 is the new nine hole golf course. To launch the new project the first spit of turf was removed by Rosi Mittermaier-Neureuther who, before her marriage, was the famous ski racer. In the municipal park there are band concerts sometimes combined with the *Schühplattler* dancing and the local theatre where plays are performed; some amusing, some historical. They are of course given in German but it is not too difficult to follow them even if one cannot understand every word that is said. The Kuhstall is a great favourite in the evenings and is where one may be entertained with a large repertoire of yodelling. As Reit is on the Austrian border many find it useful as a base to combine an Austro-German holiday.

From Reit im Winkl to Ruhpolding the road passes four lakes and a nature reserve. The lakes are the Weitsee, the Mittersee, the Lodensee and finally the Förchensee. All are attractive alpine lakes either completely or partially surrounded by areas suitable for use as bathing and windsurfing beaches. They also attract families from the nearby towns on both sides of the border who arrive in their cars and park them along the roadside or just off the highway amongst the bushes. They bring with them dinghies, surf boards, canoes, sunbeds and hampers to ensure a pleasurable day away from busy town life.

The town of **Ruhpolding** lies just off the main Alpenstrasse, although the road that runs through the town does connect up with the *Autobahn* and provides a short cut avoiding the slower but more scenic route. With this almost direct access Ruhpolding attracts visitors not only from Germany but Austria as well. This beautiful alpine town set in the Chiemgau Alps is perhaps the last place that one would expect to find English and American newspapers but in fact both the *Daily Telegraph* and the *New York Herald* are on sale here albeit 24 hours out of date. This needs to be mentioned because usually the only daily papers available in these parts are the German ones. The people who must have a paper from home have to go to Munich, Salzburg, Berchtesgaden or Bad Reichenhall to seek supplies.

The setting may be rural but the town is an elegant and popular one. The houses combine town elegance with touches associated with those found in the more remote areas and are set in well tended gardens. Built in the first half of the eighteenth century, the parish church of St George has the reputation of being one of the finest in Upper Bavaria. The interior has exquisitely carved and decorated choir stalls and pulpit. To the right of the main altar is an early thirteenth-century wooden sculpture of the *Madonna and Child*.

The large *Kurpark* is an oasis of lawns, flowerbeds, paths and trees with a lily pond and the open-air bandstand. The tourist office is also to be found in the centre of the park. The town has many fountains derived from tree trunks and adorned with carvings; some are drinking troughs. The wayside shrines always seem to have fresh flowers placed in them.

The facilities here are first class and include two outdoor swimming pools with high diving boards. Tiled surrounds give way to smooth lawns surrounded by colourful and well tended flower beds, adjacent to which is the immaculate indoor pool.

One special aspect is the way Ruhpolding caters for its young visitors. There are adventure play areas and indoor activities like painting and modelling here, with pony-riding, a miniature train on which one may ride, and a miniature town. Most of these attractions are to be found at the Märchenpark on the outskirts of the town on the banks of the Urschlauer Ache. Across the river is the Märchenwald (Enchanted Forest) with its well sign-posted woodland walks. The local mountain is the Rauschberg, whose heights can be reached by cable car from where an even wider choice of mountain walks is available.

Ruhpolding also possesses two excellent indoor riding schools and tennis halls. There are two museums: the one in the Schloss-

Ruhpolding

Strasse is housed in an old hunting lodge dating from the sixteenth century and depicts the town's history and growth through the ages. The second one is in the Friesingerstrasse and houses the art gallery as well as old painted furniture and glassware. One is constantly aware how much anything 'folk' means to this alpine resort.

After Ruhpolding the Alpenstrasse climbs and weaves its way past the Froschsee where it is joined by the B306 road and where the resort of **Inzell** is found. Like Reit im Winkl it is both a winter and summer resort and the new ice stadium built just outside the village is open all the year and provides a stark contrast to a day spent out in the warm sunshine. The village itself lies in an open sunny valley at the start of the Bavarian Alps. Plenty of amenities are on offer here with a modern bathing complex consisting of a full sized swimming pool and a separate diving pool with both springboard and highboard. There is another pool for children only. This complex has also been built just outside of the main village and is surrounded with lawns and flower beds. Also to be found here are sauna and solarium facilities.

The village is small and compact, and close by the parish church of St Michael is the newly built House of the Guest, incorporating the local tourist office as well as a library and reading room for visitors. Although small, Inzell is a lively resort and attracts visitors from near and far. Many of these are on excursions to sample the delights of the various mountain villages before going on to Berchtesgaden or Salzburg. Inzell is an ideal centre for touring and the local tour operator offers excursions to the Salzkammergut as well as places like Vienna and Venice.

Rejoin the main Alpenstrasse and almost immediately one comes to the Gletschergarten (Glacier Garden). Parking is available on both sides of the road enabling visitors to proceed on foot to view this phenomenon. Steps have been cut into the hillside for those wishing to climb to the higher part. It takes about 15 minutes for the round trip but quite frankly the best part can be reached in about 2 minutes. This is a rare opportunity to see the result of massive geological upheavals of 15-20,000 years ago, bringing rocks through the surface from far underground. They now look very smooth and grey from the movement of glaciers and are very different to the surrounding jagged rocks. A pipeline for water was built over these hills in 1617 and remained in use till 1958 but has now been sadly replaced by a more modern method.

The Chiemgau area now gives way to what is known as the Berchtesgadenerland and to reach Bad Reichenhall take the small turning via the Thumsee: a delightful lake and much loved by the local inhabitants. The marshy area has now been turned into a protected reserve for rare water plants. Perched high above is the church of St Pancras of Karlstein.

Bad Reichenhall is an elegant spa town in this modern age but has in fact been famous since Celtic times due to its vast salt deposits. Its history can be followed in the museum showing how the town drew its wealth from the salt mines as well as the life and customs that flourished here. Bad Reichenhall has provided well laid out parks with colourful flower beds; a botanical garden will attract those who lean towards horticulture. Many of the visitors that throng the streets here have come to take the waters and baths that they feel may relieve many of their ailments. Visits to the old salt workings are available during the summer both in the mornings and afternoons, decreasing to twice a week in the winter. Check locally for the times of these visits.

Bad Reichenhall has a cathedral, St Jeno, originally built at the beginning of the thirteenth century and is the largest Romanesque church in Upper Bavaria. The main entrance is decorated with alternating red and grey marble. The interior was severely damaged in a fire at the beginning of the sixteenth century and had to be replaced using the newer techniques available at that time.

The old cloisters of the adjacent monastery are open to the public on Sunday mornings and are noted for the relief embellishments found on the columns. The parish church of St Nikolaus dates from 1181 but, perhaps unfortunately, was extended in the latter part of the last century which has made the transept rather dark and gloomy for the windows have been set high up in the vaulted roof.

Two roads leave Bad Reichenhall for Berchtesgaden, the B20 and the B21. The former follows the railway while the latter after passing the Saalachsee, a long and rather narrow lake, rejoins the Alpenstrasse to climb up to the Schwarzbachwacht Pass where the scenery is dramatic. The road runs through the densely wooded valley of the river Schwarzbach behind which, on the western side, rises the stark peaks of the Reiter Alpe. On the eastern side are green alpine pastures scattered with farms, a few chalets and browsing cattle. This is the beginning of Ramsau but before actually reaching it take the turning to the right for the Hintersee. This picturesque lake has, as a background, the jagged cruel peaks of the Reiter Alpe while to the south is the mighty Hochkalter. The lake itself is surrounded by meadows and woods which in the autumn turn to a glowing gold. It is known as the Zauberwald (Enchanted Forest) and provides delightful walks along shady river banks in clear mountain air broken only by the cries of a bird, the mellow sound of bells as cattle wander in search of fresh pasture and the sound of rushing water as it flings itself headlong over the rocky terrain.

Ramsau is adored by painters and climbers alike. The small cream church with its tiny cemetery sits above the mountain torrent, crossed only by a rustic wooden bridge and surrounded by old knarled trees. One may wonder why this small remote sixteenth-century church should attract so much attention; the answer is quite simple. Josef Mohr was once the priest here and when he was a young curate at Oberndorf wrote the carol *Silent Night, Holy Night*. Many come to see for themselves the real picture that appears on so many jigsaw puzzles.

Artists, both professional and amateur, find the scenery enthralling and never seem to tire of trying to recapture on canvas the changing light on the Watzmann. The Hochkalter is famed for its blue ice glacier and the streets of Ramsau, in the early hours, ring to the clatter of heavy boots and the clinking of ice picks as mountaineers start out on their long and hard climbs. For those left behind the House of the Guest offers a reading room, library and television room. A quieter and relaxing outdoor pastime is fishing or boating. There is accommodation to suit all tastes and pockets here from hotels to farmhouses.

Finally **Berchtesgaden**. Perhaps for the uninitiated it would be wise to mention that this town is one of the most expensive to be found in Bavaria outside Munich. It attracts not only Germans but is a rest centre for the American army stationed in and around Europe. Apart from those who actually stay in the town, many more arrive by train, coach and car to spend the day and see the sights, of which there are many. The Kehlstein attracts enormous crowds with its spectacular journey by bus before the final ascent by lift through the mountain itself to the summit and the Kehlstein Haus. It is now a café although probably better known by its other name of Eagle's Nest. Many people thought, and indeed some may still do so, that this was the home of Adolf Hitler but that is not true. His home at Berchtesgaden was the Berghof at Obersalzburg where Neville Chamberlain came in September 1938. The buildings were mainly destroyed in an air raid in April 1945. It was later completely demolished and traces of habitation were removed.

The historical part of the town is the Schlossplatz; a dignified square around which are the old buildings with an arcaded gallery of the sixteenth century. The Residenz was once a monastery and was later owned by the ruling family of Bavaria, the Wittelsbachs. The last resident of this family was in fact Crown Prince Rupert who during World War I was the commander in chief of the Bavarian troops and died in 1955. During his lifetime he collected fine furniture, oriental art and fifteenth- and sixteenth-century German woodcarvings. These treasures are now on view to the public in the castle museum housed in some particularly fine Renaissance style rooms as well as the fifteenth-century canons' dormitory.

To one end of the square is the church of St Peter and St Johannes. Originally built in 1122 it was superseded by a new building during the thirteenth century and combines both Romanesque and Gothic architecture. The choir stalls, beautifully and intricately carved and the quaint niches, shaped like swallows nests used for prayers, should not be missed. Massive red marble tombs are the final resting places of some of the priors.

A really outstanding visit is to the salt mines on the Bergwerkstrasse. Trips take approximately an hour but due to its popularity it is almost essential to pre-book and so ascertain when a tour can be taken. At peak periods it may be a couple of hours away and this time can then be fully utilised. Before the tour commences warm protective clothing in the form of trousers, jacket, felt hat and a leather 'seat' (used on the long slide which descends to the lower parts of the mine where it is very cold) should be worn.

Anyone who suffers from claustrophobia is advised not to embark on this adventure. Having donned the warm but unglamorous outfits, the journey commences on a small train which conveys the visitors along galleries to where a single rail descends 1,640ft (500m) into the bowels of the earth; hence the need for the leather seat which is strapped around the waist so that, when invited to sit on the rail, the leather can act as a cushion. Groups of about ten visitors, each with arms around the person in front, swoop down the shute before emerging into a real fairytale world, where the walls shimmer and sparkle with salt crystals of varying hue (not all salt is white). An illuminated underground lake is crossed by means of a raft, and small islets with wee caverns lit by tiny bulbs all cast their magic spell. There is also a film describing the history and importance of salt over the years before one regretfully leaves this underground paradise to emerge into the everyday world again.

Last but certainly not least one can visit the loveliest and also slightly mysterious lake in Bavaria, the Königsee. It is accessible only by an electrically powered boat that glides silently through the dark still waters so reminiscent of a Norwegian fjord. The round trip takes around 2 hours but can be shortened by only going as far as St Bartholomä. The area surrounding the lake is a nature and wildlife reserve and it is for this reason that noise is discouraged although on most boat trips a horn is blown to evoke celestial echoes (at least that is possibly what it is intended to do). The tiny chapel of St Bartholomä, whose shape resembles that of a three leafed clover, was built in the eighteenth century and together with an inn and one or two chalets are a world apart from the twentieth century. Two famous names that have spent some time out here are Sigmund Freud and Max Reger. In the autumn this mosaic of greens turns into a fiery furnace of flames and gold. The lake steamer goes as far as Salet but it is possible to reach the Obersee on foot in about 10 minutes to view the Rotbach waterfall which cascades down from the Teufelshorner (Devils Horns). This is wild and remote country where the real alpine walkers and climbers commence their battle against nature. A more off the beaten track spot would be hard to find and it is therefore fitting that this remain the final destination.

Further Information
— The Bavarian Alps —

Museums and Other Places of Interest

Amerang
Schloss Amerang
Conducted tours only, approximately one per hour.
☎ (0807) 5230

Aschau
Schloss Hohenaschau
By prior appointment only, apply in writing.
☎ (08052) 932

Bad Aibling
Heimatmuseum
Wilhelm-Leibl Platz 2

Bad Reichenhall
Alte Salinenwerk
Salinerstrasse
Conducted tours only.
Open: April to October 10-11.30am, 2-4pm. In winter Tuesday and Thursday only.

Heimatmuseum
Getreidegasse 4

Bad Tölz
Heimatmuseum
Marktstrasse 48

Benediktbeuren
Frauenhofermuseum
Frauenhofer Strasse 2
Open: Monday to Saturday 10am-12noon and 2-5pm. Sunday 1-5pm.

Berchtesgaden
Schlossmuseum
Schlossplatz 2

Heimatmuseum
Schroffenbergallee 6

Salzwerk and Museum
Bergwerkstrasse 83

Chiemsee
Herzog Tassilo Museum
Frauenchiemsee
☎ (08054) 672

Schloss Herrenchiemsee (Ludwig II)
Open: daily.
Guided tours, some in English.

Dürnbach
British War Cemetery
Mainly RAF personnel.

Garmisch-Partenkirchen
Werdenfelsmuseum
Ludwigstrasse 47

Richard Strauss Villa
Zoppritzstrasse 42

Kochel am See
Freilichtmuseum Glentleiten
A mile north of Schledorf.
Open: April to October 9am-6pm.
November 10am-5pm.
Closed Mondays.

Walchenseekraftwerk
Hydro-electric works.
Apply to the *Verkehrsamt* for further information.

Franz Marc Museum
Herzogstandweg 43

Königsee
Heraldry Museum
Jennerbahnstrasse 30

Lenggries
Tiermuseum
Bergweg 12
☎ (08042) 2510

Mittenwald
Geigenbau and Heimatmuseum
(Museum of Violin-Making and
    Regional Life)
Situated in the Ballenhausgasse.
Open: daily Monday-Friday, weekends and public holidays 10am-12noon.

Murnau
Münter-Haus
Kottmüllerallee 6

Prien
Heimatmuseum
Friedhofweg 1

Art-gallerie im Alten Rathuas
☎ (08051) 3031

Rosenheim
Heimatmuseum
Mittertor
Ludwigsplatz

Inn Museum
Innstrasse
Open: Friday morning and Saturdays
until 3pm April to October only.

Rottach-Egern
Greifvogelpark - Adlerhorst
Moni Alm
Open: daily in fine weather 9am-5pm.

Ruhpolding
Heimatmuseum - Jagdschloss
Schloss Strasse 2

Bäuerlich-Sakrales Museum
Roman Friesingergasse 1

Schliersee
Heimatmuseum
☎ (08026) 8162

Seebruck
Römerhaus-Bedaium
Open: Tuesday-Friday 3-5pm, May to
September.

Seeon
Oldtimermuseum
☎ (08624) 2031

Starnberg
Heimatmuseum
Possenhofener Strasse 9

Tegernsee
Heimatmuseum
Schloss Tegernsee
Open: daily.

Olaf Gulbransson Museum
Im Kurpark
☎ (08022) 8180

Deutsche Bundesbahn (Steam Trips)
For details of dates apply to
Bayerischer Localbahn Verein
PO Box 116
8180 Tegernsee

Traunstein
Stiftung Heimathaus Traunstein
Stadtplatz 2-3

Unterwössen
Radio und Plattenmuseum
☎ (08641) 8772

Tourist Offices

German National Tourist Office
65 Curzon Street
London W1Y 7PE
☎ (01) 495 3990

Bavarian Tourist Office
Fremdenverkehrsverband
Munchen-Oberbayern
Sonnen Strasse 10
8000 Munich 2
☎ (089) 597347

Local
Amerang
Verkehrsamt
8201 Amerang
☎ (08075) 230

Aschau im Chiemgau
Kurverwaltung
Kampenwandstrasse 37
8213 Aschau im Chiemgau
☎ (08052) 392

Bad Reichenhall
Verkehrsamt
Grossmainerstrasse 12
8230 Bad Reichenhall
☎ (08651) 3258
Also at the *Bahnhof* (railway station)
☎ (08651)1467

Bad Tölz
Stadt
Kurverwaltung
Ludwig Thoma Strasse 22
8170 Bad Tölz
☎ (08041) 41495

Bad Wiessee
Kuramt
Adrian Stoop Strasse 20
8182 Bad Wiessee
☎ (08022) 82051

Bayrischzell
Kuramt
Kirchplatz 7
8163 Bayrischzell
☎ (08023) 648

Bernried
See Starnberg.

Berchtesgaden
Kurdirektion
Konigseer Strasse 2
8240 Berchtesgaden
☎ (08652) 5011

Bernau am Chiemsee
Verkehrsamt
Aschauer Strasse
8214 Bernau am Chiemsee
☎ (08051) 7218

Chieming-Ising
Verkehrsamt
8224 Chieming
☎ (08664) 245

Ettal
See Oberammergau.

Garmisch-Partenkirchen
Verkehrsamt
Bahnhof Strasse 34
8100 Garmisch-Partenkirchen
☎ (08821) 53055

Gmund
Reise und Verkehrsburo
Bahnhof
8184 Gmund
☎ (08022) 7391

Grainau
Verkehrsamt
Waxensteiner Strasse 35
8104 Grainau
☎ (08821) 81281

Inzell
Verkehrsverein
Rathausplatz 35
8221 Inzell
☎ (08665) 862

Kochel am See
Verkehrsamt
Kalmbach Strasse 11
8113 Kochel am See
☎ (08851) 338

Kreuth
Kuramt
Rathaus
8185 Kreuth
☎ (08029) 1044

Lenggries
Verkehrsamt
Rathausplatz 1
8172 Lenggries
☎ (08042) 2977

Marquartstein
Verkehrsamt
Bahnhofstrasse 3
8215 Marquartstein
☎ (08641) 8236

Mittenwald
Verkehrsamt
Dammkar Strasse 3
8102 Mittenwald
☎ (08823) 5950

Murnau
Verkehrsamt
Kohlgruber Strasse 1
8110 Murnau
☎ (08841) 2074

Neubeuern
Verkehrsamt
8201 Markt Neubeuern
☎ (08035) 2959
(Part-time office)

Oberammergau
Verkehrsburo
Schnitzlergasse 6
8103 Oberammergau
☎ (08822) 4921

Pöcking and Possenhofen
See Starnberg.

Prien am Chiemsee
Verkehrsamt
Rathaus Strasse 11
8210 Prien am Chiemsee
☎ (08051) 3031

Ramsau
See Berchtesgaden.

Reit im Winkl
Verkeshrsamt
Rathaus
8216 Reit im Winkl
☎ (08640) 8207

Rottach-Egern
Kuramt
Rathaus
Hauptstrasse 60
8183 Rottach-Egern
☎ (08022) 26740

Rosenheim
Kulturamt
8200 Rosenheim
☎ (08031) 391231

Ruhpolding
Kurverwaltung
Hauptstrasse 60
8222 Ruhpolding
☎ (08663) 1268

Schliersee
Kurverwaltung
Am Bahnhof
8162 Schliersee
☎ (08026) 4756

Seebruck
Verkehrsamt
8221 Seebruck
☎ (08667) 7133

Seeon
Verkehrsamt
8221 Seeon
☎ (08624) 2155

Starnberg
Verkehrsverein
Kirchplatz 3
8130 Starnberg
☎ (08151) 13274

Tegernsee
Kuramt
Hauptstrasse
8180 Tegernsee
☎ (08022) 3981

Tutzing
Verkehrsamt
Kirchenstrasse 9
Tutzing
☎ (08158) 2031

Übersee-Feldwies
Verkehrsamt
Feldieserstrasse 27
8212 Übersee-Feldwies
☎ (08642) 295

Unter and Oberwössen
Verkeshrsamt
Rathaus
8218 Unterwössen
☎ (08641) 8205

Regional
Bad Reichenhall
Kur und Verkehrsverein
Hauptbahnhof Nebenbau
8230 Bad Reichenhall
☎ (08651) 1467

Bad Tölz
Fremdenverkehrsgemeinschaft
Isar-Loisachtal/Tolzer Land
Gasteinformation
Landratsamt
Bad Tölz
Postfach 1360
8170 Bad Tölz
☎ (08041) 5051

Berchtesgaden
Kurdirektion
Berchtesgadenerland
Postfach 2240
8240 Berchtesgaden
☎ (08652) 5011
Information on Berchtesgaden,
Bischofswiesen, Marktschellenberg,
Ramsau, Schonau and Königsee.

Garmisch-Partenkirchen
Fremdenverkehr Werdenfelser Land
Kurverwaltung
Postfach 1562
8100 Garmisch-Partenkirchen
☎ (08821) 53093

Prien am Chiemsee
Verkehrsverband Chiemsee
Alte Rathaus Strasse 11
8210 Prien am Chiemsee
☎ (08051) 2280 or 3031

Rosenheim
Fremdenverkehrsverband Wendelstein
Landratsamt Rosenheim
Wittelsbacherstrasse 53
8200 Rosenheim
☎ (08031) 392379 or 392324

Schliersee
Kuramt
Schliersee

Postfach 146
8162 Schliersee
☎ (08026) 4069
Information on Bayrischzell,
Fischbachau Schliersee.

Schongau
Fremdenverkehrsverband
Pfaffenwinkl
Postfach 40
8920 Schongau
☎ (08861) 7773 or 211117

Starnberg
Fremdenverkehrsverband Starnberger
Funf Seen Land
Postfach 1607
8130 Starnberg
☎ (08151) 15911 13274

Tegernsee
Fremdenverkehrsgemeinschaft
Tegernseer Tal
Haus des Gastes
8180 Tegernsee
☎ (08022) 3985

Traunstein
Verkehrsverband Chiemgau
Ludwig Thoma Strasse 2
8220 Traunstein
☎ (0861) 58223

12 • The Upper Danube

T he Danube river rises in the eastern slopes of the Black Forest and flows for some 1,770 miles (2,849km) to the Black Sea. There are those who claim that in the whole of its famous course there is not a more beautiful stretch than the 35 miles (56km) near its source between Tuttlingen and Sigmaringen when the infant stream makes its winding way through the Swabian Alb. The river here is narrow — not more than 10yd wide — and shallow, because it has lost a great deal of water through a curious geological phenomenon shortly before it reaches Tuttlingen, known as the Donau Versickerung. What happens here is that up to 4,000 gal (20,000 litres) of water escape every second from the river bed through cracks in the limestone, to surface 10 miles (16km) away in the south, from whence it finds its way into the upper waters of the Rhine.

After leaving Tuttlingen the river sweeps in huge curves in a narrow valley between beetling limestone cliffs to which thick woods precariously cling; lush meadows line the stream; ruined castles crown the crags; in the spring the bright green of the foliage contrasts starkly with the white rocks, and in September and October the warm autumnal colouring of the trees creates a romantic river landscape that sets the cameras clicking and causes every painter's hand to itch. If you are an artist, bring an easel and paints.

Yet this idyllic area is totally unknown to tourists, and not greatly visited even by Germans. It is true off the beaten track country. No main road passes through it, and in some stretches of the river there is no road at all. A branch railway does run down the valley but much of the view is lost in tunnels. It can only be explored on foot. There are no large hotels, and indeed not all that many small pensions and inns and yet it is not difficult to reach. The *Autobahn* from Stuttgart to the Bodensee (Lake of Constance) passes near Tuttlingen. A railway links Stuttgart with Sigmaringen, and the railway between Freiburg and Ulm provides easy access to the small towns and villages on this stretch of the river.

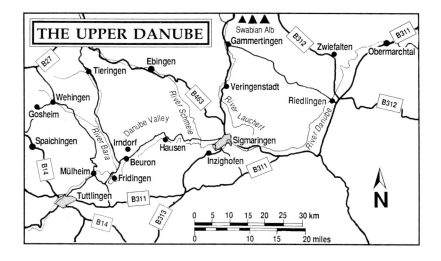

Sigmaringen

In practice there are just three places offering a choice of accommodation where you can stay. These are Sigmaringen, Tuttlingen, and
Beuron half way between them. Of these, Sigmaringen is well worth
visiting for itself. A huge castle on the rock above the river dominates
the town, and it is surprising to find this small provincial town is
graced with noble buildings and parks, worthy of a capital city. The
bewilderment of visitors will be increased when they find, placed
here and there about the town, statues of the Princes of Hohenzollern
— a name that is always associated with Prussia.

   To understand how this came about it is necessary, and interesting, to be aware of the complicated history of the German states,
principalities, kingdoms, empire, and republics — a subject that few
of us learn anything about at school! The family of Hohenzollern
originated in Swabia, not far from Sigmaringen, in the eleventh
century. In the thirteenth century it split into two main lines: the
Swabian Line, which remained based in this area and the Franconian
Line, which gained great power in the German states, ruling over the
area of Nuremberg; from the fifteenth century becoming electors of
Brandenburg, and from the eighteenth-century kings of Prussia.
After the reign of Frederick the Great, Prussia became recognised as
one of the chief European powers.

   Meanwhile the Swabian branch continued to play a more modest
but still distinguished role as aristocratic rulers in this region, remaining faithful to the Catholic faith in distinction to the Prussian

A statue of Prince Leopold of Hohenzollern
standing in front of Prussian government buildings, Sigmaringen

branch that was a leading adherent of the Protestant cause in the Reformation. In 1535 a member of the Swabian Line was created a count of Hohenzollern by the Holy Roman Emperor and obtained possession of the castle and estates of Sigmaringen. In the seventeenth century the line was elevated to the rank of Princes of Hohenzollern. Although Prince Karl, in the nineteenth century, was an enlightened ruler, his reign was disturbed by the social unrest that followed the French Revolution, and he abdicated in favour of his son, Prince Karl Anton. In 1849 Karl Anton took the decisive step of relinquishing his power in favour of the related royal house of Prussia — an action seen as a contribution towards the unification of Germany. From that date the principality of Hohenzollern became absorbed in the distant kingdom of Prussia. Sigmaringen and the surrounding territory remained part of Prussia for just over a hundred years: under the Prussian kingdom from 1849-71; under the German Empire, ruled by Hohenzollerns from Berlin, from 1871-1918; and under the Weimar Republic and the Nazi Third Reich from 1919-45. It was finally absorbed into the *Land* of Baden-Wurtemburg under the post-war constitution of the Federal Republic in 1952. The fine administrative buildings erected by the Prussian authorities bear witness to this chapter in its history, and a frontier post bearing

The castle of the Hohenzollern family dominates the town of Sigmaringen

the lettering 'Preussen Hohenzollernsche Lande' can still be seen in the town today. The town was, indeed, in its day a provincial capital of some importance, in which Prussian administrative efficiency was partnered with Swabian south German culture.

The history of the castle of Sigmaringen is equally complicated and equally fascinating. The oldest part of the building, the square tower in its centre, dates back to the twelfth century. The present shape of the structure was established by the Counts of Werdenberg in the fifteenth century. After the Swabian Hollenzollerns acquired possession of the castle it received further additions in about 1600, but 30 years later it was sacked by Swedish troops during the Thirty Years War and required considerable reconstruction. A number of embellishments in Gothic revival style were carried out in the nineteenth century, including its most obvious landmark, the octagonal and pointed helm to the central square tower. But then part of the castle was gutted by fire in 1893 and restored early in the present century. What can be seen today therefore, is a product of many different periods and its furnishings represent the domestic style of a wealthy aristocratic family in the early 1900s. It is not a homogeneous piece of architecture, nor indeed a great work of architecture of any period, but a great building that has grown with the centuries to achieve a unity of a very special kind.

The castle is open to the public (except in December and January) and presents not only a history of architectural styles but also a history of the princely family that has lived in it for so long. Prince

Karl Anton, the last Swabian Hohenzollern to rule his principality, had many connections with the royal families of Europe: a daughter married the King of Portugal; his son and successor married a Portuguese princess; his second son became king of the recently established state of Rumania; another daughter married the Count of Flanders, and became the great-grandmother of the present King of Belgium. Crown Prince Leopold was offered the throne of Spain, and although he declined the honour this provoked the Franco-Prussian War. These royal associations are all illustrated by splendid portraits on the walls of the apartments today. As a pendant to these illustrious figures from a vanished age, the last rulers of any kind to dwell in the castle of Sigmaringen were the members of the Vichy government of occupied France, who were moved here by the retreating Germans in the last months of World War II, and who must have gazed with mounting disquiet from the windows of their opulent apartments as they waited for the American army to transfer them to a different kind of captivity.

Two features of the interior call for special mention. The armoury contains weapons of every kind from the fourteenth to the twentieth centuries, and constitutes the largest private collection in Europe. The museum, built in Gothic revival style in 1867, houses a very distinguished collection of the work of Swabian painters and sculpters of the fifteenth and sixteenth centuries; in its own field this collection is unmatched anywhere.

The interest of Sigmaringen is by no means limited to its castle. It is a pleasant small town, with the nearby Wildpark Joseflust which houses many wild animals of the region in their natural habitat. It would make an admirable centre for excursions into the surrounding countryside, but before any further exploration it would be as well to describe the other places in the Upper Danube valley that might provide a base for such expeditions.

Beuron

Beuron lies in an idyllic situation in the Danube valley where a bend of the river has left sufficient flat ground for a settlement to grow up. A legend maintains that when an eleventh-century count was out hunting in this area a beautiful stag that he was pursuing laid down and indicated to him the spot where he should found a monastery. The stag certainly showed excellent taste! The monastery prospered in the hands of the Augustinian Canons, the adjoining land was acquired bit by bit or donated, and the abbey church was rebuilt in the fashionable baroque style in the eighteenth century. But then disaster struck. Although southern Germany, in general, remained Catholic during the Reformation, the influence of the French Revolution and the general secularisation of society at the end of the eighteenth century, combined with the conquests of Napoleon over the greater part of Europe, led to the acceptance in all these European countries that vast land-owning monasteries should be suppressed. Today it is hard to understand why the monks were not left to say their prayers in peace while the bulk of their property was confiscated, with or even without compensation. Perhaps this solution never appealed to the various abbots involved. Anyhow Beuron, like many others, was suppressed in 1802.

Germany today is full of great monastic buildings that were secularised in this period but now serve other purposes: Fürstenfeldbruck, near Munich, is a police college and Zwiefelten, which is described later, is a psychiatric hospital. But Beuron is a monastery again, and this is how it came about.

Early in the nineteenth century a group of idealistic German painters, who came to be called the Nazarenes, rejected the conventional art style of the period and sought to recreate an early Christian school of painting. They set up a studio and a quasi-religious brotherhood in Rome, and from this inspiration a number of Germans had joined the Benedictine monastery of St Paul's Outside the Walls in Rome. In 1862, just 60 years after the suppression, two young German monks from St Paul's moved into the ruins of Beuron. The widow of Prince Karl Hohenzollern, who now owned the site, gave them the property to enable them to refound the monastery. Barely had the work of restoration begun when the monastery found itself caught up in the quarrel between Prussia (in whose territory it now stood, as explained earlier) and the Catholic Church. This was Bismarck's *Kulturkampf*, under which all Catholic religious institutions were closed down. But after 12 years the situation improved and the monks could return. The monastery prospered, more monks joined the community and under its inspiration there grew up a new school of Christian art, which would be less sentimental and more truly religious than what had passed for religious art previously.

The artistic style of what came to be known as the Beuron School of Art is not very fashionable today, and one must regret that the original altarpiece by Josef Feuchtmayer, by all accounts a masterpiece of baroque sculpture, was destroyed in the process of redecorating the church. Perhaps it seemed too worldy for these idealistic reformers. But where one can see Beuron art in its own setting, as in the new Lady Chapel of the church or in the Saint Maurus Chapel a few miles down the river, one cannot withhold one's admiration, especially when one sees the crowds of genuine pilgrims who come to pray there.

Beuron not only founded a new school of art but revived the ancient art of Gregorian plainsong, which had fallen into neglect. Today the offices of High Mass and Compline are sung daily, in Latin, by the monks in the choir. For anyone who has any feeling for this form of worship, in which prayer is transmuted into a high form of art, this is an experience that should not be missed.

As every monk will tell you, the main purpose of their life is to pray. But they also have to work, and Beuron supports itself (and the hotel where visitors probably stay) by an efficiently and ecologically run farm. It contains monk craftsmen in almost every form of activity; it runs a printing press and a publishing house and houses an institute for the study of biblical palimpsets that has an international reputation. If you are male you can ask to stay in the guest house, where you can share, as far as you wish, something of the monastic atmosphere. Women must stay in one of the hotels or pensions in the village!

While Beuron will make a particular appeal to those who appreciate the religious atmosphere of the abbey, it is an excellent centre for any one who wants to explore the Danube valley. Wonderful walks stretch in every direction from outside your door.

The Danube Valley

The third place in the district that can offer a fair choice of hotels and inns is **Tuttlingen**. This is a larger town than Sigmaringen, and more industrial in character, with firms that specialise in the manufacture of medical instruments. It is well situated at the point where the romantic Danube valley closes in, and would provide an excellent base for exploration, especially if accomodation in Sigmaringen or Beuron is fully occupied.

As to the exploration of the Danube valley it is difficult to give advice, as it is wonderful wherever you go. Try to walk beside the river, and climb to the top of the cliffs on either side to take in the views. You should try to reach some of the castles on the peaks, though these are mostly either in ruins or in private hands. Among the most attractive are Burg Wildenstein, which is now a youth hostel, Schloss Bronnen, which is used by the Stuttgart School of Art, and Schloss Werenwag, where the Minnesinger Hugo von Weren-

The Danube between Tuttlingen and Sigmaringen

wag sang in the thirteenth century, and there are several others. An effort should be made to visit some of the caves that the action of water has worn out of the limestone. This whole area is honeycombed with caves, of which about 1,200 are registered. Some are little more than small depressions in the rock but others stretch for hundreds of yards; a dozen or so have been fitted with electric lights as show caves. Of these the most convenient to visit is the Kolbinger Höhle near Mülheim which stretches for 65yd into the rock and contains fine stalactites; it is only open to the public at weekends. There are several other caves near Mülheim, some of which should be entered only with caution. The Ziegelhöhle near Fridingen is similar to the Kolbinger Höhle but it is not illuminated; you are warned not to enter it without three good torches, of which you may expect to use up two. The Falkensteinhöhle, near the ruined castle of that name, is much smaller in size but bears signs of having been

At **Zwiefalten**, a few miles away, the art of baroque has taken wings in a flight of purest rococo. This is one of the finest of the many fine rococo churches in Germany. It was designed in 1741 by Johann Michael Fischer, one of the greatest of the architects of this period. The situation in a wooded valley at the foot of the Alb is beautiful; the exterior is imposing; the interior is a dream of white and gold, with walls flanked by stucco pillars. It is hard to believe that they are not real marble. The ceilings are painted in frescoes that seem to whirl the visitor up into the company of the saints in heaven. The statues, in contrast, are in pure white: Ezechial, on one side of the transept crossing, gazes in prophetic ecstasy at his vision of the valley of dry bones grouped round the pulpit opposite. The eye is led on, past the older pilgrimage statue of Mary in its nimbus of golden rays, through the ironwork grille, to the choir whose dark wooden stalls seem alive with movement, to reach the climax of the church in the high altar set between clusters of pink and white columns.

It would be best to visit this church on a Sunday. This is the only day on which it is open to all to walk round it as wished. On weekdays in summer there are guided tours every hour, but that is no way for a visitor to slowly absorb the atmosphere of such a building. In the winter there are not even guided tours. One can always enter the large vestibule at the west end and gaze at the rest of the interior through an ironwork grille, but this is a poor substitute for a careful and perhaps prayerful visit. One must appreciate the problems for the authorities who have the charge of a church like this. It was built for the use of a large community of monks, and was closed down in the suppression of 1803. It is now simply the parish church of the small village that surrounds it. The German state has done magnificent work and at enormous expense in restoration, which was completed only in 1984, but the state is not responsible for the day-to-day care of the building. Obviously proper care must be taken to guard the superb artistic treasures that it houses; the provision of this care may well be beyond the resources of a small village. But the consequence for a visitor, who perhaps has travelled thousands of miles to see one of the greatest buildings of its kind in Europe and who arrives on a winter weekday, is not one of which Germany or Zwiefalten can be proud. So, till this situation is improved, visit on a Sunday!

When you are at Zwiefalten there is one other visit you may like to make. The Wimsener Höhle, a mile or so from the village, is one of the most dramatic of all the caves in the Swabian Alb, and the only one that has to be visited by boat. A river rises here, giving a depth of 9ft (3m) of crystal-clear water. Boats will take you into the cave for about 100yd. It goes much further, and has been explored in conditions of great difficulty and some danger for nearly half a mile; no one knows quite how far it reaches.

This visit to Riedlingen and the churches nearby is the only excursion that has been described for which a car would be useful. In general, visitors to the nature park of the Upper Danube who have come by car are advised to leave their cars in the hotel car park, to abstain from blocking the narrow roads with their vehicles, and to make use of the excellent public transport that is available both by train and bus. If you haven't got a car, it is easy to travel to Riedlingen by train; there are buses from there to Zwiefalten and (occasionally) to Obermarchtal, but these are timed rather to the requirements of school children than to the convenience of independent travellers with a taste for rococo architecture. It is possible to walk from Riedlingen to Zwiefalten in 3 hours by pleasant footpaths, and return by bus; or to take a taxi at either place, or hire a bicycle at Sigmaringen railway station.

While you are here you will be very conscious of the fact that you are staying in Swabia. It is a long time since this has been an administrative or political area of its own, but the Swabians are, like all Germans, very conscious of their own regional identity. They have the reputation of being hard working, thrifty and inclined to introspection, and have produced many poets. It is not uncommon to find a memorial on a house in some little village recording that such and such a poet lived there — a name perhaps quite unknown elsewhere but fondly cherished in his homeland. If the visitors' German is good enough they will recognise the Swabian accent, and even the Swabian dialect. A common diminutive suffix is *-le*: a small rucksack becomes *Rucksäckle*, a small inn, *Wirtschäftle* and a little house might even be *ein kloins Häusle*. However elementary your German, you will certainly notice, and hopefully eat dishes on the Speisekarte that you will not meet elsewhere: *Maultaschen* is *Spätzle* (dumpling) filled with meat and spinach and bound with egg; a *Gaisburger Marsch* is a stew with *Spätzle*, potato, sausage, fried onions and meat gravy. There is no local wine, but the Wurtemberg vineyards are not far off and provide good wine that is not often listed in other areas.

As has been indicated, the Swabian Alb is of special interest to geologists. It is, indeed, the largest limestone range in central Europe. As well as the numerous caves and evidence of past volcanic activity, the rocks are rich in fossils. It also offers good opportunities to rock climbers; in particular the stretch of river between Beuron and Inzighofen is known as a climber's playground. Skilled climbers may reach the nests of eagles and peregrine falcons (but not to take their eggs), and find one of their few surviving breeding grounds, but visitors should beware of loose rocks. Climbers and pot holers who are attracted to this area would do well to make contact with similar German societies through their own clubs for advice before venturing alone.

Riding holidays are popular here and the gently rolling plateau of the south-eastern Alb provides good riding country. Several farms offer horses for hire. The river also offers scope for fishing and boating and canoes may be hired. There are camping sites at Sigmaringen and Hausen, and open-air swimming pools at all the chief places in the area. Flying gliders is popular and there are several good spots for launching them. In the winter you can ski all over the hills, and there are many ski lifts; the plateau is particularly suitable for Langlauf Skiwanderung.

Further Information
— The Upper Danube —

Places of Interest

Beuron
Kolbinger Höhle
Near Mulheim
Open: only between March and
November at weekends.

Sigmaringen
Schloss Sigmaringen
Open: February to November, daily
from 8.30am-12noon and 1-5pm.
Tour of castle takes about 45 minutes.

Tourist Offices

Sigmaringen
Verkehrsamt
Postfach 249
7480 Sigmaringen
☎ 07541 106 223

Tuttlingen
Verkehrsamt
7200 Tuttlingen
☎ 07462 6217 or 07462 340 6243

Information of a specialist nature about other opportunities for activity may be requested from the following organisations:

Fremdenverkehrsgemeinschaft
'Bergland junge Donau'
7200 Tuttlingen
-Möhringen

Gebietsgemeinschaft 'Schwäbsche Alb'
7400 Tübingen
An der Neckarbrücke

Geschäftsstelle Naturpark Obere
Donau
7792 Beuron 1

Schwaber International
7000 Stuttgart 1
Charlottenplatz 6

Verband Deutscher Höhlen- und
Karstforschen
7440 Nürtingen
Jusistrasse 4/2

Index

Bayreuth 133
Bech, Josef 96
Beckingen 91
Beethoven, Ludwig van 78
Befreiungshalle 165
Behrens, Peter 41
Beilstein 71
Benediktbeuern 250
Beneditktenwand 255
Berchtesgaden 235, 238, 285, 286
Berg 247
Bergen 279
Bergenthal, Wilhelm 47-8
Berghausen 54
Bergreichensteinerweg 158
Bernau 271, 272
Bernauer, Agnes 167
Bernried 206, 249
Berus 95-6
Besseringen 88
Bestwig 49
Bettingen 136
Beuron 297-9
Bély, Franz von 95
Bieberehren 146
Bigge, river 55
Biggesee 34, 35
Bilstein 55
Bingen 63, 67
Bischmisheim 99
Bischofsreuth 158
Blies, river 100
Blieskastel 100
Bochum 42
Bockenheim 108
Bodenmais 203, 204
Bogen 168
Bohemia 156, 187
Bohemian Forest 156
Bollerberg 53
Bonn 78, 211

Booth, William 12
Boppard 63
Borkum 26
Böbenthaler Kopf 119
Bödefeld 54
Böhmzwiesel 158
Brannenburg 267
Brauer, Max 14
Breckerfeld 38
Breitbrunn 276
Breitenberg 178
Brentano, Clemens 126
Brilon 50
Bronnbach 138
Brotdorf 90
Bruchhausen 50
Buchheim, L. G. 248
Burgberg 40
Burgerroth 149
Burgstall 150
Buscher, Professor Thomas 114
Busenberg 119
Bush-Woods, W. 249
Bübingen 100
Büchlberg 177, 189
Bürkel, Heinrich 116

C
Carmina Burana 253
Castell 130
Charlemagne (Karl der Grosse) 32, 50
Chieming 278
Chiemsee 267, 268, 271, 272, 276, 278, 279
Childers, Erskine 22-4
Cloef 88
Cochem 71
Cologne (Köln) 32, 34, 75-8, 81
Cond 71
Creglingen 146-50

MPC

EXPLORE THE UNEXPLORED
WITH

_____ OFF _____
THE BEATEN TRACK

With the **Off the Beaten Track** series you will explore the unexplored and absorb the essential flavour of the countries you visit.

An **Off the Beaten Track** book is the only companion you will need on your travels.

The series includes the following titles which are available:

Off the Beaten Track: ITALY
Off the Beaten Track: FRANCE
Off the Beaten Track: SPAIN
Off the Beaten Track: AUSTRIA
Off the Beaten Track: WEST GERMANY
Off the Beaten Track: SWITZERLAND

Our books are on sale in all good bookshops or can be ordered directly from the publishers.

SIMPLY THE BEST